Mo Yan in Context:
Nobel Laureate and Global Storyteller

Comparative Cultural Studies
Steven Tötösy de Zepetnek, Series Editor

The Purdue University Press monograph series of Books in Comparative Cultural Studies publishes single-authored and thematic collected volumes of new scholarship. Manuscripts are invited for publication in the series in fields of the study of culture, literature, the arts, media studies, communication studies, the history of ideas, etc., and related disciplines of the humanities and social sciences to the series editor via e-mail at <clcweb@purdue.edu>. Comparative cultural studies is a contextual approach in the study of culture in a global and intercultural context and work with a plurality of methods and approaches; the theoretical and methodological framework of comparative cultural studies is built on tenets borrowed from the disciplines of cultural studies and comparative literature and from a range of thought including literary and culture theory, (radical) constructivism, communication theories, and systems theories; in comparative cultural studies focus is on theory and method as well as application. For a detailed description of the aims and scope of the series including the style guide of the series link to <http://docs.lib.purdue.edu/clcweblibrary/seriespurduecs>. Manuscripts submitted to the series are peer reviewed followed by the usual standards of editing, copy editing, marketing, and distribution. The series is affiliated with *CLCWeb: Comparative Literature and Culture* (ISSN 1481-4374), the peer-reviewed, full-text, and open-access quarterly published by Purdue University Press at <http://docs.lib.purdue.edu/clcweb>.

Volumes in the Purdue series of Books in Comparative Cultural Studies include <http://www.thepress.purdue.edu/series/comparative-cultural-studies>

Angelica Duran and Yuhan Huang, *Mo Yan in Context: Nobel Laureate and Global Storyteller*
Elke Sturm-Trigonakis, *Comparative Cultural Studies and the New* Weltliteratur
Lauren Rule Maxwell, *Romantic Revisions in Novels from the Americas*
Liisa Steinby, *Kundera and Modernity*
Text and Image in Modern European Culture, Ed. Natasha Grigorian, Thomas Baldwin, and Margaret Rigaud-Drayton
Sheng-mei Ma, *Asian Diaspora and East-West Modernity*
Irene Marques, *Transnational Discourses on Class, Gender, and Cultural Identity*
Comparative Hungarian Cultural Studies, Ed. Steven Tötösy de Zepetnek and Louise O. Vasvári
Hui Zou, *A Jesuit Garden in Beijing and Early Modern Chinese Culture*
Yi Zheng, *From Burke and Wordsworth to the Modern Sublime in Chinese Literature*
Agata Anna Lisiak, *Urban Cultures in (Post)Colonial Central Europe*
Representing Humanity in an Age of Terror, Ed. Sophia A. McClennen and Henry James Morello
Michael Goddard, *Gombrowicz, Polish Modernism, and the Subversion of Form*
Shakespeare in Hollywood, Asia, and Cyberspace, Ed. Alexander C.Y. Huang and Charles S. Ross
Gustav Shpet's Contribution to Philosophy and Cultural Theory, Ed. Galin Tihanov
Comparative Central European Holocaust Studies, Ed. Louise O. Vasvári and Steven Tötösy de Zepetnek
Marko Juvan, *History and Poetics of Intertextuality*
Thomas O. Beebee, *Nation and Region in Modern American and European Fiction*
Paolo Bartoloni, *On the Cultures of Exile, Translation, and Writing*
Justyna Sempruch, *Fantasies of Gender and the Witch in Feminist Theory and Literature*
Kimberly Chabot Davis, *Postmodern Texts and Emotional Audiences*
Philippe Codde, *The Jewish American Novel*
Deborah Streifford Reisinger, *Crime and Media in Contemporary France*

Mo Yan in Context:
Nobel Laureate and Global Storyteller

Edited by Angelica Duran and Yuhan Huang

Purdue University Press
West Lafayette, Indiana

Copyright 2014 by Purdue University. All rights reserved.
Printed in the United States of America.

Library of Congress Cataloging-in-Publication Data

Mo Yan in context : Nobel laureate and global storyteller / edited by Angelica Duran, Yuhan Huang.
　　pages cm. -- (Comparative cultural studies)
　　Includes bibliographical references and index.
　　ISBN 978-1-55753-681-5 (paperback) -- ISBN 978-1-61249-343-5 (epdf) -- ISBN 978-1-61249-344-2 (epub) 1. Mo, Yan, 1955---Criticism and interpretation. I. Duran, Angelica, editor. II. Huang, Yuhan, 1988- editor.
　　PL2886.O1684Z74 2014
　　895.13'52--dc23
　　　　　　　　　　　　　　　　2014012989

Cover image: Copyright release by Johannes Kolfhaus, Gymnasium Marienthal.

Contents

Acknowledgments   vii

Note   ix

Introduction to *Mo Yan in Context: Nobel Laureate and Global Storyteller*
Angelica Duran and Yuhan Huang   1

Part One
Leaves

A Mutually Rewarding yet Uneasy and Sometimes Fragile Relationship between Author and Translator
Howard Goldblatt   23

The Censorship of Mo Yan's 天堂蒜薹之歌 (*The Garlic Ballads*)
Thomas Chen   37

Representations of "China" and "Japan" in Mo Yan's, Hayashi's, and Naruse's Texts
Noriko J. Horiguchi   51

Abortion in Faulkner's *The Wild Palms* and Mo Yan's 蛙 (Frog)
Lanlan Du   63

Rural Chineseness, Mo Yan's Work, and World Literature
Chengzhou He   77

Part Two
Trunk

The Realpolitik of Mo Yan's Fiction
Sabina Knight   93

Mo Yan's *Life and Death Are Wearing Me Out* in a Cultural and Visual Context
Yuhan Huang   107

Mo Yan's *The Garlic Ballads* and *Life and Death Are Wearing Me Out*
in the Context of Religious and Chinese Literary Conventions
Chi-ying Alice Wang 123

Religious Elements in Mo Yan's and Yan Lianke's Works
Jinghui Wang 139

Mo Yan's Work and the Politics of Literary Humor
Alexa Huang and Angelica Duran 153

Part Three
Roots

Cosmopolitanism and the Internationalization of Chinese Literature
Ning Wang 167

Variation Study in Western and Chinese Comparative Literature
Shunqing Cao and Miaomiao Wang 183

A Textbook Case of Comparative Cultural Studies
Donald Mitchell and Angelica Duran 195

Epilogue

Soul Searching in Contemporary Chinese Literature and Society
Fenggang Yang 215

Selected Bibliography of and about
Mo Yan's Work in Chinese and English
Angelica Duran and Yuhan Huang 221

Index 227

Acknowledgments

The editors of *Mo Yan in Context: Nobel Laureate and Global Storyteller* Angelica Duran and Yuhan Huang acknowledge gratefully the advice and support of Purdue University and Purdue University Press, especially James Mullins, dean of Purdue University Libraries; Charles Watkinson, director of Purdue University Press; and Steven Tötösy de Zepetnek, editor of the Purdue University Press series of Books in Comparative Cultural Studies. Also deserving special acknowledgment include Keith Dickson, interim chair of the School of Languages and Cultures; John Duvall, editor of Purdue's *Modern Fiction Studies* for direction and funding; Daniel Hsieh and Mark Tilton, consecutive directors of Purdue's Asian Studies; Wei Hong, director of Purdue's Confucius Institute; JoAnn Miller, associate dean of Interdisciplinary Programs; Charles S. Ross, director of Purdue's Program in Comparative Literature; Irwin Weiser, dean of the College of Liberal Arts; Fenggang Yang, director of the Purdue Center for Religion and Chinese Culture; and Michael Brzezinski, dean of Purdue's International Program. A final acknowledgment must go to the *Sino-American Symposium*, an important series of scholarly gatherings since the 1980s that alternates between the P.R. of China and the U.S., with the most recent hosted at Purdue University in 2013. Angelica Duran dedicates her efforts for the publication of the volume to Sean O'Connor, her companion in discovering "all Earths Kingdomes and their Glory" (Milton, *Paradise Lost* 11.384).

—Angelica Duran and Yuhan Huang

Note

Readers of *Mo Yan in Context: Nobel Laureate and Global Storyteller* should be aware of the style of the Purdue University Press's series of Books in Comparative Cultural Studies: the series uses no footnotes or endnotes. When used judiciously, footnotes or endnotes provide additional depth to the main discussion; however, in this volume—following the series' style guide—the contributors' texts are presented to be reader friendly for general readers and thus without footnotes or endnotes. At the same time, the editors of the volume provide depth in part through a substantial introduction and a selected bibliography, the former articulating part of the conversation in which the volume's contributors are engaged, and the latter giving signposts for further interactions. With regard to languages, the series generally follows in-text the Western sequence of First Name Surname unless, for example in Asian languages, the names are established, historical, or aka names. This is done because Western academic publishing is not consistent with surnames in other languages, which, similar to East Asian languages, use the Surname First Name sequence. However, some contributors to the volume have chosen the Chinese sequence in their texts, and two ways of in-text East Asian names reflect the contested nature of conventions as in East Asian names. Further, while the series style generally does not allow for titles with subtitles, the press decided to grant an exception, and thus the volume's title is with a subtitle (articles in the volume are without subtitles).

Introduction to *Mo Yan in Context: Nobel Laureate and Global Storyteller*

Angelica Duran and Yuhan Huang

In *The Economy of Prestige: Prizes, Awards, and the Circulation of Cultural Value* James F. English chronicles the enduring cultural entity of artistic prizes in terms of global economies, or systems, in which prizes act as cultural capital to be exchanged. While noting that prizes date "back at least to the Greek drama and arts competitions in the sixth century B.C.," English concentrates on "the modern ascendancy of cultural prizes," which he notes can "conveniently be said to have started in 1901 with the Nobel Prize for Literature, perhaps the oldest prize that strikes us as fully contemporary, as being less a historical artifact than a part of our own moment" (1, 28). The attention and prestige that a Nobel Prize endows, as well as the cultural authority that it has accumulated over more than a century, ensures attention and curiosity in each of its six categories: chemistry, economic sciences, literature, medicine, peace, and physics. The life's work and works of Nobel laureates have inevitably come to be seen as forming a kind of canon, which would surprise its creators: "the Academy members who commenced work in that first Nobel Committee of 1901 would have been terrified had they realized what they were about to set in train" (Engdahl 317). John Guillory's definition of cultural capital is especially helpful in its clear-eyed delineation of the elements which come into play, especially for literary forms of cultural capital, in order to circulate in today's global culture under construction such as access and authority and in its demonstration of the ambivalence—the simultaneous attraction and repulsion—surrounding ideologically, politically, and financially freighted cultural exchanges.

Ambivalence well describes the response to the Swedish Academy's announcement in October 2012 that it had awarded the Nobel Prize in Literature to Mo Yan (莫言). Issues of access, authority, politics, and literary merit emerged on various fronts. Usually, the media publishes a few articles about the new laureate with a pleasant exposition of the author's writing style and such. For example, the political involvement in Turkey of the 2006 Nobel Prize in Literature Laureate Orhan Pamuk was deemphasized. The comments in *The New York Times* centered mostly on his writing style: "Mr. Pamuk's prize is richly deserved. It was awarded for a body of work, fiction and nonfiction, that is driven by the conscience of imagination, as well as the conscience of memory" ("Orhan Pamuk's" <http://www.nytimes.com/2006/10/16/opinion/16mon4.html?_r=0>). Certainly, the media had plenty of praise when Seamus Heaney was awarded the Nobel in 1995, which perhaps helps to account for the few complaints that he did not write enough about the "maimed music" and "cold/ Raw silence" that came from the Irish-British clashes of the 1960s (see Heaney, "Station Island," "Casualty").

The political commentary that followed Mo Yan's 2012 Nobel is a rare but not isolated case. In a few cases, like that of Chinese-born but naturalized French citizen Gao Xingjian's Nobel in 2000 and Holocaust survivor Imre Kertész's Nobel in 2002, the award has been fraught with objections. Western media made much of the pseudonym "Mo Yan" (莫言)—which means "Don't Talk"—the writer originally named Guan Moye (管谟业) uses. Mo Yan addressed the matter of his pseudonym at the award ceremony of the Newman Prize for Chinese Literature in March 2009 at the University of Oklahoma (see "Six Lives"). Using hyperbole and referring to himself in the third person, as he has done in some of his fictional works, he stated that "back then he was thinking that he should have a pen name, since all major writers had one. As he stared at the new name that meant 'don't talk,' he was reminded of his mother's admonition from way back. At that time, people in China were living in an unusual political climate; political struggles came in waves, one more severe than the one before, and people in general lost their sense of security. There was no loyalty or trust among people ... many people got into trouble because of things they said; a single carelessly uttered word could bring disaster to one's life and reputation as well as ruination to one's family ... Whenever he [Mo Yan] felt like showing off his eloquence, his mother would remind him, 'Don't talk too much'" ("Six Lives" 26). Mo Yan was asked again to address the topic in relation to the imprisoned 2010 Nobel Peace Prize Laureate Liu Xiaobo. Media curiosity is understandable given that Mo Yan and Liu are the only two Chinese-born Nobel Prize awardees in any category who have retained their Chinese citizenship. Notwithstanding, Mo Yan commented only briefly, providing additional political responses regarding his works' merits. *The New York Times* focused nearly a third of the article "After Fury Over 2010 Peace Prize, China Embraces Nobel Selection" on similar comments Mo Yan made at the University of California–Berkeley in 2011 (see Jacobs and Lyall <http://www.nytimes.com/2012/10/12/books/nobel-literature-prize.html?_r=0>). A couple of months later, *world.time.com* keyed in on the pen name in terms of political activism and censorship, rather than literature (see Ramzy <http://world.time.com/2012/12/07/chinas-nobel-laureate-mo-yan-defends-censorship>; for a discussion on silence in literature, see Damrosch; Summit). Chinese media never dedicated as much attention to the Nobel Prize in Literature as it did following the October 2012 announcement. It is for this reason that Jing Tsu's and David Der-wei Wang's

Global Chinese Literature: Critical Essays pays attention to China's quest for the Nobel Prize at a time when Gao was the only Chinese-born writer to earn the Prize.

People's Daily, the official mouthpiece of the Chinese government, acknowledged Mo Yan as "the Chinese Mo Yan," emphasizing that the Prize "will take Chinese literature to readers worldwide. China has many excellent authors and literary works. They are insufficiently read due to the barriers of language and ideological differences. Many foreign readers know little about Chinese literature, and Chinese literature has very limited influence in the world. Awarding the Nobel Prize in Literature to Mo Yan will bring attention to Chinese writers and works, and it will also evoke interest by Sinologists, who will be able to translate and introduce Chinese literature to the world" (unless indicated otherwise, all translations are by Yuhan Huang) ("一方面，拉近了中国文学和世界各国读者之间的距离。 中国有一批优秀的作家和优秀的作品，因为语言障碍、价值观差异，中国文学在国际上的传播还不够广泛，一些外国读者对中国文学知之甚少. 诺贝尔文学奖颁给中国作家莫言，会使外国读者更加关注中国文学和中国作家，激起他们对中国文学的兴趣，而这种兴趣又会激发国外汉学家下功夫把更多的中国文学作品翻译介绍到世界上去" (Dong 3). *People's Daily* listed the three reasons for the pen name which Mo Yan provided in a press conference at Stockholm: "First, the first character in my given name, 'mo' 谟 is a combination of the two characters 'mo yan'; second, when I was young, I was very talkative and brought troubles to my family, thus my parents often taught me of the virtue of silence; third, when one speaks too much one loses one's energy in writing. Now that I have made writing my career, I will write down all that I would like to talk in words" ("关于自己的笔名，莫言介绍自己的本名叫'管谟业'，改名莫言有三个原因，一是'谟'字拆开就是'莫言'；二是小时候因为乱说话，给父母带来很多麻烦，所以他们教育我要少说话；三是人如果多说话就没精力写作了，既然选择作家这个职业，就把用嘴说出的话全都写出来" (Liu, 4). This may be the most opportune moment to note that *Mo Yan in Context* refers to the author by the Chinese phrase and pen name "Mo Yan." Our intent in this editorial choice, as with other choices, is to be as sensitive as possible to the texts and human agents that comprise this volume and to imply a rigorous concentration on the textual and cultural expressions of a specific author, not on a historical individual.

Western and Eastern readers are exposed to different motives about the Prize and about literature based on the amount and type of press attributed just to a pen name. Contributors to *Mo Yan in Context* seek to include both sets and to jostle with them in order to further global conciliation through comparative cultural studies, an emerging field whose framework and methodology have been percolating in many fields, as noted previously, and have been developed by Steven Tötösy de Zepetnek since the late 1990s (e.g., "From Comparative"). They are able to engage in such an ambitious, worthwhile aim in large part because of another aspect of modernity that has paralleled the new prize culture that English notes: globalization. Like the foundations of prize culture, this volume is fully dependent on the increased communication, access, and travel that are the hallmarks of globalization: ten of the sixteen contributors to this volume are Chinese born, with three claiming the U.S. as their long-term home. This background about the human agents behind this volume leads us to yet another caveat about another editorial choice. We co-editors have sought to lend guidance primarily in terms of overall direction and content, but not to homogenize individual voices or personas. The contributors' author profiles at the end of each article speak to the variety of the contributors' national, linguistic, and disciplinary identities.

Insofar as the benefits of the circulation of artistic production and distribution, Mo Yan's works are indeed more accessible than those of other contemporary Chinese writers with the exception of those of Gao. As such, his works had greater chances of being nominated by the "600–700 individuals and organizations qualified to nominate for the Nobel Prize in Literature" and enabling "the members of the Academy to read and assess the work of the final [15–20] candidates" ("Process" <http://www.nobelprize.org/nomination/literature/process.html>). The list of the 109 awardees of the Nobel Prize in Literature since 1901 reflects the predominant language facilities of the Academy members and their access, including the prevalence of English and regional (in this case Western) restrictions in the past century before globalization ripened: English (26), French (13), German (13), and Spanish (11) works have garnered the lion's share of the Prizes ("Facts" <http://www.nobelprize.org/nobel_prizes/facts/>). Insofar as the repercussions of Mo Yan's Prize, his works will gain further access and authority. There is also another "insofar" for cultural and literary scholars and cosmopolitanites (see Wang, Ning), to which this textual gathering around a prized literary artist is a testament. Insofar as this group is concerned, Mo Yan's Prize serves as a ripe opportunity to circulate more broadly the critical conversations in which they have been engaged for quite some time.

This critical conversation is perhaps best characterized, rather than in the terms of cultural capital, in terms of "ripeness," which in turn pays homage to the roots or root-seeking movement in Chinese literature and culture associated with Mo Yan. The term seeks to reflect an ideological imperative that arose in the 1980s and that is articulated primarily in artistic productions that are self-consciously rooted in traditional, nonstandard culture and which fixate on specific locales to gain insights into contemporary Chinese culture. Although many root-seeking authors refer to popular language and rural settings in their writings, as does Mo Yan, the search for roots is not nostalgic for customs and languages of the past or of the rural. It is instead a rediscovery of the nation's past and rethinking of its place in the contemporary context, facilitating present productivity. Han Shaogong's article "文学的根" ("The Root of Literature") defined the root-seeking movement and articulated the commonly felt sense of the importance of not forgetting, quoting the contemporary Chinese novelist Acheng (阿城): "a nation seems to be forgetful of its own past, yet it is not easy to forget" ("一个民族自己的过去，是很容易被忘记的，也是不那么容易被忘记的。") (84). Root-seeking literature seeks to ground remembrance and memory in the soil of national and folklore culture. If the root is not deep enough, the "leaves won't grow thick" (Han 77). In growing the "leaves," or the resulting expressions of strong roots, Chinese writers since the second half of the twentieth century have developed a critical body of work toward the past as well as individualistic limbs that value personal experience and independent growth.

The 2012 Nobel Prize in Literature is the well-deserved recognition of the life's work of one individual, fully matured yet still growing. Contributors to *Mo Yan in Context* attend in Part One: Leaves carefully and closely to the shimmering shadow his works have cast as world literature and in world literature; Part Two: Trunk to its nativist core; and Part Three: Roots to its cultural foundations. In Part One contributors discuss a selection of Mo Yan's short stories and novels in terms of their translation to English and the unique nature of the literary conversation Mo Yan engages in world literature. The trajectory of Parts One and Two is neither an unintentional reflection of a Western hegemonic interest nor the outcome of a too precious preservation of the logic of the vegetative metaphor that governs this volume. Rather, it is driven by the internal logic of Mo Yan's works, first shaded by the leaves of world-renown writers then blossoming into its own. In a short article on writing novels in the Chinese tradition, Mo Yan discussed his trajectory in coping with the influence of foreign world literature:

> I wrote an article for the first issue of 世界文学 / *World Literature* in 1987, entitled "Avoiding the Two Burning Furnaces." I meant that Márquez and Faulkner were two burning furnaces, while I was ice. If I came too close to them, I would melt and vaporize. Yet my avoidance was by no means complete. It was like lovers with tumultuous passion who broke up yet still thought about one another. Their [Márquez's and Faulkner's] techniques are simply too convenient to use, and I have accumulated too many stories that are similar to theirs. The momentum was great, and it takes time to divert. In the following decade, I wrote with rebellion. I wrote *The Garlic Ballads, The Republic of Wine, Big Breasts and Wide Hips*, and many other novels... It was not until 2000 when I was writing *Sandalwood Death* that I felt the ability to produce writings equal to my Western counterparts. In my creation of the three novels *Sandalwood Death*, *POW!*, and *Life and Death are Wearing Me Out*, I have retreated from Western influence and learned from Chinese folk literature and traditional writings... In the history of literature, there are two things that can save a declining art form: one is the folk, the other is the foreign. ("The Tradition" 153)

In Part Two: Trunk contributors read Mo Yan's works in terms of its most immediate Chinese literary, cultural, and social context linking the "leaves" of its literary presentations to the main body of its creation. Some of those nativist elements are near the surface, nearly raw in their presentation, such as China's controversial and difficult national family planning (计划生育) or One-child policy. Others are equally provocative, although they extend much further into the rich soil of China's religious heritage. Given government policies and current religious demographics, the religious elements of folk religion and Buddhist, Taoist, and Hindu religions which are explored in this Part may seem counterintuitive to some readers. But they should not be, given that the author himself sites "Chinese folk literature and traditional writings," redolent with such elements, as so influential.

It is the contention of this volume that the readily visible signs of Mo Yan's artistic works, towering within the literatures of the world, are rooted in cultural, literary, and critical systems, which it is the function of Part Three: Roots to demonstrate. We might here invoke the image from Mo Yan's *Life and Death are Wearing Me Out* of a poplar tree which, when "yanked" out of the ground, reveals roots "half a block long" (36). This volume proposes that rooting the cultural narratives within and about Mo Yan's works in its native China and in the West, primarily the U.S., enriches our appreciation of the variety and specificity of the discourses generated through these encounters, and may yield more generally applicable paradigms that illuminate the workings and foundations of transcultural as well as distinctly nationally and linguistically bound zones in other times and places.

The only English-language critical study of Mo Yan's works to date is *A Subversive Voice in China: The Fictional World of Mo Yan* by Shelley W. Chan. Chan's single-author book is "a thematic study of Mo Yan's fictional works within the framework of his continuity with and innovations on Lu Xun's work against the background of post-Mao China" (6). *Mo Yan in Context* is distinct from Chan's book in its multiauthorship and degree of interdisciplinarity, thus ensuring that (specialist) depth is brought to bear on its cultural and critical breadth. Extended Anglophone scholarship about Mo Yan's work appeared with articles by Howard Goldblatt, Hongtao Liu and Haiyan Lee, and Alexa Huang in the journal *World Literature Today*, shortly following his 2009 Newman Prize for Chinese Literature. As one would imagine, Mo Yan's works have received more critical attention in China: Zhang Zhizhong's single-authored volume 莫言论 (On Mo Yan) is the first volume of criticism devoted entirely to Mo Yan's work. Zhang presents detailed and incisive readings of Mo Yan's earlier stories and novels, yet covers no work later than *The Garlic Ballads*. The collected volume 莫言研究资料 (Materials for the Study of Mo Yan) remains one of the most important resources for the study of Mo Yan's work in Chinese (see Kong, Shi, Li). Instead of giving a coherent reading of a specific set of historical and cultural contexts, Materials focuses on comprehensiveness and materials for further research with its content ranging from letters of and interviews with Mo Yan in the 1980s to literary reviews published in newspapers and magazines in the 2000s. In 莫言的小说世界 (Mo Yan's Fictional World), Fu Yanxia looks closely at Mo Yan's literary style and use of literary forms. Well based on critical theories and supported by close textual readings, Fu nonetheless gives little attention to other aspects of Mo Yan's work. Chen Xiaoming's edited volume 莫言研究: *2004-2012*

(The Study of Mo Yan: 2004-2012) includes more recent interviews and reviews of Mo Yan and his work. As the title implies, the volume includes material up to the time of Mo Yan winning the Nobel Prize and thus avoids any post-Prize criticism. As Chen expounds in the preface to the volume: "The time range is strictly defined in order to avoid any conscious or unconscious afterthoughts" ("而本书的下限设定，恰恰是希望避开有意无意的后见之明") (13). Chen has good reason to distance himself from the book craze for Mo Yan–related books in China since his laureateship. Besides the republishing of Mo Yan's writings with two sets of Mo Yan collections by two of the most prestigious Chinese publishing houses in literature—eleven volumes by Shanghai Wenyi Publishing House (上海文艺出版社) and twenty volumes by Zuojia Publishing House (作家出版社)—numerous Mo Yan–related books came out in China in late 2012 and early 2013. Just to list a few: 大哥说莫言 (Big Brother on Mo Yan) penned by Mo Yan's elder brother Guan Moxian; a collection of interviews and accounts of Mo Yan's experience of receiving the Nobel Prize in Literature entitled 盛典: 诺奖之行 (Grand Ceremony: The Journey to the Nobel Prize) (see Mo Yan); Ye Kai's literary exposition 莫言的文学共和国 (Mo Yan's Republic of Letters); and 看莫言: 朋友、专家、同行眼中的诺奖得主 (Seeing Mo Yan: The Nobel Laureate in the Eyes of Friends, Experts, and Counterparts), a volume by a colleague of Mo Yan at Beijing Normal University Zhang Qinghua, co-edited with Cao Xia.

Careful afterthoughts and reflective contemplations on Mo Yan in the context of the Prize's cultural and social implications are as, if not more, important than prior criticisms. Thus *Mo Yan in Context* provides a multiauthored volume that situates Mo Yan's work in its literary, cultural, and social context, as well as within a broader view of reading and studying world literature. Natural growth—from leaves, to trunk, to roots—is opportunistic, as is this volume, in its focus on the Sino-Anglophone branches (under and above ground), more particularly the Chinese-U.S. offshoot of this literary flowering. The 2008 *Translation, Globalization and Localization: A Chinese Perspective* edited by Ning Wang and Yifeng Sun is a major contribution to the approach this volume takes. It takes to heart the practical realities and critical tendencies of current Chinese scholarship, especially in terms of the globalization in which this volume participates. Thus *Mo Yan in Context* uses a global voice both to extend its readership and to fulfill a capacious model of scholarship. Our ambitions are high: to be part of the first major wave of studies of the intersections of globalized Chinese and U.S. cultures, which is of wide interest to many scholars but difficult to transform into a resource like this one given the newness of the historical, cultural, and linguistic conditions that enable such work. This volume is responsive to the global interest in all aspects of the relationships between these two great global powers. *The Economist* made much of the similarities and differences between the long-standing term "the American Dream" of the U.S. and "the Chinese Dream" that the newly appointed Chinese general secretary and military commander-in-chief Xi Jinping used in November 2012 to describe the cultural path for "the Chinese nation" that he envisioned ("China's Future" <http://www.economist.com/printedition/2013-05-04>). Moreover, this volume is the result of the long-standing, deliberate, and successful attempts by educational institutions in the U.S. and China to foster joint research in the sciences, technology, engineering, and mathematics (STEM) fields, as well as in the humanities.

Mo Yan in Context is tethered relentlessly to Mo Yan yet extends broadly in its contexts of the interface of literature and Chinese and Western, primarily U.S., societies. Yet it in no way aspires to be comprehensive. The distinctive features of this collection of Western (primarily Anglophone) and Eastern (primarily Chinese) cultural studies are its historical breadth and inclusion of major critical scholars based in both the West (exclusively U.S. institutions) and the East (exclusively Chinese institutions). The division can be thought of as addressing the two main notions Tötösy de Zepetnek and Louise O. Vasvári define in the *Companion to Comparative Literature, World Literatures, and Comparative Cultural Studies*: "Comparative cultural studies is a combination of tenets of comparative literature and cultural studies—minus the former's Eurocentrism and the national approach—and including the ideological orientation of cultural studies" (4).

As noted, then, *Mo Yan in Context* does indeed fixate on China and the U.S. Each Part, however, provides a trenchant corrective for the potential of a nationalistic fixation: for example, in Part One alone with Chengzhou He's emphasis on the transnational nature of Mo Yan's authorial role and works and Lanlan Du's comparative study of reproductive rights in a novel by Mo Yan and another by another Nobel laureate, William Faulkner; and in Part Three with Donald Mitchell's and Angelica Duran's delineation of the globalization of religions. Additionally, the volume extends comparative literature's recent innovations in its "national approach," developed through its disciplinary conversations with world literature, which requires a specialist's sensitivity to the texts themselves. Our volume is one that reacts to rather than rejects Roland Greene's articulation of "an almost superstitious obeisance to the category of the national" (26) and that heeds Eric Griffin's caution that, "like a number of scholars who came into the profession in [the wake of the New Historicist movement of the 1980s and 1990s], I began to sense that as much as some New Historicist criticism spoke of crossing borders and committed as many of its practitioners were to unmasking the apparatuses of ideology, New Historicist critical methodologies—like those of the older historicisms they claimed to be interrogating and displacing—often failed to envision a time when the boundaries between national were substantially different from what they were in modernity" (21).

It is in part this awareness that precipitated our attention to the limiting and delimiting identities inscribed in Mo Yan's works, especially since his works emerged from a specific locale but also within an increasingly borderless world. The contributors of this volume, thus, do not eschew but rather put their specialist knowledge in careful conversation with other specialists' knowledge in the hopes of fulfilling David Damrosch's belief that "the specialist's knowledge is the major safeguard against the generalist's own will to power over texts that otherwise too easily become grist for the mill of a preferred historical argument or theoretical system" (287). Such considerations and others account for the comparative cultural studies approach that can be witnessed in this volume's value of the scholarly analogue of the popular and populist characters in Mo Yan's fictions. After the first decade of the twenty-first century, as Haun Saussy defined, "the concept of world literature" consists "chiefly of a canon, a body of works and their presence as models of literary quality in the minds of scholars and writers. But the phrase 'world literature' is not used exclusively" (291). Saussy refers to a "global literary history" that necessarily has incorporated popular and high-culture reader receptions, as well as the economic matters which Damrosch outlines in his exposition of Goethe's "newly minted [in 1827] term *Weltliteratur*" (1). Horace Engdahl suggests that Alfred Nobel, too, with business interests in many countries, was a cosmopolitanite in creating the literary prize and bequeathing to the Swedish Academy the daunting task of choosing prizewinners from the literatures of the entire world, following the intellectual tradition of "Weltliteratur" (317). This is another theoretical foundation of *Mo Yan in Context*.

Part One: Leaves leads off with Howard Goldblatt's "A Mutually Rewarding yet Uneasy and Sometimes Fragile Relationship between Author and Translator." Goldblatt elucidates with candor the uneasiness owing to internal and external reasons as well as to the successes, from personal satisfaction to wide readership, in translating from Chinese to English generally and Mo Yan's works in particular. Goldblatt's article doubles as a spirited defense of Mo Yan's selection as the 2012 Nobel Prize in Literature Laureate as based on the right reasons. The defense is text based, a task done with significant knowledge since Goldblatt is Mo Yan's English translator. Text based means understanding the process of translation, respecting reader reception and authorial intent, and referring to the work, primarily but not limited to his latest novels published in English, establishing his bona fides as a master storyteller and contemporary China's finest writer. This method contrasts with some media responses directly following Mo Yan's selection and reviews, some of which Golblatt, in turn, reviews.

In "The Censorship of Mo Yan's 天堂蒜薹之歌 (*The Garlic Ballads*)" Thomas Chen considers reader reception, literary production and circulation, and other matters of translation on a macro-scale and from a comparative literature and comparative cultural studies perspective. Chen examines literary censorship in the case of Mo Yan's *The Garlic Ballads*, a novel formerly banned in China. He gives insights into issues concerning writing and translation in contemporary China, as well as the function of Chinese news media, which have monopolized current discourse on Chinese censorship. This exposition problematizes the facile binary of a powerless writer pitted against an all-powerful state, because such categories mask the complexity of the issue. By comparing various editions of *The Garlic Ballads*, including a Chinese-language edition published in Taiwan and an English-language edition published in the U.S., Chen challenges the traditional definition of censorship, questioning the boundaries of where editing ends and where censoring begins, and the legitimacy of the titillating phrase "Banned in China."

With "Representations of 'China' and 'Japan' in Mo Yan's, Hayashi's, and Naruse's Texts" Noriko J. Horiguchi also focuses within and just beyond China's current borders. She discusses the narration of displacements and memory in the context of subjectivity and Japanese imperialism in Mainland China through her analysis of Mo Yan's, Fumiko Hayashi's, and Mikio Naruse's texts. Horiguchi demonstrates the paradox of the stories of individuals who construct subjectivities that simultaneously resist and recreate perspectives of empire and its doings. Haraguchi's analysis provides a regional (Asian) contextualization of Mo Yan's, Hayashi's, and Naruse's texts with a perspective that may help us consider literary settings more sensitively and gain particular regional context as well. Moreover, Asians and others around the globe, thus, may gain a deeper appreciation and perhaps better tools for dealing with the continuing battles—verbal and physical—over disputed Asian territories and cultural imperatives.

In "Abortion in Faulkner's *The Wild Palms* and Mo Yan's 蛙 (Frog)" Lanlan Du focuses on the operation of geo-historical settings in the hands of two Nobel Prize in Literature laureates. With the methodologies of cultural criticism, Du pairs Faulkner's novel *The Wild Palms* (also known as *If I Forget Thee, Jerusalem*) and Mo Yan's Frog, giving thematic attention to the burdens of social and governmental controls on citizens' reproductive rights. In 1939 *The Wild Palms* was revolutionary and sophisticated in its frank representation of adultery and abortion. It remains so, as Frog (2011) promises to remain in its treatment of the One-child policy. Du analyzes the two novelists' moving representations of three sets of characters: the female protagonists, the male protagonists, and the performers of abortion. Readers are guided through how these novels represent daily lives and daily communities responding to ever-changing and ever-powerful cultural forces.

While Du's study invokes Faulkner's and Mo Yan's likely authorial intentions in electing to handle such a difficult topic as reproductive rights, in "Rural Chineseness, Mo Yan's Work, and World Literature" Chengzhou He keys in on how the persona Mo Yan contributes to the current concept of Chineseness, particularly rural Chineseness. While some authors reject prize culture—or at least attempt to do so—Mo Yan has participated in ways that have been perceived as constructing the rural and the Chinese to a global reading community interested in both. He's article lends a critical eye to one branch of cultural studies focalized in *Sinophone Studies: A Critical Reader*, edited by Shu-mei Shih, Chien-hsin Tsai, and Brian Bernards. *Sinophone Studies* attends primarily to "Chineseness" and to literary works written in Chinese, from Mainland China, Taiwan, Tibet, and Japan. The collection offers important frameworks and methods to apply in Sinophone studies, a field that has experienced an upsurge since the start of the twenty-first century. Yet, while *Sinophone Studies* applies comparative methodologies and critical tools on Chinese cultural and literary elements, it does not extend to interactions between China and the West. He demonstrates the productive work that can be achieved by extending the critical perspective. He touches upon and ties together various elements in contemporary scholarship and in each of the preceding articles in Part One, thus providing a coherent path to Part Two, with its focus on key facets of China's vast cultural heritage inherent in Mo Yan's works.

Part Two: Trunk aligns Mo Yan's works with major political and religious movements in China, from ancient eras to recent times. In "The Realpolitik of Mo Yan's Fiction" Sabina Knight echoes Goldblatt when she posits that "Mo Yan won the Nobel Prize for his writing, not for political engagement" (94). Knight supports her claim by explicating the ways in which Mo Yan's art does not eschew but rather captures and transforms China's recent political movements. Knight's analyses of a variety of Mo Yan's works, including the short stories "Abandoned Child" and "White Dog and the Swing," jolt readers into remembering that all writers of world literature emerged from the crucible of personal and social struggles and joys. Mo Yan's literary *Realpolitik*—an informed and informing integration of the practical and material, rather than the explicitly ideological—becomes especially clear in Knight's deft pairing of *Red Sorghum* and *Sandalwood Death*, which press on different areas of China's collective trauma. These areas, and Mo Yan's art, are not black and white. Thus this chapter extrapolates what Jeffrey N. Wasserstrom calls in his *China in the 21st Century: What Everyone Needs to Know* the gray zone, "a subtly negotiated space where the government suffers heterodoxy as long as writers camouflage their dissent in literary metaphor" (Knight 95).

In "Mo Yan's *Life and Death are Wearing Me Out* in Cultural and Visual Context" Yuhan Huang dedicates attention to Mo Yan's novel alongside an important set of Chinese cultural artifacts: political posters. Huang reads Mo Yan's novel with a strong sense of historicity and Chinese art, examining the visual experience of the Cultural Revolution. Poster art complements the novel's description of the era's facts and aura, and demonstrates the story's cultural and historical mooring. Huang's reading of Mo Yan's personal and stylized version of history alongside the public and collective records of propaganda posters shows the ways in which propaganda has been carried out through visual experience and sheds light on the novel's seemingly idiosyncratic narrative and metaphors. This juxtaposition of one author's contemporary verbal presentation and an era's visual presentation provides an alternative access to understanding a time and space that has become distant to contemporary readers.

Contributors in the next two articles evince how Mo Yan's works can be more readily appreciated when their rich religious meanings are recognized and addressed, no easy feat for contemporary readers from either the East or West. Indeed, religious studies as an interdisciplinary field of secular study distinct from divinity, theology, or philosophy came into its own only in the second half of the twentieth century. In "*Life and Death are Wearing Me Out* and *The Garlic Ballads* in the Context of Chinese Literary and Religious Conventions" Chi-ying Alice Wang makes a signal contribution in comparative cultural studies by merging religious studies and Sinophone studies, in this case incorporating especially linguistics and literary studies. Exploring Mo Yan's novel in the context of traditional Chinese literature and religion is responsive to the overt Buddhist characters and structural overlay of the protagonist's six reincarnations in *Life and Death Are Wearing Me Out*. Wang's attention to *The Garlic Ballads* is an astute choice in that it shows other religious undercurrents to be found in a work by Mo Yan not often thought of as resting on religious foundations. A lack of religious influence in Mo Yan's works would indeed strike religious studies scholars as surprising given that Mo Yan's home county of Gaomi in Shandong Province is where the first local literary works appeared, in the eleventh to eight century BCE, in the form of the "Airs of Qi" in the earliest collection of Chinese poetry *The Book of Songs*, a major literary masterpiece and a major chronicle of religious belief. The bulk of Wang's study exposes how a three-thousand-year-old work is in conversation with these two distinct novels by Mo Yan.

We move from the context of China's ancient religious texts to that of China's current religious and popular writings with Jinghui Wang's "Religious Elements in Mo Yan's and Yan Lianke's Works." Wang explores the concepts of incarnation and atonement, and demonstrates how Chinese folk versions of these concepts are represented in two contemporary Chinese novels, Mo Yan's *Life and Death Are Wearing Me Out* and Yan Lianke's *Dream of Ding Village*. Wang describes the intratextual and extratextual parallels of these novels. After demonstrating the primary religious elements in both works, Wang opens the purview to Chinese reception of the writers of these two important works and provides an informed account of Yan's more limited reception in China and globally. Combined, Chi-ying Alice Wang's and Jinghui Wang's studies present readers with models for discussing sets of religious and social elements which inform Mo Yan's works and that are not often discussed or even considered, but that are pervasive, eloquent, and meaningful.

Part Two ends with Alexa Huang's and Angelica Duran's "Mo Yan's Work and the Politics of Literary Humor" and involves yet another topic often ignored in the few scholarly studies of Mo Yan's works and that can be lost on Mo Yan's readers whether accessing the original or translations. After providing an overview of the unique characteristics of Chinese textual humor since ancient times, Huang and Duran tease out a few kinds of humor that can be found in Mo Yan's novels. Close readings of word plays, comic scenes, and humorous elements in such works as *The Republic of Wine* and *The Garlic Ballads* demonstrate Mo Yan's keen sense of humor and his use of comic tools. The article also demonstrates how Mo Yan innovates and thereby extends a long-standing feature of Chinese writing, as is the case also with his use of politics and religion as discussed in the other articles of this Part.

Part Three: Roots complements Parts One and Two by illuminating the critical, cultural, and global theories and practices at the root of the production, reception, and circulation of Mo Yan's works as well as their themes, settings, and characters. In "Cosmopolitanism and the Internationalization of Chinese Literature" Ning Wang considers how the globalization of Chinese literature resituates the concept of world literature within the wider cultural purview of cosmopolitanism. Noting that cosmopolitanism was introduced into China much later than it was in the West and that it is still seldom discussed in Chinese literary and critical circles, Wang offers a theoretical framework from a literary and cultural perspective. In doing so, he attempts to grapple even-handedly with the internationalizing process of modern Chinese literature with regard to cosmopolitanism. This approach is exigent given the advent of globalization, the rapid development of the Chinese economy, and relevance with regard to Mo Yan's work. Wang ends with a scholarly meditation founded on decades of scholarship on the success of Mo Yan as lying in the author's appropriate and productive handling of the fundamental problems that confront contemporary China within a broad cosmopolitan context with regard to human concerns at large.

Next, in "Variation Study in Western and Chinese Comparative Literature" Shunqing Cao and Miaomiao Wang outline contemporary Chinese literary and critical scholarship, addressing the practical past, present, and likely future obstacles for enacting truly multidirectional comparative cultural studies. They do this from a Chinese scholarly context and in the service of providing provisional and promising methodologies. Cao and Wang provide an overview of the introduction and development of comparative literature in China showing that, following a course of integrative processes, Chinese scholars are reconstructing existing subjects and addressing the phenomenon of variation between literatures. They apply the critical methodology that the article's lead author, Cao, has developed in recent decades in order to assess heterogeneity and variability between literatures rather than assume a literary universalism. They outline how this direction of the research can contribute to the ongoing development of comparative literature. The final section focuses on ancient Chinese traditional literary classics and the works of Mo Yan with special attention to the Sinicization of Buddhism, thus leading to the concluding article of Part Three.

In "A Textbook Case of Comparative Cultural Studies" Donald Mitchell and Angelica Duran discuss one of the most controversial and certainly one of the most important foundations of Mo Yan's works: religion. The chief focus is on the permutations of how religious studies is understood and practiced, based on Mitchell's experience as the author of the most widely used Eastern religions textbook in the U.S., *Buddhism: Introducing the Buddhist Experience*. Mitchell and Duran contend that as Chinese literature takes its rightful place on the global stage, a singularly important factor in its reception outside of Asia is educating non-Asians about the cultural context that plays such a crucial role in Chinese fiction, including Mo Yan's. Buddhism is deeply seeded in Chinese culture, with the suppression of religious practice during part of the twentieth century comprising only a small period in China's long and rich religious heritage. Mitchell and Duran describe the development of Global Buddhism and provide examples of how it has spread knowledge about Chinese culture to indeed a global audience. Close readings of two of Mo Yan's religious figures demonstrate just some of the dynamism of reading with a religious studies eye: the Swedish, Christian Pastor Malory in *Big Breasts and Wide Hips* and "Wise Monk Yan" in *POW!*

The volume concludes with two sections distinct in form but in close conversation with the preceding articles. First is the Epilogue by Fenggang Yang titled "Soul Searching in Contemporary Chinese Literature and Society." Yang's epilogue is not an afterthought but in many ways the flowering of the explicit and implicit sociological and literary arguments that precede it. Second and finally is Angelica Duran's and Yuhan Huang's "Selected Bibliography of and about Mo Yan's Work in Chinese and English," which is also available in the series' affiliate *CLCWeb: Comparative Literature and Culture* <http://docs.lib.purdue.edu/clcweb>, the peer-reviewed, full-text, and open-access humanities and social sciences quarterly at <http://docs.lib.purdue.edu/clcweblibrary/moyanbibliography>. Yang's Epilogue lends a personal perspective on the social and cultural revolutions in China and globally that have engaged the scholars whose works are recorded in Duran's and Huang's "Selected Bibliography." The year of publication of *Mo Yan in Context* marks the anniversaries of major cultural events in China and the U.S. which had global impact. A number of articles in the volume refer to riveting historical events in China including the 4 June 1989 Tiananmen Square Incident that marked the end of its Era of Restructuring (1976-89). In the U.S., 2014 marks the tenth anniversary of the founding of Facebook (February 2004), the social network that transformed human connectivity first in the U.S. then worldwide; the quarter-century anniversary of numerous events in 1989 which speak to the global impact of U.S. culture especially in technology and the start of the presidency of George H.W. Bush when the Berlin Wall fell and when strained relationships led to U.S. military action in the Persian Gulf and Panama; and of the proposal by Tim Berners-Lee for what he described as "a large hypertext database with typed links" and what would eventually become the world wide web. The transformative and often-incendiary cultural matters that literary works at once record and contribute to are communicated in these articles perhaps because the major twenty-first-century powerhouses of China and the U.S. foregrounded in this volume have been leaders in these cultural arenas. Yang's Epilogue casts a personal and sociologist's gaze on such changes and provides an intimate record of how "Chinese souls" have responded to these dramatic social changes and to the most recent instantiation of a great spiritual awakening and thereby literary blossoming with Mo Yan's as a key example. In their Selected Bibliography, Duran and Huang focus on Mo Yan's work in order to foster future critical blossomings.

Mo Yan in Context showcases the sustained crosscultural and transcultural gazes that catapulted Mo Yan's works onto the global landscape and promise to keep them in central and peripheral view. Such vistas are difficult to maintain and must always be adjusted, so that we may give equal attention to the forest and its trees, so to speak. We end by shifting century, country, and genre to a quotation that is apt on a number of levels, from John Milton's Renaissance British epic *Paradise Lost* (1667), based on the biblical story of human creation and the human movement from a peaceful Eden to the world as we know it:

> [Adam's] Eye might there command wherever stood
> City of old or modern Fame, the Seat
> Of mightiest Empire, from the destind Walls
> Of Cambalu [capital city of Mongolian Cathay], seat of Cathaian Can
> And Samarchand by Oxus [in Uzbekistan], Temirs Throne
> To Paquin [Peking/Beijing, China] of Sinæan Kings
> ...
> In spirit perhaps he also saw
> Rich Mexico the seat of Motezume,
> And Cusco in Peru, the richer seat
> Of Atabalipa, and yet unspoil'd
> Guiana, whose great Citie Geryons Sons
> Call El Dorado (11.385-90, 406-11)

Unlike Mo Yan, Milton never won an award in his lifetime, yet today his works reside in some of the same anthologies where we now find Mo Yan's. Like Mo Yan, Milton commented on his beloved homeland throughout his literary works, which he, again like Mo Yan, often represented in artistic language that made it through governmental controls. The epigraph also personalizes the human agents invested in this volume, since Duran's work is primarily on Milton, which we note here in large part to argue for the accessibility and importance of Mo Yan, an author whose time, space, style, language, and biography are so distinct from Milton's: even a Miltonist can appreciate Mo Yan's works. The epigraph is most apt because it describes a panorama that starts in China and extends to the Americas: "Cambalu" refers the capital city of Mongolian Cathay, "Oxus" to Uzbekistan, "Paquin" to Peking, and "Geryons sons" to Walter Raleigh, who founded the Roanoke Colony in present-day North Carolina. Milton's innovation with the literary convention of the epic vista is to extend the Eastern starting point to China and the Western end point to the Americas rather than limiting the purview to Western Europe or just one's hometown. The directionality of the passage evokes hope as much of the end of *Paradise Lost* does with the East to West movement mirroring the promising dawning of a new age for humankind. The East to West movement also mirrors the directionality that Renaissance scholars termed *translatio studii* to describe the transfer of knowledge with the traditional Eastern starting point of Greece and traditional Western end points of England and Spain. Then, too, there are the details of the passage: each of these places is associated with a leader: for example, Cambalu with its Khan, Oxus with Tamir, Paquin with its kings. Thus Milton's innovation in extending the Eastern starting point to China and the Western end point to the Americas couples with his repeated association of peoples to places therefore articulating a distinctly modern, global hope for the improvement of the human condition. The point of the passage, then, is emblematic of one of the main points of this volume, an instantiation of a brave, significant, critical, communally constructed connection of East and West in which we invite readers to participate as global citizens.

Works Cited

Cao, Shunqing, and Miaomiao Wang. "Variation Study in Western and Chinese Comparative Literature." *Mo Yan in Context: Nobel Laureate and Global Storyteller*. Ed. Angelica Duran and Yuhan Huang. West Lafayette: Purdue UP, 2014. 183–93.

Chen, Thomas. "The Censorship of Mo Yan's 天堂蒜薹之歌 (*The Garlic Ballads*)." *Mo Yan in Context: Nobel Laureate and Global Storyteller*. Ed. Angelica Duran and Yuhan Huang. West Lafayette: Purdue UP, 2014. 37–49.

Chen, Xiaoming (陈晓明), ed. 莫言研究: *2004-2012* (The Study of Mo Yan: 2004-2012). Beijing: Huaxia chubanshe, 2013.

"China's Future: Xi Jinping and the Chinese Dream." *The Economist* (4 May 2014): <http://www.economist.com/news/leaders/21577070-vision-chinas-new-president-should-serve-his-people-not-nationalist-state-xi-jinping>.

Damrosch, David. *What Is World Literature?* Princeton: Princeton UP, 2003.

Dong, Yang (董阳). "中国当代文学走入世界" ("Chinese Contemporary Literature Goes to the World"). *People's Daily* (13 October 2012): 3.

Du, Lanlan. "Abortion in Faulkner's *The Wild Palms* and Mo Yan's 蛙 (Frog)." *Mo Yan in Context: Nobel Laureate and Global Storyteller*. Ed. Angelica Duran and Yuhan Huang. West Lafayette: Purdue UP, 2014. 63–76.

Duran, Angelica, and Yuhan Huang. "Selected Bibliography of and about Mo Yan's Work in Chinese and English." *Mo Yan in Context: Nobel Laureate and Global Storyteller*. Ed. Angelica Duran and Yuhan Huang. West Lafayette: Purdue UP, 2014. 221–25.

Duran, Angelica, and Yuhan Huang. "Selected Bibliography of and about Mo Yan's Work in Chinese and English." *CLCWeb: Comparative Literature and Culture* (*Library*): <http://docs.lib.purdue.edu/clcweblibrary/moyanbibliography>.

Engdahl, Horace. "Canonization and World Literature: The Nobel Experience." *World Literature: A Reader*. Ed. Theo D'haen, César Domínguez, and Mads Rosendahl Thomsen. London: Routledge, 2012. 316-28.

English, James F. *The Economy of Prestige: Prizes, Awards, and the Circulation of Cultural Value*. Cambridge: Harvard UP, 2005.

"Facts." *nobelprize.org* (2014): <http://www.nobelprize.org/nobel_prizes/facts/>.

Fu, Yanxia (付艳霞). 莫言的小说世界 (The Fictional World of Mo Yan). Beijing: Zhongguo wenshi chubanshe, 2012.

Goldblatt, Howard. "Mo Yan's Novels Are Wearing me Out: Nominating Statement for the 2009 Newman Prize." *Special Section: Newman Prize—Mo Yan. World Literature Today* 83.4 (2009): 28-29.

Goldblatt, Howard. "A Mutually Rewarding yet Uneasy and Sometimes Fragile Relationship between Author and Translator." *Mo Yan in Context: Nobel Laureate and Global Storyteller*. Ed. Angelica Duran and Yuhan Huang. West Lafayette: Purdue UP, 2014. 23–36.

Guan, Moxian (管莫贤). 大哥说莫言 (*Big Brother on Mo Yan*). Jinan: Shandong renmin chubanshe, 2013.

Guillory, John. *Cultural Capital: The Problem of Literary Canon Formation*. Chicago: U of Chicago P, 1993.

Han, Shaogong (韩少功). 文学的根 (*Root of Literature*). Jinan: Shandong chubanshe, 2001.

He, Chengzhou. "Rural Chineseness, Mo Yan's Work, and World Literature." *Mo Yan in Context: Nobel Laureate and Global Storyteller*. Ed. Angelica Duran and Yuhan Huang. West Lafayette: Purdue UP, 2014. 77–90.

Heaney, Seamus. "Casualty." *Fieldwork*. By Seamus Henay. New York: Farrar, Straus and Giroux, 1979. 13-16.

Heaney, Seamus. "Station Island." *The Hudson Review* 36.2 (1983): 257-64.

Huang, Alexander. "Mo Yan as Humorist." *Special Section: Newman Prize—Mo Yan. World Literature Today* 83.4 (2009): 32-35.

Huang, Alexa, and Angelica Duran. "Mo Yan's Work and the Politics of Literary Humor." *Mo Yan in Context: Nobel Laureate and Global Storyteller*. Ed. Angelica Duran and Yuhan Huang. West Lafayette: Purdue UP, 2014. 153–64.

Huang, Yuhan. "Mo Yan's *Life and Death are Wearing Me Out* in a Cultural and Visual Context." *Mo Yan in Context: Nobel Laureate and Global Storyteller*. Ed. Angelica Duran and Yuhan Huang. West Lafayette: Purdue UP, 2014. 107–22.

Jacobs, Andrew, and Sarah Lyall. "After Fury Over 2010 Peace Prize, China Embraces Nobel Selection." *nytimes.com* (11 October 2012): <http://www.nytimes.com/2012/10/12/books/nobel-literature-prize.html?_r=0>.

Knight, Sabina. "The Realpolitik of Mo Yan's Fiction." *Mo Yan in Context: Nobel Laureate and Global Storyteller*. Ed. Angelica Duran and Yuhan Huang. West Lafayette: Purdue UP, 2014. 93–105.

Kong, Fanjin (孔范今), Zhanjun Shi (施战军), and Xiaobing Lu (路晓冰), eds. 莫言研究资料 (Materials for Mo Yan Study). Jinan: Shandong wenyi chubanshe, 2006.

Liu, Hongtao, and Haiyan Lee. "Mo Yan's Fiction and the Chinese Nativist Literary Tradition." *Special Section: Newman Prize—Mo Yan. World Literature Today* 83.4 (2009): 30-31.

Liu, Zhonghua (刘仲华). "莫言斯城率真对记者" ("Mo Yan Talks to the Press Openly at Stockholm"). *People's Daily Overseas Edition* (7 December 2012): 4.

Milton, John. *Paradise Lost*. *John Milton: The Complete Works*. Ed. John Leonard. New York: Penguin, 1998.

Mitchell, Donald, and Angelica Duran. "A Textbook Case of Comparative Cultural Studies." *Mo Yan in Context: Nobel Laureate and Global Storyteller*. Ed. Angelica Duran and Yuhan Huang. West Lafayette: Purdue UP, 2014. 195–212.

Mo Yan (莫言), ed. 盛典: 诺奖之行 (Grand Ceremony: The Journey to Nobel Prize). Wuhan: Changjiang wenyi chubanshe, 2013.

Mo Yan. "Six Lives in Search of a Character: The 2009 Newman Prize Lecture." Trans. Sylvia Li-chun Lin. *World Literature Today* 83.4 (2009): 26-27.

Mo Yan (莫言). "中国小说传统: 从我的三部长篇小说谈起" ("The Tradition of Chinese Fiction: A Talk about Three of My Novels"). 用耳朵阅读 (Reading with Ears). Beijing: Zuojia chubanshe, 2012. 149-56.

"Orhan Pamuk's Nobel Prize." *nytimes.com* (16 October 2006): <http://www.nytimes.com/2006/10/16/opinion/16mon4.html?_r=0>.

"Process of Nomination and Selection." *nobelprize.org* (2014): <http://www.nobelprize.org/nomination/literature/process.html>.

Ramzy, Austin. "China's Nobel Laureate Mo Yan Defends Censorship." *world.time.com* (7 December 2012): <http://world.time.com/2012/12/07/chinas-nobel-laureate-mo-yan-defends-censorship>.

Saussy, Haun. *Comparative Literature in an Age of Globalization*. Baltimore: The Johns Hopkins UP, 2006.

Shih, Shu-mei, Chien-hsin Tsai, and Brian Bernards, eds. *Sinophone Studies: A Critical Reader*. New York: Columbia UP, 2013.

Summit, Jennifer. *Lost Property: The Woman Writer and English Literary History, 1380-1589*. Chicago: U of Chicago P, 2000.

Tötösy de Zepetnek, Steven. "From Comparative Literature Today toward Comparative Cultural Studies." *CLCWeb: Comparative Literature and Culture* 1.3 (1999): <http://dx.doi.org/10.7771/1481-4374.1041>.

Tötösy de Zepetnek, Steven, and Louise O. Vasvári. "About the Contextual Study of Literature and Culture, Globalization, and Digital Humanities." *Companion to Comparative Literature, World Literatures, and Comparative Cultural Studies*. Ed. Steven Tötösy de Zepetnek and Tutun Mukherjee. New Delhi: Cambridge UP India, 2013. 3-35.

Tsu, Jing, and David Der-wei Wang, eds. *Global Chinese Literature: Critical Essays*. Leiden: Brill, 2010.

Wang, Chi-ying Alice. "Mo Yan's *The Garlic Ballads* and *Life and Death Are Wearing Me Out* in the Context of Religious and Chinese Literary and Conventions." *Mo Yan in Context: Nobel Laureate and Global Storyteller*. Ed. Angelica Duran and Yuhan Huang. West Lafayette: Purdue UP, 2014. 123–37.

Wang, Jinghui. "Religious Elements in Mo Yan's and Yan Lianke's Works." *Mo Yan in Context: Nobel Laureate and Global Storyteller*. Ed. Angelica Duran and Yuhan Huang. West Lafayette: Purdue UP, 2014. 139–52.

Wang, Ning. "Cosmopolitanism and the Internationalization of Chinese Literature." *Mo Yan in Context: Nobel Laureate and Global Storyteller*. Ed. Angelica Duran and Yuhan Huang. West Lafayette: Purdue UP, 2014. 167–81.

Wang, Ning, and Yifeng Sun, eds. *Translation, Globalization and Localization: A Chinese Perspective*. Clevedon: Multilingual Matters, 2008.

Wasserstrom, Jeffrey N. *China in the 21st Century: What Everyone Needs to Know*. Oxford: Oxford UP, 2013.

Yang, Fenggang. "Soul Searching in Contemporary Chinese Literature and Society." *Mo Yan in Context: Nobel Laureate and Global Storyteller*. Ed. Angelica Duran and Yuhan Huang. West Lafayette: Purdue UP, 2014. 215–20.
Ye, Kai (叶开). 莫言的文学共和国 (Mo Yan's Republic of Letters). Beijing: Peking UP, 2013.
Ye, Kai (叶开). 野性的红高粱: 莫言传 (The Wild Red Sorghum: A Biography of Mo Yan). Nanchang: Ershiyi shiji chubanshe, 2013.
Zhang, Qinghua (张清华), and Xia Cao (曹霞), eds. 看莫言: 朋友、专家、同行眼中的诺奖得主 (Seeing Mo Yan: The Nobel Laureate in the Eyes of Friends, Experts, and Counterparts). Wuhan: Huazhong U of Science and Technology P, 2013.
Zhang, Zhizhong (张志忠). 莫言论 (On Mo Yan). Beijing: Zhongguo shehui kexue chubanshe, 1990.

Author's profile

Angelica Duran teaches English, comparative literature, and religious studies at Purdue University. Her interests in scholarship include comparative literature, disability studies, and Renaissance British literature. In addition to numerous articles and chapters, Duran's single-authored book publications include *The Age of Milton and the Scientific Revolution* (2007) and her edited volumes include *A Concise Companion to Milton* (2007) and *The King James Bible across Borders and Centuries* (2014).

Author's profile

Yuhan Huang is working toward her PhD in comparative literature at Purdue University with a project on literature and art during the Chinese Cultural Revolution. Her interests in scholarship include documentary film and photography, word and image, and art history.

Part One
Leaves

A Mutually Rewarding yet Uneasy and Sometimes Fragile Relationship between Author and Translator

Howard Goldblatt

Abstract

In "A Mutually Rewarding yet Uneasy and Sometimes Fragile Relationship between Author and Translator" Howard Goldblatt discusses the literary merits of Mo Yan's works to situate his selection as the 2012 Nobel Prize in Literature laureate. The account is text based, a task done with significant knowledge since Goldblatt is Mo Yan's translator to English. Text based means understanding the process of translation, respecting reader reception and authorial intent, and referring to the work primarily, but not limited to Mo Yan's latest novels published in English, establishing his bona fides as a master storyteller. This method contrasts with some media responses directly following Mo Yan's selection and reviews, some of which are, in turn, reviewed.

I have heard talk in recent months that the author of those internationally acclaimed novels we have been hearing about was in reality a US-American, Howard Goldblatt, and that he is, in fact, the real Mo Yan. I categorically deny that. Mo Yan is a Chinese novelist who received three gold medals, US $1.2 million, and a handshake from King Carl XVI Gustaf of Sweden. But wait a minute. Which Mo Yan are people referring to? That Chinese author of a dozen or so novels, many of which were labeled hallucinatory realism by the academy? Or maybe the Swedish Mo Yan, who lives most of her life as Anna Gustafsson Chen? Or how about the Japanese Mo Yan, an engaging fellow otherwise known as Tomio Yoshida? Then there are the two French Mo Yans, Noël Dutrait and Chantal Chen-Andro; a Norwegian Mo Yan who wrote to me as Brith Sæthre; and even an Italian Mo Yan, Patrizia Liberati. I'd be remiss if I did not at least give a shout-out to the American Mo Yan ... well, we are back to the original rumor.

In December 2012 the newly elevated Chinese Nobel laureate invited those several avatars to join him at his expense in Stockholm for the annual conclave. Beyond the excitement of actually dressing up for this most celebratory of ceremonies and participating in the week-long festivities surrounding it, we less famous Mo Yans were given an opportunity to compare notes, discuss issues of fidelity, literariness, and even marketing in relation to our versions of such novels as *Red Sorghum*, *Big Breasts and Wide Hips*, and more. It did not quite pan out, in part because all those unfamiliar tongues kept getting in the way, and because we saw the experience more as play than work. Much has been written in China and elsewhere lately about how Mo Yan's translators actually earned the prize for the Chinese novelist. I am sure that cannot please him, and he has reason to be unhappy. The novels for which he was nominated and selected for the prize are his creations. Or are they? He once responded to a question of mine in regard to one of his translations with something like: "Do what you want. I can't read what you've written. It's your book." See what I mean? We know that only one Swedish Academy member reads Chinese, so they had to rely on other Mo Yans to determine the Chinese Mo Yan's worthiness for selection. But this cannot be the first time. How many Italian readers were there among them when they selected playwright Dario Fo? Russian for Joseph Brodsky? Hungarian for Imre Kertész? Chinese (again) for Gao Xingjian? I do not mean to diminish the accomplishments or qualifications of any winners of this coveted prize; rather, I want to acknowledge the critical role a writer's translators play, especially when the talk rolls around to "language."

Some writers have a cordial, rewarding relationship with their translators and some do not. Mo Yan has never been especially vocal in his support or disapproval of those of us who not only love but also translate his novels into many languages, yet he has referred to some of us publicly and seems to be friendly with most. He has insisted that a writer must not write for the translator—unfortunately that happens—and, to his credit, he does not. I imagine that, like many writers, he would be happier if a decent Google translation program could put us "stylists" out of business, but if that were the case, then only Scandinavian writers would win Nobel Prizes from here on out. We do not want that, despite the pleasure we get from reading Henning Mankell, Jo Nesbø, Håkan Nesser, and, of course, Tomas Transtromer, the Swedish poet who actually did win the prize the year before we—I mean, Mo Yan—won. I imagine that most people who are not translators do not think much about the role of translators in literary production generally, or about the individual translators of works they read. And why should they? We are supposed to be invisible. There really is no compelling reason to be concerned about whether or not the translator gets his or her due, since the beauty of a translated work, it seems, accrues to the original author and the warts to the translator. Sometimes, of course, that's not true. The renowned translator of Spanish and Portuguese literature Gregory Rabassa was complimented by Gabriel García Márquez, who is reported to have said that the English translation of his *One Hundred Years of Solitude* was superior to the original, a revelation that may or may not have pleased the translator (see Rabassa 96). Here I am reminded of a comment by the humorist James Thurber, who, when told by a French reader that his stories read better in French than in English, replied: "Yes, I tend to lose something in the original" (*The World of Translation* 151).

Why the spotlight on translators? Because I am one and because my peers and I make foreign writing available to new audiences. How we do that, both in terms of method and results, is a hotly debated topic in some circles, although all will agree that while translation is an imperfect way to gain accessibility to writing from other cultures, it is *a* way and almost always *the* way a writer gains an international reputation. Now to the laureate himself. By now everyone knows that Mo Yan is a fifty-nine-year-old novelist living and writing in northern China. But back in 1987, he was a peasant-born, largely self-educated member of the People's Liberation Army and a modestly published writer of considerable potential. That year, he published five linked novellas, which were subsequently released as the novel 红高粱家族 (*Red Sorghum Clan*). Then came a cinematic adaptation of *Red Sorghum* by the then-unheralded director Zhang Yimou: it won the Berlin Film Festival's Golden Bear Award, was nominated for an Oscar, and Mo Yan was on his way to becoming an international celebrity.

In 1989 I was a newly transplanted and largely unknown professor of Chinese at the University of Colorado. I stumbled upon a Taiwanese edition of *Red Sorghum Clan*, read it, and knew at once that it needed to be available in English. In 1993 Viking published my translation of *Red Sorghum*. I was confident that Mo Yan's writing would have propelled him into the top ranks of Chinese writers at any time, but appearing as it did, at the height of an introspective historical moment in China, about a decade after the nation-crippling Cultural Revolution, it captured that zeitgeist as no other had. For Mo Yan and his peers, reeling from a quarter-century of incessant political campaigns, a three-year famine, a couple of wars (India and Vietnam), and an economy held hostage by politics, the future held out little promise; it was a minefield, for which only the past offered a roadmap.

The British historian C. V. Wedgewood has written that "history is lived forward but is written in retrospect. We know the end before we consider the beginning, and we can never wholly recapture what it was to know the beginning only" (35). While that might make sense to you and me, to a novelist, I suspect, it is merely a challenge. By reimagining the space in which history occurs and then imposing his or her own understanding of behavioral norms, the historical novelist, who re-creates the past from below, becomes the chronicler of that other history, the one not written but lived. For the post–Cultural Revolution generation of writers, who dug into China's past, ancient and recent, a sense of mission was at the heart of their historical re-creations, almost a quest for national salvation. In pondering the excesses of the Cultural Revolution, in particular, young intellectuals agonized over the question: How could so many ordinary people have been so caught up in blind revolutionary fervor, which caused them to have done so many bad things to each other, family and friends included? Was it an aberration or was there something in the Chinese character that so easily turned millions of people into bloodthirsty mobs? The search for answers to these questions drove scores of budding young novelists to the far reaches of rural China to examine the "roots" of the national character. What they found was often unsettling: the ritualization of cruelty, a façade of benevolence and caring that often masked a deep-seated distrust of others, and a patriarchal system that stifled originality, among others. The biggest loser in the quest was the sanctity of recorded history, a corpus of materials that seemed out of step with the perceived realities of this scarred generation, whose members would surely agree with Voltaire's observation that "a fair-minded man, when reading history, is occupied almost entirely with refuting it" (Voltaire qtd. in Fusilier 51).

Prominent among this group of writers was, as we have seen, Mo Yan, whose re-creations of early twentieth-century Chinese history, then and now, but especially the war years, evoke a powerful sense of futility and loss. *Red Sorghum* merges myth and reality, biographical and historical incidents, heroic and mundane activities. This ambivalence makes a case for cultural degeneration while drawing attention to the way the past is reconstructed. It is a novel of family, myth, and memory, centering on the dark days of war with Japan in the 1930s, yet moving backward and forward in time via compelling omniscience by the first-person narrator. It is a work that embraces contradictions, dwelling on the author's northeastern homeland that stands as a metaphor for all of China, both its virtues and its defects. Here is how the narrator of *Red Sorghum*, Mo Yan's alter ego, describes his feelings for his birthplace: "I had learned to love Northeast Gaomi Township with all my heart, and to hate it with unbridled fury. I didn't realize until I'd grown up that Northeast Gaomi Township is easily the most beautiful and most repulsive, most unusual and most common, most sacred and most corrupt, most heroic and most bastardly, hardest-drinking and hardest-loving place in the world" (4). *Red Sorghum* ushered in a new era of literary endeavor in post-Mao China. It was also groundbreaking in its modernist narrative technique, one of constant defamiliarization. A novelist of a different order, Amy Tan, stumbled upon the work and wrote that Mo Yan's "imagery is astounding, sensual and visceral. His story is electrifying and epic" (back cover of *Red Sorghum*).

There is, some have said, a bit of a ghoulish streak in Mo Yan, who often finds no better vehicle for his rich, colorful (literally; see Huang), imagistic language than disturbing scenes. Here from *Red Sorghum*:

> Full purple lips, like ripe grapes, gave Second Grandma—Passion—her extraordinary appeal. The sands of time had long since interred her origins and background. Her rich, youthful, resilient flesh, her plump bean-pod face, and her deep-blue, seemingly deathless eyes were buried in the wet yellow earth, extinguishing for all time her angry, defiant gaze, which challenged the world of filth, adored the world of beauty, and brimmed over with an intense consciousness. Second Grandma had been buried in the black earth of her hometown. Her body was enclosed in a coffin of thin willow covered

with an uneven coat of reddish-brown varnish that failed to camouflage its wormy, beetle-holed surface. The sight of her blackened, blood-shiny corpse being swallowed up by golden earth is etched forever on the screen of my mind. (307)

Purple, blue, yellow, black, reddish-brown, golden, all in a single thought. *Red Sorghum* was only the beginning. In the novels that followed, Mo Yan continued to reinvigorate and recast the art of historical fiction, frequently echoing the view of Edward Gibbon, who, in *The Decline and Fall of the Roman Empire*, wrote, "History ... is little more than the register of crimes, follies and misfortunes of mankind" (105). As the 1980s came to a close, although the demons of China's recent past had not been fully purged, her people in general and her writers in particular had at last begun to turn their attention to the road ahead. Just in time for the 4 June 1989 blood-letting at Tiananmen Square, one of those historical moments, like the 4 May 1970 massacre at Kent State in U.S. history, when public dissent became a capital offense! By then, Mo Yan had witnessed how China's past had infiltrated its present, as the brutalities of landlords of earlier times were replaced by a worse brutality practiced by former peasants newly elevated to positions of power and influence.

The actual event that led to Mo Yan's next novel, 天堂蒜薹之歌 (*The Garlic Ballads*), was an uprising in the Shandong countryside by peasants who had been cheated out of their garlic crop by corrupt officials. The novel is often magical, disturbing in the story told yet magnetic in the means of telling. Passionate and angry, panoramic yet brilliant in its specificity, the novel was kept out of distribution by a government fearful that its publication would be too incendiary during the growing unrest in the days leading up to 4 June 1989. Considered by some to be an essentially ideological novel, *The Garlic Ballads* is unambiguous evidence that while Mo Yan may not be one who believes that a work of fiction can by itself bring about public or personal improvement, he does believe in the humanistic power of art. Set in fictional Paradise County, the novel is tied both to rural China and her literary traditions by a blind minstrel's ballads, which not only open and foretell developments in each chapter, in much the same manner as premodern novels and stories, but also, through the involvement of the balladeer in the story, highlight the tragic consequences of the characters' sometimes heroic, sometimes inexplicably reckless, actions. And in a reprise of the lament in *Red Sorghum*, that is, in the author's own words, a "nagging sense of our species' regression," the balladeer articulates a sense of despair over a growing impotence, either natured or nurtured, of the Chinese peasant: "Paradise County once produced bold, heroic men, [he sings]. / Now we see nothing but flaccid, weak-kneed cowards / With furrowed brows and scowling faces: / They sigh and fret before their rotting garlic" (143).

This is a novelist for whom narrative power easily accommodates the grotesque and the fantastic. When, for instance, the leader of the uprising, Gao Ma, discovers the corpse of his pregnant lover, who has hanged herself, we share in the grisly scene:

> After clambering unsteadily to his feet, Gao Ma toppled over again, just as seven or eight gaily colored parakeets flew in through the open window, made passes above and below the roof beams, then playfully hugged the walls, brushing past Jinju's hanging corpse. The silkiness of their feathers made them appear bare-skinned. Jinju's body swung gracefully, causing the doorframe to creak ... Clutching the doorframe, he straightened up slowly, like a bent tree reaching for the sky ... The sight of her sagging belly made the sickeningly sweet taste in his throat stronger than ever. Mounting a bench, he fumbled with the knot in the rope—shaky hands, feeble fingers. The strong, acrid, and garlicky smell of her body hit him full-force; so did the sickeningly sweet taste in his throat. He could discern a slight difference between the smell of her blood and his. A man's blood is blazing hot, a woman's icy cold. A woman's blood is clean and pure, a man's dirty and polluted. Parakeets flitted under his armpits and between his legs, their malicious squawks making his heart skip a beat. (175)

From there, Gao Ma and the pregnant corpse of his lover embark upon a dialogue that precedes a scene of raw blood and gore, as Gao Ma slaughters the strangely situated parakeets. Written over a month-long explosion of energy, passion, and rage, the novel underscores the author's own admission that "I may look like a writer, but deep down I'm still a peasant" (Kakutani <http://www.nytimes.com/2002/04/19/movies/books-of-the-times-tale-of-a-tibetan-clan-told-by-an-idiot.html>).

The Garlic Ballads was followed by a metafictional novel that attacked China's vaunted Epicureanism by linking it to cannibalism; 酒国 (*The Republic of Wine*) is easily the most incisive and trenchant social satire any modern Chinese writer has created. For readers, *The Republic of Wine* packs a real wallop, like the colorless liquor distilled in Mo Yan's home province. Few contemporary works have exposed and satirized the political structure of post-Mao China, or the enduring obsession of the Chinese with food, with the wit and venom of this explosive novel. None approaches its structural inventiveness. Nothing in the previous novels prepares readers for the surprises to be found in this cornucopia of comedy, ingenuity, and technical dexterity (see Huang and Duran). Mo Yan's purpose dawns upon us gradually as we discover a fictional structure unlike anything we are likely to have seen before, perhaps Laurence Sterne's *Tristram Shandy* offering the closest parallel. In the end, it is a complex allegory not only about the Chinese character but also about the larger issues of how we define truth, reality, imagination, and creativity. And, oh, that little matter of cannibalism, recalling Jonathan Swift's *A Modest Proposal*. Here is how Mo Yan's protagonist, a hapless special investigator named Ding Gou'er, reacts to the sight of what he assumes is a cooked little boy at a welcoming banquet at the official residence of the local boss in a mining community where, reputedly, children are being raised as food for the jaded palates of corrupt officials:

> Ding Gou'er's ... eyes blurred and the lovely butterfly that had returned to its cocoon began to squirm again. Feelings of dread pressed down on him like a boulder, weighing heavily on his shoulders until he felt that his ...

skeleton could crumble at any moment. He was face-to-face with a bottomless, foul-smelling cesspool that would pull him down into its obliterating muck and keep him there forever. But ... the boy gushing perfume, a tiny son joining ranks with his mother, sitting amid a fairy mist the shape and color of a lotus flower, raised his hand, actually raised his hand toward me! His fingers were stubby, pudgy, meaty and so very lovely. Wrinkles on his fingers, three circular seams; the back of his hand sporting four prominent dimples. The sweet sound of his laughter wound round the fragrance hanging in the air. The lotus began to levitate, carrying the child along with it. His round little belly button, so childish and innocent, like a dimple on a cheek ... The cooked little boy smiled at me. You say this child is actually a famous dish ... I hear the piteous wails of little boys in the steamers. I hear them wailing in crackling woks, on chopping blocks, in oil, salt, soy sauce, vinegar, sugar, anise powder, peppercorns, cinnamon, ginger, and cooking liquor. They are wailing in your intestines, in the toilets, and in the sewers. They are wailing. (78)

You get the idea, although the scene continues for a while, with an encyclopedic litany of accusations that keep readers spellbound.

As the novel progresses, the disparate sections begin to merge, until "Mo Yan" himself assumes the persona of Ding Gou'er in a Joycean stream-of-consciousness epilogue that recaps the highlights of a physical and psychological odyssey and alludes to a string of political campaigns that have plagued China for decades. Having been ingested into the maw of a cannibalistic society and digested in the twists and turns of its intestinal network, the writer-protagonist is evacuated into the vile porridge of an outdoor privy while an anthropophaginian feast takes place on a pleasure boat just beyond his reach. *The Republic of Wine* is a *tour de force* of literary imagination and offers, I might add, about as much fun as a translator can have.

In 1996 Mo Yan published an immense novel of nearly half a million characters, 丰乳肥臀 (*Big Breasts and Wide Hips*), in which he revisits the historical period of his grandfather's generation, focusing on a woman, her nine children (eight daughters, all from different fathers, and a son sired by a foreign cleric), and the men they marry, once again calling into question the official black-and-white histories fed to members of his generation in school. As the title suggests, the book is dominated by a powerful matriarchy of strong, voluptuous women. Mo Yan is unflinching in his portrayal of the clan's struggles to survive poverty through the decades, while writing with a vibrant style that embraces fantasy and surrealism. Resplendent with the grotesque, bristling with black humor, and visceral in its treatment of sex, violence, and death, *Big Breasts and Wide Hips* is a searing vision of rural China.

Big Breasts and Wide Hips was followed in English translation by yet another sweeping recreation of modern Chinese history, 生死疲劳 (*Life and Death Are Wearing Me Out*). It is the transmigratory story of a landlord who is executed in 1950 by the rebellious masses in the rural township of Gaomi. Reborn six times via the Buddhist cycle of life and death, samsara—as a donkey, an ox, a pig, a dog, a monkey, and a boy who turns out to be one of several narrators—he provides unusual windows into the march of progress in contemporary China. With parallel and recollected narratives in typical Mo Yan fashion, the plot moves at a rapid and often hilarious pace toward the ... well, toward the beginning. Honored with two major prizes—the 2008 Hongloumeng Prize as the best Chinese novel and the inaugural Newman Prize for his achievements in Chinese literature—the novel entertains, educates, and fulfills readers—domestic and international.

While Mo Yan's novel from the early twenty-first century, 四十一炮, was somewhat overlooked in Chinese, its English translation, *POW!*, published in 2012, has proved to be among his most popular and most critically effective in the U.S. As we know, the Chinese like to say they will eat anything on four legs except a table. Mo Yan's *POW!* makes a good case for that. What he did for alcohol in *The Republic of Wine* he does here for meat—its sometimes ghoulish production, its gluttonous consumption, and its obsessive social role. And meat is the prism through which contemporary China and many of its contentious issues are viewed. By turns accusatory, comical, and fantastic, this latest riveting novel by one of China's most popular writers has already further embellished his international reputation. The timing of the novel's appearance in the United States and the United Kingdom was serendipitous, given reports out of China revealing the prevalence of adulterated pork sold on the open market, recently resulting in the pollution of rivers by more than 10,000 dead, toxic pigs. Mo Yan seems almost prescient in calling attention to the cavalier greed of those who will descend to any moral and ethical depth in order to make money via predatory capitalism.

The latest of Mo Yan's novels to be published in English is a terrifying work, 檀香刑 (*Sandalwood Death*), a work in which the now internationally acclaimed author shows both the truly dark side of recent Chinese history (precisely, the Boxer Rebellion of more than a century ago), and, however fragilely, the possibility of love among witnesses to unbearable brutality. Set, as always, in his native Shandong Province, the novel centers on an executioner and the gruesome devices used to torture and dispatch individuals who have offended the court, the foreign invaders, or the rich and powerful. The violence in this and much of Mo Yan's oeuvre is both a representation of twentieth-century realities and a metaphor for the historiographic process. Mo Yan sees not only darkness and evil in China's past, but, like so many of his contemporaries, is wary of the all-powerful "great men" and agonizes over the degenerative effects China's past has produced in her present. A land of heroes has become, in the words of our blind balladeer of *The Garlic Ballads*, home to "flaccid, weak-kneed cowards with furrowed brows and scowling faces" (141).

Sadly, the initial media focus on Mo Yan's selection as the 2012 Nobel Prize in Literature laureate had nothing to do with what actually made him the laureate. The announcement was met with shrill outbursts that his selection was a "catastrophe" by Romanian Nobelist Herta Müller, with the urging of expatriate Chinese dissident

Liao Yiwu, reckless remarks that he is a government "patsy" by Salman Rushdie, who likely has never read a word the Nobelist has written, the sophistry of otherwise rational individuals such as China scholar Perry Link, and outsider calls from the likes of the controversial artist Ai Weiwei for Mo Yan to use his newly won leverage as a soapbox to demand change. He was criticized for belonging to the eighty-million-member Communist Party; for his membership in the Writers Association, a government-sponsored guild to which virtually all writers in China belong, and in which he holds an honorary vice-chairmanship; and for only once asking for Liu Xiaobo's release from prison, equating the drumbeat of calls for him to do more, and more, and more with the forced repetition of slogans during the Cultural Revolution. In the weeks and months since, the situation has changed dramatically, in part owing to the excellent reviews of his latest offerings in translation. Virtually every reviewer has referred to the controversy, more or less in passing, and then has concluded that Mo Yan was indeed a worthy recipient of the literature prize. The verbal histrionics and intemperate remarks in op-eds, long articles, and a host of published cheap shots are a reminder that it sometimes makes sense to get the facts before popping off.

In one of the more bizarre criticisms, Mo Yan's muckraking roman à clef 蛙 (Frog), an exposé of the costs of the Party's family planning (计划生育) or One-child policy, has been attacked for its appearance at a time when the Party is reexamining the issue, as opposed to, say, a decade ago, when it was fully sanctioned. Of course, he could not have published the novel a decade ago, when the policy was still in effect; but the more important issue is Mo Yan's critique here not of misguided individuals or the Chinese character but of the formers of national policy, past or present. What critics have called cowardice or accommodation is in reality a bold act.

Mo Yan has been reviled most severely for his views of and statements on censorship (see Chen). For him, censorship, including self-censorship, is part of the system under which he and his fellow writers work and is accepted as such by most, to a greater or lesser extent, so long as it serves the country, and not just bureaucrats and their ilk, and is not capriciously implemented. That may be a hard pill for some in the West to swallow, but not necessarily by writers within China's borders. While there are proscriptions against openly defaming the Party, advocating the overthrow of the government, or calling for Taiwanese or Tibetan independence, writers need not worry about heavy-fisted censors redacting their texts in accord with perceived heresies. Mo Yan writes in a gray area in which he avoids direct, overt criticism of established institutions and policies while revealing social pathologies and what he characterizes as a devolution of attitudes and behaviors in the Party. Although not alone in this, he does it better than most. In the end, he is unapologetic in regard to his stances and statements and insists: "Everything I have to say is in my writing" (Mo Yan, "Nobel Lecture" <http://www.nobelprize.org/nobel_prizes/literature/laureates/2012/yan-lecture_en.html>).

With the indulgence of my readers, I shift my attention away from Mo Yan the novelist writing in Chinese for a moment and back toward those of us who deal with him through Western eyes—you, me, and a good number of his critics. Mo Yan's work has often resonated among reviewers with Western models. García Márquez, Sterne, and Borges are frequently mentioned. Others include Pirandello, Rabelais, and, Mo Yan's favorite Western writer, William Faulkner (see Du), almost always in approbation of Mo Yan's art and seldom with the intent of holding him up to Western standards. Until John Updike, that is. In a long, characteristically articulate yet mixed review in *The New Yorker* of *Big Breasts and Wide Hips* and a second novel, *My Life as Emperor*, by Mo Yan's contemporary Su Tong, Updike, choosing not to take either work on its own terms, deplores the facts that "the Chinese novel had no Victorian heyday to teach it decorum," that Mo Yan's metaphors are "abundant and hyperactive," and that the principal characters of both novels are "immature weaklings" (87).

Normally, all I or any of my authors—and there have been more than twenty of them—ask is that they be dealt with on their own terms. No one disputes the view that the act of literary translation creates losses for readers of the translated text. For some, however, the losses in the reception of foreign literature have more to do with what the work itself is not than what it has become in a new language. That, as it turns out, appears to be Mr. Updike's stance. For him, as for other critics, these works are redeemed only when they can be viewed as sociohistorical or nakedly political texts. The "message" in these novels by mature, popular, respected novelists, for Updike, is that "bad societies offer no incentive to grow up" and that "free spirits in China are still short of enjoying free speech" (87). This is fiction as history or screed, not what one would expect from a novelist, at least a good one, much less a prize-winning one.

Much of Mo Yan's language, alluded to by the Nobel Committee as hallucinatory, is a response to the rigid, formulaic, and ideology-bound discourse that monopolized Chinese literary productions for decades in what was called socialist realism; Mo Yan uses literary language in service of his revisionist view of official Communist history and in the dissection of his own race. He is, for instance, convinced of the metaphorical power of depicting sexual acts—which domestic critics often find objectionable and is mischaracterized as gratuitous by Updike and other detractors—that permeate his fictional world. In this, Mo Yan is more rather than less representative of recent creative writing in China. It would be surprising if that were not the case, given the unremittingly violent nature of China's past century. If sex is a powerful fictional metaphor, violence serves as a powerful fictional reminder of the human capacity to inflict pain on other people. Mr. Updike is right when he characterizes Mo Yan's novel as a "stew of slaughter, torture, famine, flood, and, for the peasant masses, brutalizing overwork" (87). It is just that he sees that as something bad! To his credit, Updike reminds readers that this is translated fiction, that someone else has been involved in making it available outside of China, and if I've seemed whiningly unfair to him or slavishly devoted to the work of a Chinese novelist who has brought me enjoyment and satisfaction, if not fame and fortune, I apologize.

Now that Mo Yan's international visibility has reached new heights, the appearance of his work in many societies will certainly lead to increased attention to the translators and publishers of his work in other languages. So how does the author view the relationship with his translators? In a protracted interview given in China in 2007, published in book form as 说吧，莫言 (Speak, Mo Yan), available only in Chinese, he deals favorably with the cooperative ventures with some of his translators. In his Nobel Lecture, the only reference to his translators had to do with the title of *Life and Death Are Wearing Me Out*: "I've been told that my translators have had fits trying to render it into their languages" (<http://www.nobelprize.org/nobel_prizes/literature/laureates/2012/yan-lecture_en.html>). That was certainly true in my case, and although both the publisher and I are pleased with the title on several fronts, it must be seen as an interpretation rather than a literal translation of part of a Buddhist phrase that means something on the order of "living and dying are exhausting; desire is born of greed" (see Chi-ying Alice Wang on this and other Buddhist phrases and concepts). I think my fellow translators generally hewed more closely to the original, with less evocative results. But in a speech Mo Yan gave in 2013 to a Chinese university audience, he spoke of the author-translator relationship in greater detail. I quote at length from a translation made in China:

> At present, more and more Chinese novels are being translated into foreign languages and disseminated far and wide. This, however, touches upon a problem—the point of departure for an author: Who are writers writing for, really? Are they writing for themselves, or are they writing for their readers? If they are writing for their readers, are they writing for Chinese readers or for foreign readers? In order for a novel to be translated into a foreign language there must be a translator. In this case can't we say the writer is writing for his translator? This trend of writing for one's translator is absolutely unsupportable. Notwithstanding the fact that literature must pass through a translator's translation to reach the world, must undergo their creative efforts, the personal artistic style of an author who thinks of their translator when they are writing is bound to be cheapened, and the eloquence and impenetrability of their work is bound to be simplified for the ease of translation. Therefore, when a writer is writing, they can think of whomever they so choose, but whatever happens they shouldn't think of the translator; they can't forget anyone, but they must forget the translator. It is only when it is thus that he can write novels with his own style, with a Chinese style. (Mo Yan, "Good Literature")

Mo Yan can say that because he does not write for us the translators or us foreign readers. I suspect that, knowing no foreign language or the ins and outs of reading tastes in other countries, he wouldn't know how to do so, even if he were so inclined.

On the other side of the issue is for whom translators translate. Is it our job to please writers who do not know the language into which their translators are working, to stay as close to the original as possible? The answer, of course, is no. The author writes not for himself nor for his translator, but for his readers. And that is for whom we must translate, our readers. Normally, this is not an issue. But sometimes it is, and I have, in the past, revealed instances in which an author was displeased with some of my renderings. I made it clear then, and will do so again now, that so long as I do not err in my translation of a word, a phrase, or something longer, I am duty bound to write in such a way as to faithfully reproduce what the author meant—to be precise, my interpretation of what the author meant—and not necessarily what he wrote. A fine point, perhaps, but an important distinction.

A translator's relationship with his/her author is not always a happy one. Some writers, of course, appreciate and understand the author-translator relationship. The symbiosis between the creator and the re-creator is not well understood by readers of either text. When it is smooth, healthy, mutually rewarding, as, for instance, between Umberto Eco and his Italian translator, William Weaver, the results are exemplary. When the relationship becomes destructive, as with Jorge Luis Borges (who was a translator himself) and the US-American Norman Thomas di Giovanni, it can have a terrible outcome. I have had extraordinarily good luck with most of the novelists I work with, in particular, Mo Yan, who has proved to be supportive and generous in regard to the English translations of his works. He is well aware of the impossibility of one-to-one correspondence between Chinese and English, as well as other languages into which his work is rendered; is forthcoming in revealing obscure cultural and historical aspects of his work; and comprehends the fact that a translation can complement, not supplement, the original. Most authors are happy to place their trust in a translator's hands, for they realize that translation, in Eugene Eoyang's words, "revitalizes a work of the past and makes it part of the present," that it extends the life of a work, and that it can reveal things hidden in the original text (77).

As translators, we are encouraged by words of praise from literary figures, including Borges himself, who has written that "perhaps the translator's work is more subtle, more civilized than that of the writer: the translator clearly comes after the writer. Translation is a more advanced stage of civilization" (Borges qtd. in Wechsler 9). Or Pushkin: "The translator is a 'courier of the human spirit'" (Pushkin qtd. in Barnstone 126). Not all are so generous: in an article about Mo Yan's Nobel, Kevin Bloom wrote referring to Bashevis Singer that the latter said that "'There is no such thing as a good translator,' Singer once said, seemingly oblivious to the likelihood that his readership would have peaked in the low double digits—including friends and family—had this long-suffering literary caste refused to indulge him. 'The best translators make the worst mistakes'" (<http://www.dailymaverick.co.za/article/2012-10-12-found-in-translation-mo-yan-wins-literature-nobel#.UzA_PF7qJ9k>). Yes, the relationship between author and translator, while mutually rewarding, can be uneasy and fragile, but in the end it is the relationship that makes world literature possible and, incidentally, frees the rest of us from having to live our lives as Mo Yan.

Works Cited

Barnstone, Willis. *The Poetics of Translation: History, Theory, Practice*. New Haven: Yale UP, 1995.

Bloom, Kevin. "Found in Translation: Mo Yan Wins Literature Nobel." *daily maverick.co.za* (12 October 2012): <http://www.dailymaverick.co.za/article/2012 -10-12-found-in-translation-mo-yan-wins-literature-nobel#.UzA_PF7qJ9k>.

Chen, Thomas. "The Censorship of Mo Yan's 天堂蒜薹之歌 (*The Garlic Ballads*)." *Mo Yan in Context: Nobel Laureate and Global Storyteller*. Ed. Angelica Duran and Yuhan Huang. West Lafayette: Purdue UP, 2014. 37–49.

Du, Lanlan. "Abortion in Faulkner's *The Wild Palms* and Mo Yan's 蛙 (Frog)." *Mo Yan in Context: Nobel Laureate and Global Storyteller*. Ed. Angelica Duran and Yuhan Huang. West Lafayette: Purdue UP, 2014. 63–76.

Eoyang, Eugene. *The Transparent Eye: Reflections on Translation, Chinese Literature, and Comparative Poetics*. Honolulu: U of Hawai'i P, 1993.

Fusilier, Richard. "Facts, Allegations and Judicial Notice." *Journal of Historical Review* 3.1 (1982): 48–51.

Gibbon, Edward. *The Decline and Fall of the Roman Empire*. New York: P. F. Collier and Sons, 1900.

Hilton, Isabel. "Let a Thousand Flowers Bloom." *The Los Angeles Times Book Review* (7 April 2002): 3.

Huang, Alexa, and Angelica Duran. "Mo Yan's Work and the Politics of Literary Humor." *Mo Yan in Context: Nobel Laureate and Global Storyteller*. Ed. Angelica Duran and Yuhan Huang. West Lafayette: Purdue UP, 2014. 153–64.

James, Jamie. "Bad Boy: Why China's Most Popular Novelist Won't Go Home." *The New Yorker* (21 April 1997): 50-53.

Kakutani, Michiko. "Books of the Times: Tale of a Tibetan Clan, Told by an Idiot." *The New York Times* (19 April 2002): <http://www.nytimes.com/2002/04/19 /movies/books-of-the-times-tale-of-a-tibetan-clan-told-by-an-idiot.html>.

Mo Yan. *Big Breasts and Wide Hips*. Trans. Howard Goldblatt. New York: Arcade, 2004.

Mo Yan. *The Garlic Ballads*. Trans. Howard Goldblatt. New York: Viking, 1995.

Mo Yan (莫言). "好的文学应该让人看到自己" ("Good Literature Should Allow One to See Oneself"). Lecture. Beijing: Beijing Normal U, 2013.

Mo Yan. *Life and Death are Wearing Me Out*. Trans. Howard Goldblatt. New York: Arcade, 2008.

Mo Yan. "Nobel Lecture: A Storyteller." Trans. Howard Goldblatt. *nobelprize .org* (2012): <http://www.nobelprize.org/nobel_prizes/literature/laureates/2012 /yan-lecture_en.html>.

Mo Yan. *POW!* Trans. Howard Goldblatt. London: Seagull, 2012.

Mo Yan. *Red Sorghum*. Trans. Howard Goldblatt. New York: Penguin, 1994.

Mo Yan. *The Republic of Wine*. Trans. Howard Goldblatt. New York: Penguin, 2000.

Mo Yan. *Sandalwood Death*. Trans. Howard Goldblatt. Norman: U of Oklahoma P, 2013.
Mo Yan (莫言). 说吧, 莫言 (Speak, Mo Yan). Taipei: Maitian, 2007.
Rabassa, Gregory. *If This Be Treason: Translation and Its Dyscontents. A Memoir*. New York: New Directions, 2005.
Red Sorghum (红高粱). Dir. Yimou Zhang (张艺谋). Beijing: Xi'an Film Studio, 1987.
Tan, Amy. Book cover endorsement. *The Red Sorghum*. By Mo Yan. Trans. Howard Goldblatt. New York: Penguin, 1994.
Updike, John. "Bitter Bamboo: Two Novels from China." *The New Yorker* (9 May 2005): 84-87.
Wechsler, Robert. *Performing without a Stage: The Art of Literary Translation*. North Haven: Catbird P, 1998.
The World of Translation. Ed. American Center of PEN. New York: PEN American Center, 1987.

Author's profile

Howard Goldblatt taught Chinese literature at the University of Colorado and the University of Notre Dame. He is an award-winning translator of numerous works of contemporary Chinese fiction by Huang Chunming, Alai, Mo Yan, and others. His translations contribute to giving Anglophone readers insights into contemporary Chinese fiction.

The Censorship of Mo Yan's 天堂蒜薹之歌 (*The Garlic Ballads*)

Thomas Chen

Abstract

In "The Censorship of Mo Yan's 天堂蒜薹之歌 (*The Garlic Ballads*)" Thomas Chen examines literary censorship in China by analyzing the various editions of the formerly banned novel by Mo Yan. Chen analyzes the binary of a powerless writer pitted against an all-powerful state. By comparing the various editions of *The Garlic Ballads* published in Chinese and English, Chen challenges the traditional definition of censorship and questions the boundaries of where editing ends and where censoring begins and whether there is such a thing as an uncensored original text. In our age of transnational capitalism, one must reflect critically on the fetishism of censorship and the commodification of the titillating phrase "Banned in China."

"Banned in China" is a label that sells well internationally, and the reasons are obvious: it piques the interest, sometimes prurient, of readers who want to know what is forbidden in the "Forbidden City." To those in some nations, it reaffirms the notion of a "Red China" where freedom of speech and of the press is unheard of, and it conjures up the only possible escape for Chinese writers who are censored: being read and published elsewhere (especially the Western world) through translations. The banning of Yan Lianke's 2005 为人民服务 (*Serve the People!*), a novella in which a woman and her lover desecrate Mao objects such as statuettes and *The Little Red Book* for sexual excitement, would seem to indicate that the words and images of Mao Zedong could still not be taken in vain in the twenty-first century. The absence of the works by Chinese-born French national Gao Xingjian, the 2000 Nobel Prize in Literature Laureate, in his country of origin would indicate a nationalist sensitivity that affects literary availability. So what does it exactly mean to be banned in China today? What are the actual dynamics of literary censorship in post-Mao China? And what is censorship?

In the 1990s the theorization of literary censorship was nuanced, for example, in collections edited by Robert Post and Richard Burt (*The Administration*). The debates they engendered and perspectives they presented, the most important of which revolve around the constitution of subjectivity, have not, however, been applied to contemporary Chinese literature. This lack is felt all the more acutely because of the proliferation of cases of Chinese censorship, especially internet censorship and the attention to these cases by Western news media. After winning the Nobel Prize in 2012, Mo Yan addressed the question of censorship in the Chinese edition of the *New York Times* ("Mo Yan Heads" <http://cn.nytimes.com/china/20121206/cc06moyan-press/>). He stated that he is against censorship in general while acknowledging that no conditions of total freedom or total censorship are possible because the relationship between censorship and the practice of literature is a complicated one mediated by the extent to which the writer is "free inside" ("内心是否自由") to overcome one's own political and class stance. Another part of his answer can be derived from the censorship he portrays in *The Garlic Ballads*.

The Garlic Ballads (天堂蒜薹之歌) was inspired by a historical event, 苍山蒜薹事件 (the 1987 Cangshan Garlic Incident) in Mo Yan's native province of Shandong. According to the official account by the provincial Communist Party newspaper (省委机关报) *Mass Daily* (大众日报), there was an overproduction of garlic in Cangshan County that year and, coupled with the indiscriminate fees and fines levied by the "market administration" (市场管理) that obstructed sales, the price of garlic dropped dramatically (see Wang, Dazhong <http://www.dzwww.com/2009/hrh/40/1987/200908/t20090825_5035128.htm>). On 27 May 1987, a big market day in the Cangshan County seat, "acquisition points" (收购点) stopped purchasing garlic from the farmers, who then dumped their rotting garlic in front of the county seat government building. A riot ensued: people broke into and wreaked havoc on the government offices.

The Garlic Ballads was first published in book format under the title 天堂蒜薹之歌 by the Writers' Publishing House in April 1988 (henceforth *Garlic* 1988). The novel was banned in China a year later, however, because of another "incident," the 4 June 1989 Incident of Tiananmen Square, for "its sympathetic representation of an antigovernment riot" (Kraus 132). Four years later, it was unbanned, reissued in December 1993 by Beijing Normal University Press under a different title, 愤怒的蒜薹 (henceforth *Garlic* 1993) (The Garlic of Wrath; the title is a reference to *The Grapes of Wrath* by John Steinbeck, the 1962 Nobel Prize in Literature Laureate). Meanwhile, in Taiwan a version called 天堂蒜薹之歌 appeared in 1989 (henceforth *Garlic* Taiwan 1989). However, the sequence of publications of the novel does not end there. Mo Yan wrote the novel's final (for now) version when he revised it at the end of the 1990s, and now the Chinese version again goes under the title 天堂蒜薹之歌 (*The Garlic Ballads*), published by Shanghai Literature and Arts Publishing House (henceforth *Garlic* 2009). Therefore, the analysis of the aforementioned four

Chinese-language editions of the novel helps to elucidate the impact of censorship and its relation to the text. The novel has also been translated to Dutch, French, German, Hebrew, Italian, Korean, Spanish, Swedish, among other languages, including English by Howard Goldblatt (henceforth *Garlic* U.S. 1995). I include only Chinese-language and U.S. editions because the former are in the original language of the novel and the latter has received the most global media attention.

One of the most distinctive details differentiating the various editions occurs at the very end of the novel: "Author's addendum: this book is purely fictional; if unfortunately it has similarities to a certain incident in real life, this is a random coincidence; the author does not bear responsibility for the feelings and health of those who automatically jump to conclusions" (unless indicated otherwise, all translations are mine) ("作者附记：本书纯属虚构，假如不幸与现实生活中的某个事件有相似之处，则系偶然巧合，作者不为自动对号入座者的心情和健康负责" [*Garlic* 1988, 298]). The note is followed by the dates of composition: 10 August to 15 September 1987. This supplement is found in the first three book editions of the novel: *Garlic* 1988, *Garlic* Taiwan 1989, and *Garlic* 1993. To the novel's first readers, Mo Yan's note could not help sounding tongue-in-cheek: the Cangshan Garlic Incident of 1987 had caused a stir nationwide and, especially given the dates of composition, it would not be difficult for Chinese readers to make the connection. Aside from this, Mo Yan's reference to the "feelings and health" of readers is an indirect commentary on a literary-political debate that persisted from Mao Zedong's 1942 "在延安文艺座谈会上的讲话" ("Talks at the Yan'an Conference on Literature and Art") into the 1980s: the debate on how much responsibility authors should bear for the "social effects" that their works produce, whether the authors' intentionality should be taken into account, and the traits of "healthy" literature versus "spiritual pollution" for the socialist society. We can understand Mo Yan's caution in making these allusions when the book first appeared in 1988 and when it resurfaced in Chinese bookstores in 1993 after a four-year ban. The aforementioned supplement is absent from *Garlic* U.S. 1995, and we might presume the reason to be that all the oblique references would be lost on Anglophone readers. But it is also missing from the latest Chinese edition: *Garlic* 2009 replaces it with a separate "afterword" in which Mo Yan affirms that his novel is based on the real-life Cangshan Garlic Incident, which "impelled me to put aside the family novel I was working on, and in 35 days I wrote this novel filled with indignation" (促使我放下正在创作着的家族小说，用了三十五天的时间，写出了这部义愤填膺的长篇小说" [329]).

We might be tempted at this point to make the following claim: after two decades of censorship and the author's fear of censorship, Mo Yan is brave enough or the creative environment in China has relaxed enough for him to discard the mask that the censorship apparatus made him wear and to attest to the truth. This line of thinking might lead us to call *Garlic* 2009 the authoritative text, the text unmarred by censorship. But some of us, certainly, would argue that the first edition, *Garlic* 1988, is the originary text. And there will be others, surely, who cast their vote for *Garlic* 1989. After all, how can there be free speech under the communist regime before or after the the crackdown following the 4 June 1989 Tiananmen Square Incident, (六四天安门事件)? Only in Taiwan will a Chinese author dare to speak fully his/her mind. The matter of the "uncensored original" must be kept in abeyance for the moment as we proceed to the second, and related, textual detail that deserves scrutiny. When we open up *Garlic* U.S. 1995, we are struck by a quotation placed before page one: "Novelists are forever trying to distance themselves from politics, but the novel itself closes in on politics. Novelists are so concerned with 'man's fate' that they tend to lose sight of their own fate. Therein lies their tragedy. —Josef Stalin" (*Garlic* U.S. 1995 n.p.) This epigraph is unique to this edition, but with qualifications. *Garlic* 1988 and *Garlic* Taiwan 1989 have the same quotation but attribute it as "words of a famous person" ("名人语录") and *Garlic* 1993 and *Garlic* 2009 drop it altogether. On this issue, there is, in fact, another published version of *The Garlic Ballads* that precedes all book editions. The story appeared in print in the first issue of the literary journal *October* in 1988 (十月, henceforth *Garlic October* 1988). In this new candidate for an "uncensored original," the quotation is also attributed to Stalin as it is in *Garlic* U.S. 1995.

Surely, the attribution to Stalin was too sensitive to be included in subsequent Chinese editions, and so the censor crossed out the Soviet dictator's name and replaced it with something more innocuous. But apparently this substitution was not enough for Chinese authorities. In the 1993 reissued edition the quotation is completely sublated, the author forced to voice subtly the "censored" quotation. That is why, we lament, Mo Yan can manage only this statement in the foreword to *Garlic* 1993: "I've always believed that a novel should distance itself from politics, but sometimes the novel itself closes in on politics" (我一贯认为小说还是应该离政治远些，但有时小说自己逼近了政治) [1]).

In restoring the Stalin quotation from *Garlic October* 1988, Goldblatt and/or the editors and/or the publishers at Viking Penguin and/or anyone else who played a role in producing *Garlic* U.S. 1995 must have believed that he/they were restoring the intention of a suppressed author. Imagine our shock, then, when we read in Mo Yan's "afterword" ("代后记") to *Garlic* 2009 that the quotation was a complete fabrication. Mo Yan did not have access to Stalin's papers and he simply made up the epigraph: "After the novel was published, many people asked me: When and where did Stalin say these words? How come I've searched through Stalin's Complete Works and cannot find their source? These words were spoken by Stalin, with his pipe tapping on my forehead and in all earnestness, to me alone in my dream. He hadn't time to include them in his Complete Works, which is why you won't find them there" ("小说发表后，许多人问我：这段话，是斯大林在什么时候，在什么地方说的？为什么查遍斯大林全集，也找不到出处？这段话是斯大林在我的梦中，用烟斗指点着我的额头，语重心长地单独对我说的，还没来得及往他的全集里收，因此您查不到" [*Garlic* 2009, 329]).

Outrage and accusations against the author committing "reverse censorship" on Stalin are fortunately forestalled by cooler heads, who note that in *Garlic October* 1988 the epigraph appears immediately before the text of the narrative begins. The quotation, thus, is part of the fiction. Perhaps we will then begin to consider explanations other than censorship for the transformations of this quotation across the various Chinese editions, such as lessening misunderstanding, which is what I believe Mo Yan is doing in the aforementioned excerpt from *Garlic* 2009's afterword, where, it should be noted, the quotation also appears in full. But is this the final verdict? No: where editing and revising end and where censoring begins is not always easy to pinpoint on the spectrum of writing. And now my interrogation has a new target: by placing the Stalin quotation four pages before the text of the narrative, what have Goldblatt and/or the editors and/or the publishers at Viking Penguin and/or anyone else who played a role in producing *Garlic* U.S. 1995 actually done with the intentions of the author? Has the publishing of *Garlic* U.S. 1995 under the triumphant red, white, and blue flag of freedom of speech and of the press allowed the censored author to say things he could not say in Red China? Or a better question that dismisses authorial intention and a still unthawed Cold War mentality altogether: what new product have they created out of Mo Yan's novel? Could this be an instance of the "fetishism of censorship" that, as Richard Burt has astutely remarked, "involves the commodification of small differences meant to increase the text's value?" (29).

The differences of *Garlic* U.S. 1995 overflow the pages themselves. The front flap of the dust jacket of *Garlic* U.S. 1995 states that Mo Yan's novel was a "visceral tale of brutal beauty, one so inflammatory that it was banned in his homeland." When *Garlic* U.S. 1995 came out, *Garlic* 1993 had been unbanned for two years. But the past participle "banned" allows for this semantic loophole. Of course, one can also defend Viking Penguin by pointing out that *Garlic* 1988 was still banned in 1995: it was *Garlic* 1993 that had been unbanned. But once we start suspecting *Garlic* 1993's faithfulness to an urtext, can we exempt *Garlic* U.S. 1995 from such doubts? In the end, however, can we fault the U.S. publisher for not making fine distinctions in promoting the novel? Complexity does not fit within a book blurb: what sells are clear oppositions such as propagandistic and subversive, censored and free.

A comparison of a section from two editions of the novel complicates the opposition between being subversive and being tamed. Each chapter in the book begins with a ballad sung by the blind Zhang Kou. His ballads express both sympathy for the plight of the garlic farmers and criticism of how authorities exacerbate their conditions. The following are two versions of what he sings at the beginning of Chapter 16: "'Arrest me if that's what you want ... / Someone read the Criminal Code aloud for me— / Blind lawbreakers get lenient treatment— / I won't shut my mouth just because you put me in jail'—'You don't shut your mouth, I'll seal it for you!' a policeman in white said furiously, raising the two-foot-long electric prod in his hand.

The end of the prod crackled while spitting green sparks. 'I'll seal your mouth with electricity!' The policeman stabbed Zhang Kou's mouth with the electric prod. The incident occurred in a tiny lane around the corner from the county government compound on the twenty-ninth of May, 1987" ("'你要抓你就抓 / 俺听人念过 '刑法' / 瞎眼人有罪不重罚 / 进了监牢俺也不会闭住嘴巴' —'你不闭住嘴巴，俺给你封住嘴巴！'一位白衣警察怒气冲冲地说着，把手中二尺长的电警棍据起来。电警棍头上'喇喇'地喷着绿色的火花。'俺用电封住你的嘴巴！' '警察把电警棍戳在张扣嘴上。这是一九八七年五月二十九日，发生在县府拐角小胡同里的事情" (*Garlic* 1988, 232); and "Arrest me if that's what you want ... / Someone read the Criminal Code aloud for me— / Blind lawbreakers get lenient treatment— / I won't shut my mouth just because you put me in jail ... —from a ballad by Zhang Kou sung after being touched on the mouth with a policeman's electric prod. The incident occurred in a tiny lane around the corner from the county government compound on the twenty-ninth of May, 1987" (*Garlic* U.S. 1995, 221). Without looking at the citations, one would surmise that the second version has been censored. Who else but nervous censors would soften Zhang Kou's getting stabbed in the mouth with an electric prod that shoots green sparks to "being touched on the mouth with a policeman's electric prod"? Imagine our disbelief, then, when we note that the second version is found—and found only—in *Garlic* U.S. 1995: all Chinese editions have the first version. How do we explain this? One could expect *Garlic* Taiwan 1989 to contain this passage and even *Garlic* 2009 because of its distance of twenty years from the Tiananmen and Cangshan Garlic Incidents. But how does one account for the presence of this graphic dramatization of censorship in *Garlic October* 1988, *Garlic* 1988, and *Garlic* 1993? Why was this dramatization of censorship not censored in China? And why is it absent—and absent only—from *Garlic* U.S. 1995? Could the omission or rather the substitution be an editorial choice either by the translator, the editor, or the publisher? Even if any one of these were to provide an answer, it still leads to the question of where does editing end and censoring begin?

A dramatization of censorship occurs at the beginning of Chapter 19 as well.

County Chief, your hands aren't big enough to cover heaven! / Party Secretary, your power isn't as weighty as the mountain! / You cannot hide the ugly events of Paradise County, / For the people have eyes— / —At this point in Zhang Kou's ballad a ferocious policeman jumped to his feet and cursed, "You blind bastard, you're the prime suspect in the Paradise County garlic case! We've got you dead to rights!" He kicked Zhang Kou in the mouth, cutting off the final note. Blood spurted from Zhang Kou's mouth; several white teeth hit the floor. Zhang Kou climbed back into the chair; the policeman sent him back to the floor with another kick. Garbled speech spilled from Zhang Kou's lips, scaring the interrogators, even though they hadn't understood a word of it. The chief interrogator stopped the policeman from kicking him a third time, as another man bent down and sealed Zhang Kou's mouth with a plastic gag. (*Garlic* U.S. 1995, 259)

县长你手大捂不住天 / 书记你权重重不过山 / 天堂县丑事遮不住 / 人民群众都有眼— / —张扣唱到这里，一位虎背熊腰的警察忍无可忍地跳起来，骂道："瞎种，你是'天堂蒜薹案'的头号罪犯。老子不信制服不了你！"他跳起来，一脚踢中了张扣的嘴巴。张扣的歌声戛然而止。一股血水喷出来，几颗雪白的牙齿落在了审讯室的地板上。张扣摸索着坐起来，警察又是一脚，将他放平在地。他的嘴里依然呜噜着，那是一些虽然模糊不清但令警察们胆战心惊的话。警察抬脚还要踢时，被一位政府官员止住了。一个戴眼镜的警察蹲在张扣身边，用透明的胶纸牢牢地封住了他嘴巴。(*Garlic* 2009, 286-87)

The previous passage appears in all editions of the novel starting with *Garlic* 1993. While the ballad is the same as the one in *Garlic October* 1988, *Garlic* 1988, and *Garlic* Taiwan 1989, it is described only as the "ballad excerpt from Zhang Kou's interrogation" (张扣受审时歌唱断章) in *Garlic* 1988 (272). Could we then deduce that the depiction of police brutality was too sensitive for the China of 1988 and, apparently, for *Garlic* Taiwan 1989, given Taiwan's own recent history of bloody suppressions under Kuomintang martial law? Could we surmise that only starting in 1993 was the creative environment relaxed enough for this passage to pass censorship? But then we wonder why kicking and sealing Zhang Kou's mouth crosses the fine line of censorship, while jamming an electric prod in his mouth does not. Could the two different ballad descriptions be a matter of revision, Mo Yan editing the passage in order to make it better art, rather than a case of suppression or transgression? After all, accusing the county chief and party secretary of obstructing justice, present from the first edition, is not exactly toadying to officialdom.

Further examination of other details of the previous passage problematizes the definition of censorship. In *Garlic* U.S. 1995, only police interrogators are in the room with Zhang Kou, and it is inside an interrogation room that the brutality takes places—although this is not stated clearly in the translation—and it is the "chief interrogator" who stops a policeman from kicking Zhang Kou a third time. In the Chinese version, however, the man is described as a "政府官员" ("government official"). The designation is significant because the interrogation and beating are not conducted by police-toughs but presided over by an official from an unspecified level of government. If such a substitution of "chief interrogator" for "government official" occurred between two Chinese editions, we would cry foul at censorship. But surely Goldblatt is not a censor, and we attribute the modification instead to a choice of translation. And the differences do not end there: the Chinese text is not, as Goldblatt translates it, "another man bent down and sealed Zhang Kou's mouth with a plastic gag" (259). A more literal translation would be "a policeman wearing glasses squatted next to Zhang Kou and with transparent tape firmly sealed his mouth." Might Mo Yan be actually suggesting, in this dramatization of censorship, that "censorship" is not always so obtrusive as a "plastic gag?" Perhaps he is pointing out that censorship might not always take the blatantly violent forms of bans but that it might be more subtle and insidious in its operations, as barely noticeable as transparent tape? These are nuances of meaning unavailable from *Garlic* U.S. 1995, where censorship is the thug who knocks books off bookshelves and kicks writers in the mouth.

Goldblatt is a translator within the system of the U.S. and the global publishing industry, and translation is a noble task, one which (so far) no Chinese (national) specialist has taken up in terms of Mo Yan's work. But if we are to use the traditional definition of censorship as "an act of external interference with the internally generated communicative, expressive, artistic, or informational preferences of some agent" (Schauer 150), then we necessarily have to group the task of translation into this demonized category. Criticism itself also becomes suspect. If we follow this definition, then "censorship was structurally complicit with what is often taken to be its opposite—namely, criticism" (Burt, "(Un)Censoring" 22). On the other hand, are we ready to limit censorship to acts of only the "government," however broadly the government may be construed? Then we would have to do away with Banned Books Week, that cherished celebration since 1982 on U.S. liberals' calendars, for doubtlessly the perpetrators are stodgy educators and backwater parents removing classics like *Huckleberry Finn* or *Harry Potter* from grade school libraries.

Perhaps limiting the discussion to texts in China can prove helpful. Can we centralize Chinese censorship upon the Party State? Yes, some would argue: although the writer acts as his or her own self-censor and the publishing house editor acts as a censor, these practices of censorship can ultimately be traced to one authoritarian Power. But even in a one-party state, can we locate Power in a center whether that center be depicted as the President or the President + the Premier or the Politburo Standing Committee or, since we are talking about Power over cultural production, the PSC + Judiciary + Ministry of Public Security + Ministry of Culture + Ministry for Information Security + Central Propaganda Department + State Administration of Press, Publication, Radio, Film and Television? If we have trouble describing Power within some center, however expansive or amorphous that center may be, what can we say about the Power to censor and about censorship? Studies of censorship in contemporary Chinese literature would do well to heed Judith Butler's call that "descriptions of censorship presuppose a more general theory of the subject of power" (247). Our subjectivities are constituted not prior to power (including censorious power) but through power. There is no preformed subject in which censorship intervenes from the outside.

We need to extend our dissection of censorship beyond a Foucauldian analytics of the anatomy of power. In the age of transnational capitalism, suppressed speech has much currency in the global economy. All industry executives know how well subversion in the East (Near or Far) sells in the West. Who is not curious about *Reading Lolita in Tehran* (2003), which became a #1 *New York Times* bestseller? More to the point, *Shanghai Baby* (2001) (上海宝贝 [1999]) was an "international bestseller" (front cover) and was "banned and burned in China" (back cover). "Free speech" and "censorship" lose their cachet and their respective marketability if they are not labeled and divided. The fetishism of censorship is doubly profitable: only in the West can a free work be produced and only in the West can the original or the whole of a work banned or censored elsewhere be purchased. The more one scrutinizes the intricacies of censorship in a global context, the more one can readily see the logic of Burt's claim that "it operated in terms of complicity and collaboration between censors, authors, and critics rather than in terms of radical oppositions between dumb censors and intelligent literary writers" (Burt, "(Un)Censoring" 21).

In the foreword to the reissued edition of the novel after a four-year ban, *Garlic* 1993, Mo Yan calls attention to censorship: "Because I wrote this book, some people in a certain county got somebody to send me word that, if I dare step foot on their territory, they will ... I took much exception to this" ("因为写了这本书，某县的一些人托人带话给我，说我只要敢踏上他们的地盘，他们就要 ... 我听了很不以为然" [1]). Here we see new players in the censorship game: not a Party fearful of losing its "monopoly on power," not a publisher fearful of getting its ISBNs revoked, but, presumably, some local officials (and their hired thugs) who did not appreciate Mo Yan's portrayal of the incident in Cangshan County. And presumably the threat did not stop and leave the rest to Mo Yan's imagination. Mo Yan, however, left the rest to readers' imagination. There is no need for the threat to be spelled out, especially after the Chinese artist Ai Weiwei's 1990 visual images of police brutality for his outspokenness, including "Brain Inflation" (which Ai is careful to distinguish as atypical). The threat, a form of censorship, in Mo Yan's retelling to readers becomes also a dramatization of censorship. He needs not and, it is implied, dares not specify "some people," "a certain county," and "somebody," and his ellipsis points to his suffering of elision.

The major dramatization of censorship, however, occurs within the narrative of the novel itself, although again not in all of its editions. In *Garlic* U.S. 1995, one comes across a scene in the final chapter that is not found in the earlier editions: the blind minstrel Zhang Kou on a side street by the county government office building, is singing this time about censorship: "The common folk have a bellyful of grievances, but they dare not let them out. For the moment they open their mouths, electric prods close them fast" [*Garlic* U.S. 1995, 274]) ("老百姓满腹冤恨不敢说话，一开口就给咱戳上电棍" [*Garlic* 2009, 303]). Several policemen approach him and warn him once again: "'No more songs about garlic, do you hear me? Which do you think will give out first, your mouth or the electric prod?'" (*Garlic* U.S. 1995, 277) ("'记住，唱什么都可以，就是不要唱天堂蒜薹之歌。是你的嘴硬还是电棍硬?'") [*Garlic* 2009, 306]). After the policemen leave, Zhang Kou shouts: "'You black-hearted hyenas, do you really think you can shut me up so easily? Sixty-six years is long enough for any man to live!'" (*Garlic* 1995, 278) ("'你们这些人面兽心的畜生，想封了我的嘴？！我张扣活了六十六岁，早就活够了'" [*Garlic* 2009, 307]). He continues to sing the garlic ballads. Several days later, his body is found in the side street, his mouth stuffed with mud.

The provenance of this scene, as well as the rest of the chapter, is a bit of a puzzle until we learn from the "Translator's Note" following the end of *Garlic* U.S. 1995 that "Parts of Chapter Nineteen and all of Chapter Twenty have been revised, in conjunction with the author" (287). We might then suppose that this dramatization of censorship, along with the martyring of Zhang Kou, was much too subversive either for the Chinese censor or for pre-1995 Mo Yan. That is why the scene appears only in the U.S. edition and then in the revised edition of *Garlic* 2009: the creative atmosphere relaxed gradually in China only after 1993. Yes, the various Chinese editions of the novel are the results of negotiations of what could and could not be published at particular times in the Chinese political or literary culture. But there may be another sense in which "negotiations" is apt. Could we see in the final chapter's dramatization of censorship, which appears in print for the first time in the U.S. translated edition, a negotiation—with all the business connotations of the term—through which the author, a writer in reformed China who no longer under state patronage needs to fend for himself in the globalized economy—wins a contract with Viking Penguin? Could we say that the depiction of the singer silenced forever was not so much suppressed by an authoritarian government as inspired by the Anglophone, primarily U.S., market? Is Zhang Kou the easily consumable symbol of the Chinese artist-cum-victim exercising his would-be First Amendment rights only to be squashed by a repressive regime? Like Mo Yan's *Garlic Ballads*, Zhang Kou's garlic ballads were "banned in his homeland."

We can answer yes or no or maybe, but one thing is certain: Mo Yan himself is a player and sometimes also a playwright of the drama of censorship (see He). The author ends the novel—or rather, all editions of the novel save one—with newspaper coverage of the garlic incident from the fictional *Masses Daily* (群众日报; my translation is meant to mimic the real-life *Mass Daily* [大众日报]), comprised of a news story, a commentary, and an editorial. It is a thinly veiled fiction. The title of the news story from *Masses Daily* reads: "Serious bureaucracy and dereliction of duty brought about consequences. Those mainly responsible for the Tiantang 'Garlic Incident' dealt with severely" ("严重官僚主义和工作失职酿成恶果 天堂蒜薹事件"主要责任者受到严肃处理" [*Garlic* 2009, 318]) with the lead sentence "CCP's Cangtian municipal committee's decision: discharge Tiantang county committee Party vice-secretary Zhong Weimin from his post, suspend and investigate county committee Party secretary Ji Nancheng; the provincial Party committee and the provincial government hereby announce to the entire province" ("中共苍天市委决定：撤销仲为民天堂县委副书记职务，县委书记纪南城停职检查；省委、省政府就此通报全省" [*Garlic* 2009, 318]).

And this is the official account of the Cangshan Garlic Incident from *Mass Daily*: "CCP's Linyi prefectural committee deals severely with those mainly responsible for the Cangshan 'Garlic Incident' brought about by serious bureaucracy and dereliction of duty: discharges Cangshan county committee Party vice-secretary Li

Changcun from his post and recommends his dismissal as county commissioner; suspends and investigates county committee Party secretary Yang Guosheng. The Shandong provincial Party committee and provincial government hereby announce to the entire province" ("中共临沂地委对由于严重官僚主义、工作失职酿成苍山"蒜薹事件"的主要责任者给予严肃处理：撤销李常存苍山县委副书记职务，并建议撤销其县长职务；县委书记杨国胜停职检查。山东省委、省政府就此通报全省" [Wang, Dazhong, http://www.dzwww.com/2009/hrh/40/1987/200908/t20090825_5035128.htm>]). Further, in the first three editions of the novel—*Garlic* October 1988, *Garlic* 1988, *Garlic* Taiwan 1989—it is Zhang Kou who hands the newspaper to the "author." The following is an excerpt of Zhang Kou's song that begins the last chapter of the first three editions: "If you ask the cause behind this case / Let me first smoke a cigarette of yours / After smoking I still won't talk / But give you a copy of *Masses Daily* for you to read—ballad excerpt sung to this book's author by the blind Zhang Kou" ("要问这案缘和由 / 先让俺抽您一支高级烟 / 抽了香烟俺也不开口 / 送一张《群众日报》您自己看—瞎子张扣对本书作者演唱片段 [*Garlic* 1988, 287]). In the first three editions, which do not have the scene of Zhang Kou's martyrdom, the blind singer becomes cautious at the end. He is censored and by ending his novel with the official newspaper account of the Garlic Incident, Mo Yan implies that this version will be the one preserved in the historical archives. His novel, on the other hand, against all odds of censorship, is the only site of the counterarchive that preserves the blind singer's songs.

There is a slight but important modification to the aforementioned excerpt in *Garlic* 1993. The lyrics are the same, but now the ballad is an "excerpt sung to this book's author by the blind Zhang Kou's disciple" ("瞎子张扣的徒弟对本书作者演唱片段" [*Garlic* 1993, 265]). In this edition, we see the hint of his eventual transition from circumspect cigarette mooch to martyr of the later editions. The cowardly disciple also poses no competition to Mo Yan's monopoly on the counternarrative. The newspaper chapter is the culmination of Mo Yan's novel. For the previous 200,000 characters (or nearly three hundred pages in *Garlic* U.S. 1995), Mo Yan has been singing of the garlic farmers, their toil and sweat in the fields, the consolation of a bumper harvest, and the long distance they have to trek to bring their garlic to the acquisition points only to be fined and stymied by officials who could not care less about them or their garlic rotting in the summer heat until their indignation catches fire, raging through the county government offices. Juxtapose this story with the formulaic, whitewashed, ideologically paralyzed account in the official newspaper, and one can easily see Mo Yan's design. Both the official corruption and the very language of officialdom are excoriated, its distance from the language and reality of "the masses" condemned. In the context of the work as a whole, the newspaper coverage, far from being a kowtow to the authorities at the end of the novel, functions to foreground the Chinese government's failure to represent, linguistically and otherwise, the people.

However, the entire *Masses Daily* chapter is missing from one edition of the novel: *Garlic* U.S. 1995. Why? Was it a matter of space? Out of consideration for the Anglophone, primarily U.S., reading public? The irony of ending a tale of love and injustice with three news articles in the stilted, convoluted language of Party ideology might go over the heads of a U.S. audience, might it not? It might not, but then the bigger question is: is this omission a form of censorship, too? David Damrosch is correct about the mediation that occurs with translation: "To use translations means to accept the reality that texts come to us mediated by existing frameworks of reception and interpretation. We necessarily work in collaboration with others who have shaped what we read and how we read" (295). But does "mediation" soften the actual import of the process a bit too much? If an editor dumbs down a foreign work for Anglophone consumers because they would not appreciate its nuances of effect or meaning, is this censorship that sharply affects global readers? Where does editing end and censoring begin?

Note

Thomas Chen gratefully acknowledges Richard Curt Kraus for assistance with research. This chapter is dedicated to the memory of Michael Henry Heim: humble translator, devoted teacher, ceaseless inspiration.

Works Cited

Burt, Richard. "(Un)Censoring in Detail: The Fetish of Censorship in the Early Modern Past and the Postmodern Present." *Censorship and Silencing: Practices of Cultural Regulation*. Ed. Robert C. Post. Los Angeles: The Getty Research Institute, 1998. 17–41.

Burt, Richard, ed. *The Administration of Aesthetics: Censorship, Political Criticism, and the Public Sphere*. Minneapolis: U Minnesota P, 1994.

Butler, Judith. "Ruled Out: Vocabularies of the Censor." *Censorship and Silencing: Practices of Cultural Regulation*. Ed. Robert C. Post. Los Angeles: Getty Research Institute, 1998. 247–259.

Damrosch, David. *What Is World Literature?* Princeton: Princeton UP, 2003.

Dazhong wang (大众网). "苍山县发生蒜薹事件" ("The Garlic Incident Breaks Out in Cangshan"). *Mass Daily* (23 December 1986): <http://www.dzwww.com/2009/hrh/40/1987/200908/t20090825_5035128.htm>.

He, Chengzhou. "Rural Chineseness, Mo Yan, and World Literature." *Mo Yan in Context: Nobel Laureate and Global Storyteller*. Ed. Angelica Duran and Yuhan Huang. West Lafayette: Purdue UP, 2014. 77–90.

Kraus, Richard Curt. *The Party and the Arty in China: The New Politics of Culture*. Lanham: Rowman & Littlefield, 2004.

Mao, Zedong. *Mao Zedong's "Talks at the Yan'an Conference on Literature and Art": A Translation of the 1943 Text with Commentary*. Trans. Bonnie S. McDougall. Ann Arbor: The U of Michigan P, 1980.

Mo Yan (莫言). 天堂蒜薹之歌 (*The Garlic Ballads*). *October* 1 (1988): 135–216.
Mo Yan (莫言). 天堂蒜薹之歌 (*The Garlic Ballads*). Beijing: Zuojia chubanshe, 1988.
Mo Yan (莫言). 天堂蒜薹之歌 (*The Garlic Ballads*). Taipei: Hung-fan, 1989.
Mo Yan (莫言). 愤怒的蒜薹 (*The Garlic Ballads*). Beijing: Beijing shifan daxue chubanshe, 1993.
Mo Yan. *The Garlic Ballads*. Trans. Howard Goldblatt. New York: Viking, 1995.
Mo Yan (莫言). 天堂蒜薹之歌 (*The Garlic Ballads*). Shanghai: Shanghai wenyi chubanshe, 2009.
"Mo Yan Heads to Sweden for the Awards Ceremony, Avoids Discussing Xiaobo Liu" ("莫言赴瑞典领奖避谈刘晓波"). *cn.nytimes.com* (2012): <http://cn.nytimes.com/china/20121206/cc06moyanpress/>.
Post, Robert C., ed. *Censorship and Silencing: Practices of Cultural Regulation*. Los Angeles: The Getty Research Institute, 1998.
Schauer, Frederick. "The Ontology of Censorship." *Censorship and Silencing: Practices of Cultural Regulation*. Ed. Robert C. Post. Los Angeles: The Getty Research Institute, 1998. 147–68.
Yan, Lianke. *Serve the People!* Trans. Julia Lovell. London: Constable, 2007.

Author's profile

Thomas Chen is working toward his PhD in comparative literature at the University of California–Los Angeles. His interests in scholarship include modern and contemporary Chinese-language literature and film. His publications include "Ridiculing the Golden Age: Subversive Undertones in Yan Lianke's *Happy*" (*CLT: Chinese Literature Today* [2011]) and "An Italian Bicycle in the People's Republic: Minor Transnationalism and the Chinese Translation of *Ladri di biciclette/Bicycle Thieves*" (*Journal of Italian Cinema & Media Studies* [2014]).

Representations of "China" and "Japan" in Mo Yan's, Hayashi's, and Naruse's Texts

Noriko J. Horiguchi

Abstract

In "Representations of 'China' and 'Japan' in Mo Yan's, Hayashi's, and Naruse's Texts" Noriko J. Horiguchi discusses the narration of displacements and memory in the context of subjectivity and Japanese imperialism. Horiguchi's analysis of Mo Yan's, Fumiko Hayashi's, and Mikio Naruse's texts is located in the perspective of Japanese imperialism, and Horiguchi demonstrates the paradox of individuals' stories which construct their subjectivity that simultaneously resists and recreates perspectives of empire and its doings. Horiguchi's analysis provides a regional (Asian) contextualization of Mo Yan's, Hayashi's, and Naruse's texts in a perspective that may help to consider literary settings more sensitively and gain particular regional context as well. Moreover, Asians and others around the globe, thus, may gain a deeper appreciation and perhaps better tools for dealing with the continuing battles—verbal and physical—over disputed Asian territories which may otherwise be viewed as negligible.

Mo Yan (1955–) and the Japanese woman author Fumiko Hayashi (1904–1951) may seem to share little in common besides their callings as writers. Their lives and texts, however, intersect in several ways. Both Mo Yan and Hayashi come from lower socioeconomic strata: Mo Yan from a peasant family and Hayashi from a family of peddlers. In addition, their formal education was short or irregular: Mo Yan's formal schooling was interrupted in the fifth grade until the end of his military service, and Hayashi's formal education was often interrupted owing to her parents' transient lifestyle. There are also similarities in their adulthoods: Mo Yan was assigned to a temporary position at a factory and subsequently joined the army, and Hayashi worked in factories and served in the Japanese army as a war reporter in the late 1930s. Further, Mo Yan's and Hayashi's texts are related thematically. Place is a major motif in Mo Yan's works, most of which are set in the Eastern coastal Shandong Province. This setting acts as a stable geographical locus within which chaotic personal and national dramas occur and bears the traces of change. In *Red Sorghum*, Mo Yan depicts a family's struggles in three generations, first as distillery owners making sorghum wine and then as resistance fighters during the second Sino-Japanese War (1937-45). The narrator starts the novel with a strong attachment to the land: "I had learned to love Northeast Gaomi Township, easily the most beautiful and most repulsive, most unusual and most common, most sacred and most corrupt, most heroic and most bastardly, hardest drinking and hardest loving place in the world" (4). In *Big Breasts and Wide Hips*, Mo Yan opens his narrative on the eve of the Sino-Japanese War and begins its chronology around the time of the Boxer Rebellion (1899-1901), both of which call attention to large-scale episodes related to land as national space. Mo Yan sharpens his focus on the dynamism of place in the final section of *Big Breasts and Wide Hips*, when the protagonist, Shangguan Jintong, returns to his hometown of "Dalan, the capital of Northeast Gaomi Township" in the 1980s, after his fifteen-year imprisonment (457): "His eye caught a new line of houses on the northern bank of the river, and by a new concrete bridge not far from the old stone one ... The township government moved its offices and the school away, and the old Sima family compound had been taken over by Big Gold Tooth" (467). He is keenly aware of even minor changes in the landscape of his childhood and young adulthood.

While much is made of Mo Yan's fixation on his fictionalized home-township, commentary on the place's history usually centers, and rightly so, on its status as a cultural center for Confucianism, Taoism, and Chinese Buddhism. In China's more recent past and perhaps more at the fore of the contemporary Chinese population's considerations is the role of the Shandong Province as Japanese territory from 1919 to 1921 then 1937 to 1945. That area of Chinese land comprised part of what the Japanese call 外地 (*gaichi*), the outer territories of Japan. Relevant here is that setting ties intimately with another important theme in the works of Mo Yan and Hayashi, namely gender and specifically women's roles. Shelley W. Chan points out that Mo Yan focuses on "minor figures" who wander through at the bottom and periphery of society. These characters appear to challenge political orthodoxy and free themselves from "ideological dogma within a highly politicized grand narrative" (Chan 19). Hayashi's writing has also been read as a personal and apolitical depiction of women at the socioeconomic margin: "Hayashi's fictional world was 'of the people' [民衆的] (*minshûteki*), but not from a sense of ideological commitment or political correctness. Hayashi painted her portraits small: descriptive depictions of everyday life [庶民の生活] (*shomin no seikatsu*)" (Ericson 88).

And yet, both authors wrote political allegory late in their careers. Mo Yan engages in historical dialogues and reconstructs memory in highly imaginative ways. *Red Sorghum* and *Big Breasts and Wide Hips* merge family histories and modern Chinese national history (Chan 19). In *Big Breasts*, nationalism is exemplified in the characters' struggle under the atrocious conditions against Japanese aggression during the second Sino-Japanese War. The narrator, Shangguan Jintong, suffers violent death at the hands of the Japanese, and "granddad" and "grandma" engage in a guerrilla attack resulting in the annihilation of the Japanese invaders. As David Der-wei Wang explains, "all the morally perfect characteristics of the Chinese nation and tradition" in Mo Yan's texts seem to lie in mothers (492). Although Mo Yan focuses on male characters and male narrators (some chapters in *Big Breasts and Wide Hips* being exceptions), mothers and grandmothers are of extreme importance as figures of power. Mo Yan calls attention to his celebration of femininity in *Big Breasts and Wide Hips* by dedicating the work to his mother and praising mother figures: "Readers often ask after finishing this book, 'is the mother in the book the author's mother?' I am positive of the answer, 'yes. It is my mum, and I also hope that it is also your mum. The mother in the book has endured unthinkable pains, worked hard in the most difficult times and has managed to live on. She extends her kindness to those who are in need, and cherishes life. These qualities are exactly those of our mothers'" (see Mo Yan in Kong, Shi, Lu 32).

Hayashi and her characters belong to the generation of Mo Yan's grandmother. Like her literary characters, she participated in the discourse that both resisted and reproduced the Japanese empire, and she narrates stories of women who move through, occupy, and re-create political spaces in the context of Japan's imperial competition with the West. The Japanese empire invaded vast regions of Japan's neighboring nations, including China, encompassed them into a modern capitalist system, and transformed the lives and views of the colonized people. This empire building also transformed the lives and views of the Japanese, and Hayashi provides some views from the perspective of a Japanese woman. The realization that a woman can be an aggressor while also being a victim of the same system is driven home in Hayashi's texts: although they live at the economic margin of society and outside the institutionalized womanhood of Japan, they participate in the state's central discourse that contributed to the Japanese empire's colonization of its neighboring nations.

naichi (内地 [homeland]) in Hayashi's *Diary of a Vagabond*

In her 1927 novel 放浪記 (Diary of a Vagabond, first serialized from 1928 to 1930 in the journal 女人芸術 [nyonin geijutsu])—translated in part in 1997 by Joan E. Ericson as *Be a Woman: Hayashi Fumiko and Modern Japanese Women's Literature*—Hayashi suggests that her heroine constructs her subjectivity by identifying with the decentralized, unstable, and disjunctive home and native place, rather than the centralized, stable, and united empire of Japan. The heroine of the novel who constantly moves as a loner declares that she has "neither home nor homeland" (*Diary* 251; unless indicated otherwise, all translations are mine). Her wandering is predicated on the loss of home and an inability to re-create its sweetness. Against the the Civil Code (promulgated in 1896; effective 1898) that prescribed women's role to the home, a constant state of movement replaces any fixed space for the heroine. Unable to find residential or financial stability, she floats adrift as a vagabond in the *naichi* of the 1920s.

The heroine seems unfit as a member of the family system 家 (*ie*): she lives outside the institutionalized womanhood of "good wife, wise mother" and has no desire to get married or bear children. She thus stands in sharp contrast to Mo Yan's women figures such as the mother Shanggang Lu in *Big Breasts and Wide Hips*, who gives birth to eight daughters and one son, and the many women characters in 蛙 (Frog) who are punished for their desire to bear multiple children or capitulate reluctantly to the family planning (计划生育) or One-child policy. Hayashi's heroine deviates from the life course prescribed by Japanese state discourse. The notion that women's role is to nurture Japan's soldiers as children 赤子 (*sekishi*) of the emperor carries insufficient weight for her. She rejects the notion and function of the individual family and the united family nation/empire of Japan that nurtures its subjects. Neither a nurturing mother nor a wife, she has no function as an integral part of Japan.

The heroine who is homeless in her native land and decentered from the nation-state in *naichi* identifies not with the central discourse on Japanese women but with the sexually, economically, ethnically, and racially exploited female body. Throughout the novel, excruciating working conditions in the factory, long working hours, and meager pay threaten the heroine's physical health and livelihood and lead her to question the position and conditions of the lower socioeconomic class. The laboring female body is also sexually commodified for the exchange value of the market economy. Belonging to the class that sells the sexualized bodies of its women for economic gain, the heroine also identifies with the ethnically and racially colonized people of society. Her physical proximity to colonials in the factory dormitory in *naichi* links them in adversity: "It was sad to sleep beside the women from Karafuto and Kanazawa with our three pillows next to each other" (88). With an acute sense of helplessness, the heroine finds no grand narrative of salvation in *naichi*: "There is neither beautiful thought nor good thought ... There is no room to restore my small honor. What a strange and excruciating way of life!" (309, 380).

Entrenched in the state of the marginalized, the heroine directs her anger at the mainstream and wishes for the explosion of a society that confines her body. Although she narrates the destitution of the lower classes and race/ethnicity on the fringes of society, she also aspires to re-create the periphery of Japan, such as Hokkaidō, as a utopia for the socially marginalized and exploited. The heroine also envisions a utopia outside Japan as an unexplored place of salvation for her. Further, she aspires to create home and family in a physically distant space: "When living becomes suffering, I think of home. People often say that they want to die in their home" (285); and "the so-called warm household with family is ten thousand ri [3.9 km] away" (315). This conveys movement within place with the portable diary representing its narrator as a vagabond.

gaichi (外地 [outer territory]) in Hayashi's Northern Bank Platoon

Many of the articulated and unarticulated desires and needs of the heroine moving within *naichi* in Diary of a Vagabond assume different physical forms—and correspondingly different fulfillments—in *gaichi* in Hayashi's 1939 北岸部隊 (Northern Bank Platoon). Whereas the heroine in *naichi* in Diary of a Vagabond as one of the marginalized in society lives in a state of suffocation and fear, the heroine in *gaichi* in Northern Bank Platoon finds security by becoming a family member of the empire and worthy of dying for it. It is in a distant China as *gaichi* under Japanese occupation in the late 1930s that the sense of family she envisions materializes as the family in Northern Bank Platoon.

Following the beginning of the Second Sino-Japanese War in 1937 and after the attack on Bukan (武漢) beginning in 1938, the Ministry of Information formed the "Pen Squadron," which sent writers to the war front with the military's financial support and protection. The first Pen Squadron consisted of twenty-two writers, and Hayashi was one of only two women in it. Some writers wrote about the sacrifices of soldiers at the request of the military, others on assignment were war correspondents, but participation in the Pen Squadron was based on will rather than coercion (see Takahashi 165). As a war correspondent for *The Tokyo Daily News* in 1938, Hayashi was the first Japanese woman to enter Nanjing, the capital of Jiangsu Province in eastern China (south of Mo Yan's home province of Shandong) after it fell to Japanese troops. Hayashi's war report Northern Bank Platoon was written as a journal from 19 September to 28 December 1938, and her other report 戦線 (Battlefront) takes the form of correspondence in the same year, depicting life at the battlefront for a week. Both works resemble Diary of a Vagabond in combining forms of poetry with prose. In contrast to the Diary, however—which denies any grand narrative of good, beauty, or truth in *naichi*—in Northern Bank Platoon Hayashi creates and affirms them in *gaichi*. The heroine celebrates "the beauty and cruelty of this battlefield ... It's cruel, and also sublime and lofty" (294). Whereas the heroine in the Diary acts through the multiple identities of the economically, ethnically, and racially marginalized and colonized peoples of the Japanese empire, the heroine in Northern Bank Platoon reconstructs her identity as a pure and patriotic Japanese by recreating the dichotomy of Japan and China as separate entities. Paradoxically, it is only in the Chinese *gaichi* that the narrator of Northern Bank Platoon gains a national identity as Japanese. By marching with the Japanese soldiers on Chinese soil, the heroine identifies herself with them: "I accompanied Yosuko [揚子江] Northern Troop ... The color of my face is soiled black with dust and grime, and I am no different from the soldiers" (300). The narrator further defines herself: "I am a noncombatant and, moreover, a woman. But as a Japanese woman, I want to burn and etch the way of the Japanese soldiers' battle firmly onto my mind's eye ... My eyes are wide open with utter astonishment at the patriotic passion that has filled my body" (234). Further, the heroine feels a deep alliance with the nurses who are equated with sacred mothers of soldiers on the battlefield. The patriotism that overwhelms her body is also shown in her desire to be part of the family empire: "It seems as though every soldier is always worried about his homeland. Until they achieve heroic and incomparable deaths magnificently, they always think of their homeland. They are good husbands, fathers, and older and younger brothers" (308).

Unlike the men who exploit women's sexualized and commodified bodies in *naichi* in the Diary, the men in *gaichi* in Northern Bank Platoon are conscientious family men who are devoted to their homes and homeland: "Soldiers are all kind and gentle ... pure" (256). This representation is striking, given that the Japanese government was establishing and operating military "comfort" stations (hubs of enslaved prostitutes to serve the military) in occupied territories, including China. Although fear, insecurity, and deprivation are recurrent themes for the heroine in the Diary, the narrator in Northern Bank Platoon marching with soldiers attains confidence, security, and fulfillment by gaining national identity as Japanese. This is achievable specifically in the space of Northeast China as *gaichi*: "I will never forget, for the rest of my life, the feeling of love for the country ... I don't care about my house in Tokyo" (241). Of special note is that her very national identity reduces her affection for *naichi*: "I want to stay behind" (214). The heroine's collaboration in *gaichi* in Northern Bank Platoon signifies her quest to gain power within the empire rather than beyond it. As a result, Hayashi's writing becomes part of the forces of aggression and the atrocities of Japanese imperial expansion.

naichi and *gaichi* in Hayashi's novel *Floating Clouds* and Naruse's film adaptation of the novel

Now I turn to Hayashi's novel 浮雲 (*Floating Clouds*, 1949-1951) and Mikio Naruse's (1905-1969) 1955 adaptation of the novel to film and examine how they reframe migrant women in the language of space and time and how the literary and visual narratives function as the medium of memory to re-create the Japanese imperial past in the present. Hayashi's *Floating Clouds* received critical acclaim and popular attention, and Naruse's film was praised as "best film" in 1955, the year it was released: "*Floating Clouds* remains Naruse's most well-known film in Japan ... the film that brought Naruse the greatest recognition" (Russell 10). Both the novel and film are notable for depicting the heroine Yukiko's mobility and the malleability of space. Yukiko moves from Shizuoka to Tokyo in prewar *naichi*, she is posted to Dalat, French Indochina, in prewar *gaichi*; returns to Tokyo in the immediate postwar era; travels northwest to Ikaho; and then moves to Yakushima, a semitropical island at the southern end of Japan, where she dies.

As an unmarried woman and typist in Japan in prewar *naichi*, Yukiko struggles economically in the lower and peripheral strata of society. As a migrant, she is antithetical to the domesticated woman who supports the family within her sanctioned space of home. With no stable home or family background, she is no candidate for the status of "sacred wife and mother" in either prewar or postwar Japan. Since Yukiko is not respected as a "pure" woman, she is forced repeatedly to serve her brother-in-law Iba sexually in prewar Tokyo. Raped and exploited, she endures bitter and suffocating conditions resonating with women and men characters of Mo Yan's *Big Breasts and Wide Hips*. She is stymied in recapturing or re-creating the warmth of either a home or a homeland either for herself or for future generations. Yukiko is freed, however, from the restrictions she experiences in the homeland of Japan when she earns a position as a typist at the Ministry of Agriculture, which provides her with the opportunity to leave the space of prewar *naichi* and enter *gaichi*, French Indochina, which had fallen under the control of the Japanese empire in 1942. Yukiko's life changes from one of economic and physical repression to one of freedom, comfort, and security when she travels to Dalat, stays in a French-style mansion occupied by Japanese bureaucrats, and enters the open space of woods with her lover Tomioka, a bureaucrat from the Ministry of Agriculture. The sanctioned positions of these characters stand in contrast to the misused state positions in Mo Yan's political critique from the many petty officials in *Life and Death Are Wearing Me Out* to the overzealous abortion provider Aunt in Frog. It is her body in motion beyond the border of *naichi* but still within the space of the empire of Japan that makes the changes possible.

In Naruse's film adaptation of Hayashi's novel, the French-style mansion and the dining setting and the act of eating are narrated visually as Japan's identification with one of the Western imperial powers, France, and with the colonization of Indochina—colonization in which Yukiko participates and from which she benefits. In the film, the whiteness of the setting of the dining table—white tablecloth, white wine, and Yukiko's white dress—signifies not only the freshness and newness of her experience, but also the Japanese empire's initial identification with Western imperialism, its subsequent displacement of the "white" Western imperial power, and its assertion of control over the darker-skinned native Annamese symbolized by the maid Niu, who serves the food. Another sign of whiteness occurs in a natural rather than artificial setting, in the scene in the woods. Adorned in a "white, thin, silk skirt," according to the screenplay by Yōko Mizuki (81), Yukiko appears in an open wooded space that is filled with bright white light. Tomioka kisses her and leads her into the woods. In the open and expansive space, Yukiko leaps in joy. Some may be reminded of the different color motif in the scene of the compliance of Jiu'er (also known as Grandma and Dai Fenglian) to what is essentially rape in Yimou Zhang's 1987 film version of Mo Yan's *Red Sorghum*, where reds and yellows dominate.

In Naruse's film, scenes show how Yukiko tastes her share of the benefits of Japan's colonization of "Asia." Yukiko could not have associated with such bureaucrats in Tokyo, but in Dalat she stays at a mansion as a Japanese colonizer and breaks bread with them. She participates in the state apparatus and its social conventions, which exploit the natural and human resources in *gaichi* and use neighboring Asian nations, ethnicities, and races as the inferior servants of the Japanese empire. Specifically, it is the language of space and a mobile body which create Yukiko as an agent who acts on the nation-state's imperialist discourse of the Japanese empire. Whereas her body was restricted economically and marginalized in her homeland of Japan, Yukiko is able to experience the luxury of upper-class society in prewar *gaichi*. The unmarried Yukiko's wandering outside domestic space and then moving from Tokyo to the *gaichi* may appear to signal her departure from the center to the periphery, from living inside the system of the nation and its history to existing outside it. Some critics, including Noriko Mizuta, consider Yukiko's experience to be personal, apolitical, and ahistorical. Mizuta contends that Yukiko entertains the possibility of freedom because she is in *gaichi* and thus "outside the institutions of Japan" and "outside Japanese history" (Mizuta 346).

It is true that as a marginalized woman in *naichi*, Yukiko has nothing to do with the Japanese state: she travels to Indochina out of her own wish to leave Japan. Just as she did in Tokyo, Yukiko works in the same low-income service sector in Indochina; however, she does so under military auspices as a typist for the Ministry of Agriculture and Forestry, a government institution at the margin of the Japanese government system in contrast to the Ministry of Education and the Home Ministry, which dominated the state discourse on women. French Indochina was on the geographic periphery of the Japanese empire, but it was the building of an economic base through the exploitation of natural resources and labor that made possible the expansion of Japan and its development abroad. In this sense, the state discourse brought about its subjects' movement toward the periphery. Conversely, people's movement toward the periphery supported the discourse of the state, and this is a necessary component of strengthening the empire. For Yukiko, her movement to Indochina at the periphery of *gaichi* is an act of connecting to the discourse of the state, a national contribution impossible for her to achieve in Tokyo, the center of *naichi*. In other words, by moving to the periphery of Japanese occupied territory, Yukiko participates in the discourse that reconstructs Japan. Her personal experience and interpersonal relationships evolve in a setting created by the discourses of the state and the geopolitical expansion of the empire.

Recreation of prewar *gaichi* in postwar Japan

In postwar Japan, however, Yukiko's position as a migrant and as a person standing outside the institutionalized, family-based womanhood of prewar *naichi* is reestablished. With no stable home, Yukiko roams through the lower city of Tokyo until she finally moves into the dark, confined, shabby storage room of a hardware store. Behind the store stretch the burnt fields, black markets, narrow winding roads, and rundown hotels of postwar Tokyo. These devastated spaces are the backdrop for Yukiko's body and represent the immediate postwar period, when almost 60% of all housing in Tokyo and Osaka was destroyed by air raids. Although she has no prospect of marrying Tomioka, she continues her uncertain relationship with him, becomes pregnant, has an abortion, and suffers repeated surgeries owing to post-abortion complications (on abortion in Mo Yan's work, see Du). Yukiko's physical condition mirrors the effects of postwar national politics on women's bodies. Her abortion takes place within the particular historical and political context of post-war Japan, which produced an intersection of national and professional interests in legalizing and liberalizing abortion. More specifically, Yukiko's abortion reflects the desire of the Japanese elites and the Allied Powers to secure economic growth and avoid remilitarization of postwar Japan by limiting the seemingly out-of-control population growth caused by the repatriates and the baby boom (see Norgren 36-43).

Yukiko's body is violated and weakened: her approximation of the geographic Japanese center again paralleling her poor treatment at the hands of her brother-in-law Iba earlier in the story. Her experience of physical invasion also overlaps with the history of the U.S. occupation of Japan. Yukiko becomes a prostitute for a U.S. soldier and the exchange value of her body manifests itself in the products from the U.S. that the soldier Joe brings to her room: a transistor radio, chocolates, and Coca-Cola. These U.S. items are distinct and meager in their nature and literary use from those in *Big Breasts and Wide Hips*: "American cotton," "a sleek black Chevrolet sedan," an "American Jeep," "American submachine guns," "U.S. warplanes," and such (82, 154, 171, 203). As Yukiko struggles physically and materially, she entertains the memory of war rather than peace, and she feels nostalgia for the lost time and space of Japan's pre-war *gaichi*: "Remembering the wash of colors and sights that was French Indochina, Yukiko thought, I want to see that place once more" (*Floating Clouds* 163).

To rebuild a relationship with Tomioka and to recover the health of her body weakened by the abortion and its aftermath, Yukiko must re-create in postwar Japan the sense of physical freedom and empowerment she experienced as a Japanese colonizer in French Indochina. She therefore insists on accompanying Tomioka when she learns that he has been given a position at the Ministry of Agriculture on remote Yakushima, a semitropical island at the southern end of Japan. As if in accord with Yukiko's wish to re-create the old village in Dalat, the village on Yakushima "was exactly like an Annamese hamlet in French Indochina" (283). In the choices she makes at the end of her life as a migrant, Yukiko therefore seeks a final, harmonious resolution of her personal conflicts in nostalgia for the modern Japanese empire and encapsulates the story of the modern empire in her personal story. In *Floating Clouds*, Yukiko's nostalgia for the lost colony of the Japanese empire is accompanied by her sense of remorse and responsibility for the egoistical, aggressive, and destructive policies and actions of the former Japanese colonizers: "Were not the Japanese—who were suddenly rummaging about among the treasures of other people that had taken them centuries to develop—nothing but robbers? ... The long history of these tea fields that had been carefully managed for so many years made her [Yukiko] feel ashamed of the high-handed tactics that the Japanese had used to take over everything—even these fields—in a short amount of time" (38, 98).

The novel represents both remorse and a sense of responsibility on the part of a sexually violated and socially marginalized woman in *naichi* who benefitted from the Japanese empire's colonization of neighboring Asian nations in *gaichi*. Thus Yukiko not only notices the Japanese exploitation of natural resources and labor in Indochina but also identifies with those who were tried at the Tokyo War Tribunal in 1946. In conversation with Tomioka, Yukiko refers to the "war trial" broadcast on the radio and comments on moral "responsibility" with respect to the Japanese colonization of Indochina: "You and I are involved too, in these trials ... I want to hear the facts about the war" (286). Yukiko recognizes that "the facts" of Japan's colonization policy and actions are owing to not only the male-centered grand narrative created by the bureaucrats, politicians, and military officials but also the collaboration of low-ranking civil servants like Tomioka at the geographical periphery of the empire—and of socially and economically marginalized women such as Yukiko herself. Yet as Mariko Asano Tamanoi points out, "The past to be remembered does not cover only facts; it also covers the images into which those facts have already been transformed. Hence the facts that do not fit in such images may have been forgotten" (20). In the film, there is one brief scene that features a military truck in the woods. The emphasis, however, is on the expansive natural space in which Yukiko walks hand in hand with Tomioka and jumps for joy. These images of nature and of dream-like retreat encourage the audience to remember Indochina as a lush natural world in contrast to the grating facts of Japanese military aggression, economic exploitation, and imperial expansion.

Naruse's film as a medium of memory assists in remembering a past that marginalizes Yukiko. The film is also a strategy that enables the state and people to forget the facts of the expansion and aggression of the Japanese empire. But we must also remember that the power of the Japanese state, which once dominated ordinary Annamese people and in which Japanese women participated, helped Yukiko gain a sense of freedom and power. In the film, both Yukiko and the Japanese empire live, grow, flourish, weaken, and die. As images of Yukiko in Indochina are inserted as flashbacks into her life in postwar Japan, phenomena pass by like "a floating cloud—appearing [and] disappearing" (Hayashi, *Floating Clouds* 303). We who live today, however, continue to narrate the prewar and postwar eras—and re-create the past in memory—by interpreting such narratives. This is often the case with viewing *gaichi* from the important, but limited, native point of view. There is a danger with art whether textual or cinematic to focalize uncritically rather than to acknowledge the breadth that artists like Mo Yan and Hayashi possess and signal in their works.

Narratives about unmarried migrant Japanese women focus on their gender- and class-specific marginalized experience as women characters in *naichi* and gloss over their participation in Japan's colonization of neighboring nations in *gaichi*. As one of the most recognized visual narratives in postwar Japan, Naruse's film frames Yukiko's experience of material comfort, physical freedom, and power as an occupying colonizer in Indochina in the prewar era as something unreal. This dream-like experience of nonreality is signaled in the film by inserting discontinuous shots of Yukiko and Tomioka in the woods in Dalat into the narrative of their lives in the postwar era. But if Yukiko's experience in Indochina was dream-like, the expansion of the Japanese empire was a nightmarish reality for the Annamese who were invaded and exploited. If *gaichi* in the prewar era continues to be created and interpreted as a temporary and unrealistic dream, the question of how and why the "reality" of those who were colonized came into being may not be tackled.

In conclusion, the texts I analyze here provide a regional (Asian) contextualization of Mo Yan's, Hayashi's, and Naruse's texts in a perspective that may help to consider literary settings more sensitively and gain particular regional context as well. Moreover, Asians and others around the globe, thus, may gain a deeper appreciation and perhaps better tools for dealing with the continuing battles—verbal and physical—over disputed Asian territories which may otherwise be viewed as negligible. In Mo Yan's and Hayashi's texts, and in the latter's adaptation to film by Naruse, we read the re-creation and interpretation of memory. In Hayashi's texts, some of the narrators and characters can be read as disruptive minorities who question the majority and the norm and who live outside the political institutions of Japan. And yet, with the focus on the time and spaces of "Japan" and "China" as sites of historical and political intervention and negotiation, I show the politics of the personal stories of women who moved between *naichi* and *gaichi* in the prewar and postwar eras of the not-so-distant past. Hayashi's literary and Naruse's visual texts reconstruct the memory of the victimization of women in *naichi*, a memory that has turned to nostalgia for the same past that also victimized not only Japanese women but also the colonized nations and ethnicities in Mo Yan's China.

Note

The above article is a revised excerpt from Noriko J. Horiguchi, *Women Adrift: The Literature of Japan's Imperial Body* (Minneapolis: U of Minnesota P, 2011) and a revised version of "Migrant Women, Memory, and Empire in Japan in Naruse Mikio's Film Adaptations of Hayashi Fumiko's Novels," *U.S.-Japan Women's Journal* 36 (2009): 42–72. Copyright releases to the author.

Works Cited

Chan, Shelley W. *A Subversive Voice in China: The Fictional World of Mo Yan.* Amherst: Cambria P, 2010.

Du, Lanlan. "Abortion in Faulkner's *The Wild Palms* and Mo Yan's 蛙 (Frog)." *Mo Yan in Context: Nobel Laureate and Global Storyteller.* Ed. Angelica Duran and Yuhan Huang. West Lafayette: Purdue UP, 2014. 63–76.

Ericson, Joan E. *Be a Woman: Hayashi Fumiko and Modern Japanese Women's Literature.* Honolulu: U of Hawai'i P, 1997.

Floating Clouds (浮雲). Dir. Mikio Naruse (成瀬 巳喜男). Tokyo: Tōhō, 1955.
Hayashi, Fumiko (林 芙美子). 放浪記. 1927. (Diary of a Vagabond). Tokyo: Shinchōsha, 2000.
Hayashi, Fumiko (林 芙美子). 浮雲 (*Floating Clouds*). Tokyo: Shinchōsha, 1953.
Hayashi, Fumiko. *Floating Clouds*. 1951. Trans. Lane Dunlop. New York: Columbia UP, 2006.
Hayashi, Fumiko (林 芙美子). 北岸部隊. 1939. (Northern Bank Platoon). 林芙美子全集 (Complete Works of Fumiko Hayashi). By Fumiko Hayashi. Tokyo: Bunsendô, 1977. Vol. 12, 211-334.
Kong, Fanjin (孔范今), Zhanjun Shi (施战军), and Xiaobing Lu (路晓冰), eds. 莫言研究资料 (Materials for the Study of Mo Yan). Jinan: Shandong wenyi chubanshe, 2006.
Mizuki, Yôko (水木洋子). シナリオ浮雲 ("Screenplay *Floating Clouds*"). Ed. Chiyota Shimizu (清水千代太). Tokyo: Kinema junpō sha, 1954. Vol. 106, 79-105.
Mizuta, Noriko. "In Search of a Lost Paradise: The Wandering Woman in Hayashi Fumiko's *Drifting Clouds*." *The Woman's Hand: Gender and Theory in Japanese Women's Writing*. Ed. Paul Gordon Schalow and Janet A. Walker. Stanford: Stanford UP, 1996. 329-51.
Mo Yan. *Big Breasts and Wide Hips*. Trans. Howard Goldblatt. New York: Arcade, 1996.
Mo Yan (莫言). 蛙 (Frog). Shanghai: Shanghai Literature and Art P, 2012.
Mo Yan. *Red Sorghum: A Novel of China*. Trans. Howard Goldblatt. Harmondsworth: Penguin, 1994.
Norgren, Tiana. *Abortion before Birth Control: The Politics of Reproduction in Postwar Japan*. Princeton: Princeton UP, 2001.
Red Sorghum (红高粱). Dir. Yimou Zhang (张艺谋). Beijing: Xi'an Film Studio, 1987.
Russell, Catherine. *The Cinema of Naruse Mikio: Women and Japanese Modernity*. Durham: Duke UP, 2008.
Tamanoi, Mariko Asano. *Memory Maps: The State and Manchuria in Postwar Japan*. Honolulu: U of Hawai'i P, 2009.
Takahashi, Takaharu (高橋隆治). 戦場の女流作家達 (Women Writers on the Battleground). Tokyo: Ronsôsha, 1995.
Wang, David Der-wei. "The Literary World of Mo Yan." *World Literature Today* 74.3 (2000): 487-94.

Author's profile

Noriko J. Horiguchi teaches modern Japanese literature and cinema at the University of Tennessee. Her interests in scholarship include postcolonial studies, gender studies, and cultural studies. In addition to numerous articles, Horiguchi's book publications include *Women Adrift: The Literature of Japan's Imperial Body* (2011).

Abortion in Faulkner's *The Wild Palms* and Mo Yan's 蛙 (Frog)

Lanlan Du

Abstract

In "Abortion in Faulkner's *The Wild Palms* and Mo Yan's 蛙 (Frog)" Lanlan Du explores the two novelists' representations of the historically persistent and socially significant theme of abortion. Faulkner depicts the male protagonist's fear of female fertility and tackles the issue of abortion as a matter of individual choice with the withering of romantic love, wretched poverty, and maternal death corresponding with the popular discourse of a mid-twentieth-century U.S. that depicted abortion as tragic. On the other hand, Mo Yan focuses more on the impact of national biopolitics on women bodies and agonized would-be mothers within China's national birth control policy, which has made abortions legal but coercive, thus exploring the dilemma China faces in pursuit of modernity.

Nearly a quarter of a century before being awarded the 2012 Nobel Prize in Literature, Mo Yan cited the 1949 Nobel Prize in Literature Laureate William Faulkner as one of the chief Western figures who influenced his fictional creations: "Every once in a while I turn the page of Faulkner's books. What he wrote in the books seems unimportant to me now. Up until now I have not gone through any of his books from the beginning to the end. When I read his books, I feel like talking to an old folk in our village. Our talk is casual and random, but I can always benefit from the communication with him" (unless indicated otherwise, all translations are mine) ("每隔上一段时间，我就翻翻福克纳的书。他在书里写了些什么对我来说已经不重要了。至今我也没把他老人家的哪一本书从头到尾读完过。我看他的书时，就像跟我们村子里的一个老大爷聊天一样，东一句西一句，天南地北，漫无边际。但我总是能从与他的交流中得到教益" ("会唱歌的墙" 193). By referring to Faulkner as one of "two burning furnaces" (Inge 19)—the other being the 1982 Nobel Prize in Literature Laureate Gabriel García Márquez—Mo Yan captures his admiration for and intimate spiritual communication with Faulkner. The two Nobel

Prize laureates have much in common: both have created extensive worlds set in fictional communities very much based on their hometowns, one in Yoknapatawpha County and the other Gaomi Township, Shandong Province. Both use original narrative forms in representing their dominant themes: their works consistently renew the potential of the novel through extraordinary experimentation. In *The Wild Palms* and 蛙 (Frog), respectively, the bravery of the narrative forms Faulkner and Mo Yan employ is matched by that of the narrative topic of reproductive rights in the particular geographical time and space familiar to the authors and challenging to their societies, especially given the social restraints on sexuality and the control of female bodies. In the study at hand, I analyze *The Wild Palms* and Frog and the two writers' representations of the historically persistent and socially significant theme of abortion.

Women characters' pregnancies and their responses

In both *The Wild Palms* and Frog, some women characters are represented as excessively active and possessing a power threatening to male characters. In *The Wild Palms*, Charlotte Rittenmeyer's marriage with her well-to-do Catholic husband Francis "Rat" Rittenmeyer is described as a continuation of patriarchy in her early life: "She had a father and then four brothers exactly like him and then she married a man exactly like the four brothers" (70). Women get married, have children, take care of their husband and children, and then die. Charlotte is apparently unhappy with her marriage and its byproduct, motherhood, so she elopes with her lover Harry Wilbourne, gives up the traditional family, and leaves her husband and daughters behind. At twenty-seven years old and four months away from being a full-fledged doctor of medicine, the impecunious Harry is unable to shoulder the financial burden of his love affair. Rat's financial offer to help represents the impossibility of Charlotte's full break from her traditional female role in her nuclear family.

Charlotte does not fit into the traditional schema of Western romantic love in other ways, as she rather than her male lover is the "subject of the passion" (Gwin 147), she resists the trappings of a traditional marriage, and she pursues her sexual desires. By depicting Charlotte as a woman who has active female desire, Faulkner subverts the traditional binary model of male/active and female/passive sexuality. It is Charlotte who is the virile partner and who strips herself before Harry can do it for her. On the train to Chicago, she takes the initiative to get undressed and "almost rapes him" (Pitay 122). If the flood of the Mississippi river in the "Old Man" narrative of *The Wild Palms* is more a historical fact, then the fluidity of female sexuality in "The Wild Palms" narrative is conveyed metaphorically to denote its overwhelming power upon the male character. Charlotte's excessive sexual desire flows like a flood threatening Harry's sense of safety. Charlotte is not only a sexual aggressor in her adulterous relationship with Harry but also the leader. Because Charlotte is the main breadwinner for the couple for a time, Harry considers her "not only a better man and a better gentleman than I am, she is a better everything than I will ever be" (113). Her masculinity, particularly her willingness to make money, intimidates Harry, who is "always agonized by his entanglements with economic necessity" (Dobbs 828). Charlotte's assumption of male characteristics, such as shouldering the breadwinning, coordinates with her rejection of other conventional notions of femininity including maternity. Her rejection of motherhood is chiefly because of her belief in the purity of passion. She believes that romantic love will not die as long as lovers live in a perpetual honeymoon-like life and that only those who are unworthy of it will suffer from the deadening of love: "They say love dies, between two people. That's wrong. It doesn't die. It just leaves you, goes away, if you are not good enough, worthy enough. It doesn't die; you are the one that dies" (71).

Charlotte's and Harry's rejection of family routines and the stagnancy of familiar surroundings is mirrored by their geographical wanderings through New Orleans, Chicago, Wisconsin, Utah, San Antonio, and the Mississippi Gulf Coast. Charlotte attempts to maintain their strong passion by telling Harry that children "hurt too much" (182), which lends a sense of foreboding since, because of the use of narrative flashback, readers already know that she undergoes a botched abortion. Her aversion to motherhood makes clear that her later call for an abortion is her own choice. Faulkner's choice in the matter, however, is distinct from his characters'. He utilizes the high risk of maternal death in illegal abortions—the only kind available in the U.S. at the time—and has Charlotte pay the expensive price of death for maintaining the purity of passion. Charlotte is thus a functional character serving the purpose of advancing the male character Harry's development. Harry develops from the weak passive lover who is unable to take the initiative in a sexual relationship, even before his relationship with Charlotte, to a man who undergoes an epiphany after the failed abortion. When Charlotte tells him she is pregnant due to a contraceptive accident (she omits using her douche), he does not pin the blame on her. Then, rather than perform an abortion immediately after her request, Harry initially refuses and initiates their move to Texas so he can gain successful employment to support the child. In Texas, he continues to resist and offers to make whatever sacrifices are necessary for the child; he even considers setting "up as a professional abortionist" (175).

Both Charlotte and Harry are unwilling to welcome the baby because they desperately fear the entire set of parental roles and economic responsibilities. Charlotte's stated motivation to make the choice of abortion is to prevent the baby from experiencing poverty like them. Harry at first refuses to perform the abortion because he abhors the idea of killing his own child, not the idea of abortion *per se*. Therefore he takes the initiative to search for an abortion pill in a brothel, although in vain. He is then unsuccessful in finding a way to support a family. In the grim social reality of the late 1930s, he is lucky to find a job as a writer for pulp magazines. Harry's job is a sacrifice of his and Charlotte's obsessive relationship, as the time and low pay leave him busy and distracted: "Now he knew why he would sit before an unfinished page in the typewriter, believing he was thinking only of the money" (Faulkner 107). So Charlotte's pregnancy and failed abortion serve as the stimuli for Harry to understand his personal limitations and realize the consequences of their illicit love. No matter how hard he and Charlotte try to escape social confines, they cannot fully cling to their pure passionate love. Yet, late in the novel, after Charlotte has died and he has been accused of murder, Harry refuses to commit suicide and makes the choice to grieve.

Mo Yan's Frog depicts Tadpole's second wife Little Lion (Xiao Shizi 小狮子) as a sexually aggressive woman, based on her strong desire to become a mother, as opposed to Charlotte, who so fervently flees motherhood. After the pitiful death of Tadpole's first wife, Tadpole's aunt, Wan Xin, serves as a matchmaker between Tadpole and Little Lion, who mentors Little Lion in their work of birth control. As time passes by, Little Lion finds herself unable to conceive a child and becomes fanatic in her dream of motherhood. She laments her job assisting Wan Xin, a countryside obstetrican-gynecologist whose job is to enact the family planning (计划生育) or One-child policy, including aborting many fetuses. When she sees an adorable mixed-blood baby in a stroller during a walk with her husband, Little Lion expresses such great admiration and intimacy for the child that the child's mother becomes uncomfortable and gives her a hostile look. Tadpole reminds Little Lion of social decorum and asks her to watch out for her behavior next time, which enrages Little Lion: "Little Lion felt very wronged. She first cursed those wealthy people who had more than one child at their own will and those men and women who strived to have as many babies as they could after getting married to foreigners; then she began to be regretful, blaming herself for following Aunt to implement so strictly the family planning policy, which could have caused her infertility because they have disobeyed God's will by aborting so many fetuses that it has incurred God's wrath and hence caused her barrenness; she then wished me to impregnate a foreign woman so as to have many mixed-blood babies" ("小狮子很感委屈，先是骂了一通那些肆意超生的富人和那些与外国人结婚后便拼命生养的男人和女人；接着变自怨自艾，后悔当年跟着姑姑执行严酷的计划生育政策，引流了那么多婴儿，伤了天理，导致老天报应，是自己不能生养；然后又希望我也去找一个洋妞结婚，生一堆混血小孩") (209). Out of her fervent desire, she finally tempts Tadpole to provide his sperm to a surrogate mother, Chen Mei, to bear the child for her. Mo Yan's depiction of Little Lion's aggressiveness seems to reveal more her desire to be a mother rather than its impact on the male protagonist.

If Faulkner's Charlotte rejects traditional motherhood to pursue her own passion, Mo Yan's women characters form a sad collective of women fervently desiring to be mothers. As Michel Foucault argues, the governing of collective human life, health, and welfare has become a key objective of modern states. China is no exception. After the founding of the People's Republic of China, the government actively encouraged mothers to have more children, so there was a drastic population increase in the 1950s, resulting in a problematic imbalance between the population, resources, and the environment. Consequently, the 1960s and the first half of 1970s saw a tentative and intermittent attempt by the government to reduce the birth rate. Since 1978, birth planning has been a national policy. The One-child policy has been executed compulsively since 1980, gradually leading to a quick decline in fertility. Although the tensions between the government and citizens have eased now because the popular fertility culture since the 1990s began to converge with state birth propaganda, the situation in previous decades was tense.

In the decades before the 1990s, the natural right of Chinese women to be mothers conflicted with national biopolitics and contravened an essentially pronatalist Chinese fertility culture. Moreover, most Chinese families had a deeply rooted mindset about giving birth to a male child to carry on the family line. They opposed the new national birth limitation on the grounds of such traditional fertility ethics. In Frog, Mo Yan focuses on the tensions of rural citizens and this form of state intervention. It delves deeply into some rural families' defiance when the state's birth policy was executed with relentlessness. For the female characters in Mo Yan's fictional Gaomi, the greater the adherence to the national birth control policy, the stronger the female characters' desires to become mothers.

Wang Renmei, the first wife of the narrator Tadpole, is deeply influenced by the traditional fertility culture. After giving birth to a daughter, she dreams of getting pregnant again to give birth to a son. She is unable to conceive, however, because Wan Xin inserted an intrauterine contraceptive device (IUD) into her. But she subsequently has her IUD taken out stealthily. As with Charlotte's unintentional omission of contraception in *The Wild Palms*, Wang Renmei's intentional one results in a successful pregnancy. Her pregnancy puts both her husband and Aunt in awkward positions: her husband's military career is jeopardized and her Aunt's job of birth control seems less convincing. While Wang Renmei is a strong character, she capitulates under the extreme pressure by the chief representatives of society to abort her pregnancy. As a resolute practitioner of the birth control policy, Aunt forces Wang Renmei's maternal family to hand her over by intimidating them and their neighbors, threatening to pull down their houses. Wang Renmei gives up her right to second motherhood then pays the expensive price of her life. A very significant point here is that Wang Renmei is ignorant of the fact that she had been implanted with an IUD after the first labor. This lack of consent is a blatant violation of women's right of reproduction. Although birth planning is a way for China to coordinate economic development and population growth, forced contraception, sterilization, and abortion are illegal. Frog articulates a strong opposition to these illegal practices through the death of Wang Renmei.

Mo Yan depicts other rural women figures, who, like Wang Renmei, possess a fervent desire to be mothers. They make use of every means available to evade the national restraints on childbirth. Geng Xiulian and Wang Dan are two other rural women characters that lose their lives trying to have a second child. They are chased down and forced to abort their second pregnancies by Aunt and her followers. The unique characteristics of these women and Little Lion sensitively portray the psychological effects of an exaggerated form of national biopolitics on women in rural China. Unable to conceive a baby for a long time, Little Lion becomes extremely sexually aggressive in her eagerness to get a firstborn, while the sexuality of these two other women characters is not explicitly described. What unifies these women characteres' desperate attempt to conceive and give birth is their strong desire to have a male heir for the family, which serves patriarchal ideology more than it does female sexuality. If Charlotte in *The Wild Palms* dies because of her free choice (pro-choice) abortion, pregnant women characters in Frog die because of crude physical coercion. Mo Yan focuses more on the impact of national biopolitics on female bodies than does Faulkner, who focalizes individual choice and implied social mores. In some instances, China's national family planning policy has made abortions legal but coercive for millions of women. By depicting their fervent desire to be mothers and the poignant agonies of those Chinese women who have been forced to have abortions, Mo Yan thoroughly explores the dilemma China faces in the pursuit of modernity: the necessity of birth control and its inhumane consequences out of extreme execution of the national policy.

Narratives of male responses to female fertility

The two parallel narratives—"The Wild Palms" and "Old Man"—that Faulkner uses in *The Wild Palms* highlights the theme of male characters' fear of female sexuality and fertility, although from different male vantage points. The often incompetent lover Harry is whirled about so violently in the flood of Charlotte's passion that he capitulates to her will to perform an abortion on her, even though it is illegal and even though he had not completed his medical training, and thus instrumentally contributes to the tragic ending of their romantic love. His final captivity in Parchman Prison in the final chapter of "The Wild Palms" section results from his incompetence in balancing romantic love and social reality. Harry's inability is highlighted through contrast from the protagonist of the "Old Man" narrative of *The Wild Palms*. The unnamed tall convict featured in the "Old Man" narrative struggles actively in his battle against a natural flood that he finds himself in inadvertently. He provides food and shelter for a pregnant woman caught in the flood, but he rejects the notion of romantic love, thus staying out of the control of the mysterious female principle. Harry is apparently less resourceful than the tall convict, given that the tall convict contributes to bringing a new life into the world under highly adverse circumstances. Like Harry, the tall convict displays fear for female fertility, expressed in his view of the pregnant woman's body as monstrous and threatening. The nameless pregnant woman under the tall convict's gaze is reduced to her reproductive organs, too fleshly to be accepted. Terrified by female fertility, the tall convict willingly returns to prison because he believes it is the safest all-male world without the control of women. He prefers to "return to that monastic existence of shotguns and shackles where he would be secure from it" (130). By depicting both male protagonists' fear of female fertility, Faulkner seems to express the patriarchal dread of female sexuality and maternity. In treating abortion as the dire consequence of female hypersexuality in "The Wild Palms" and the pregnant female body as a dread in "Old Man," both sections have a very clear misogynistic line in relation to women's roles in reproduction.

The "Wild Palms" narrative demonstrates Harry's inability to innovate a new, dominant or equal role for himself within a romantic relationship. He suffers from ennui: "I am bored. I am bored to extinction. There is nothing here that I am needed for. Not even by her. I have already cut enough wood to last until Christmas and there is nothing else for me to do" (96). Faulkner describes two elements that encroach on Harry's relationship with Charlotte: money and respectability. Harry is trapped not only in Charlotte's excessive love but also in the economic struggles of the 1930s. Economic necessities constantly intrude into the realm of their romantic love. Although the lovers try desperately to escape the social confines of life and struggle to enter "a transcendental realm of romantic love" (Dobbs 816), their aspirations always conflict with grim reality. They cannot escape the worldly reality of a capitalist U.S. and are the victims of the economic crisis of the time. Destitute, they drift to the South, and then wander off aimlessly to different places. Although they fanatically fear a settled existence, the problem of feeding and caring for a family mires Harry. While Charlotte works for a time dressing store windows, he is domesticated in his job: he stays home writing stories for pulp magazines, beginning his stories with "I had the body and desires of a woman yet in knowledge and experience of the world I was but a child," "if I had only a mother's love to guard me on that fatal day" (103), and "at sixteen I was an unwed mother" (104). Harry writes his fictional stories as if he were a woman.

The novel seems to attribute Harry's lack of strong masculinity to an underdeveloped state of adolescence. Pliant and immature, Harry does not know how to cope with the active and assertive Charlotte until her pregnancy. The pregnancy initiates the possibility that he may grow up, so to speak: when Charlottes asks him to perform an abortion on her, he initially refuses. His failure in the forestalled abortion, however, indicates the failure of that potential. As Joseph J. Moldenhauer notes, Harry later explains his failure in these terms: "A miser would probably bungle the blowing of his own safe too. Should have called in a professional, a cracksman who didn't care, didn't love the iron flanks that held the money" (297). But the analogy is not an adequate explanation. Harry's dilemma precludes a successful abortion. The reason for the failure lies in his compulsive need to punish himself and Charlotte for their life of what he believes all the while to be a sin (Moldenhauer 312).

In Frog, Tadpole is reluctant to have a second baby, despite the prospect of having a boy, because he might be expelled from the army, a state institution that would frown upon the violation of another state institution, the national family planning policy. At hearing the news of his wife's second pregnancy, he hurries back to his hometown to persuade his wife to have an abortion. Although tortured by a contradictory mind, he still follows his aunt to compel his wife to have an abortion, thus being the instrumental cause of her death during the operation. The familial alliance compounds the force of the pressure for the female figure to agree to an abortion. Like thousands of husbands who are entangled by the national birth control policy, Tadpole is stuck in the plight of whether or not to have the baby, unable to experience happiness in his wife's conception. Afterward, he is riven by guilt. Here Mo Yan highlights the great impact of political intervention on men as well as women.

The performers of abortion

Birth control is often interwoven with issues of love, marriage, and parenthood. In *The Wild Palms*, Faulkner discusses the individual lovers' plight through the popular discourse of abortion at the time as basically dangerous, unnatural, unethical, and above all illegal. Although there was a birth control movement in the U.S. led primarily by Margaret Sanger between the 1910s and 1930s as a cure to the social ills of prostitution, domestic abuse, and venereal disease, abortion in the U.S. at that time was unavailable due to few providers and high financial costs. In the 1930s, only therapeutic abortions were legal; that is, "abortion was legal when it was done by a qualified medical doctor, in a hospital certified by the American Hospital Association, and when it was done to prevent mental or physical damage to the women" (Eldred 144). Charlotte is no exception in turning to illegal abortion and in her physical danger. Perhaps Harry is no exception either as a practitioner of abortions: he performs two abortions, one successful, the other bungled, and both illegal. The first abortion is on Billie Buckner, the mine manager's wife. He bungles the second operation because he cannot make his moral integrity subservient to Charlotte's ideal. After his unsuccessful search for a job, he realizes gradually that "to have the child would be to mock the very fiber of their defiance" (Galharn 143). By violating his moral principle and agreeing to perform the abortion, Harry discards an essential part of himself, "casting away the last vestiges of his personal and professional honor" (Harrington 82). Harry had ruined the Rittenmeyer's nuclear family and in Faulkner's poetic justice he therefore is prohibited from obtaining one of his own. Faulkner's poetic justice is thus not far from the divine justice that Little Lion articulates in Frog about her infertility due to her assisting Aunt with abortions.

In Frog, Aunt, unlike Harry, shows little hesitation and firmly performs abortions to enforce the national family planning policy. Foucault argues for two basic forms of biopower: the discipline of the individual body and the regulatory control of the population. The discipline of the individual body is exercised on the micro level, supervised by ideological apparatuses such as family, school, church, hospital, and prison, whereas the population is controlled at the macro level by state regulation. In Frog, Mo Yan does not narrate on the micro level how Aunt is transformed gradually into a qualified person conforming to the social norms, but rather presents her a part of the apparatus, and a part that goes wrong. As a Party member, Aunt firmly believes in the official discourse of family planning and becomes a practitioner infamous for her merciless enforcement of the One-child policy: "For those who give birth by abiding by the family planning policy, Aunt takes a bath and burns incense to deliver the baby; for those who get pregnant by violating the policy, Aunt never lets the baby survive. Aunt says so while making a chopping gesture in the air" ("对那些计划内生育的，姑姑焚香沐浴为她接生；对那些超计划怀孕的—姑姑对着虚空猛劈一掌—决不让一个漏网" (87). Aunt punishes those who violate the policy: she chases pregnant women despite their fragile physical condition, forcing them to jump into the river, hide in a cellar, drift to other places, or even lose their lives under her severe punishment.

The birth control policy was made at a time when the Chinese government found it difficult to provide decent health care, education, housing, and nutrition for the ever-growing population. It has alleviated the nation's and world's resources. However, the national policy, like any national policy, has loopholes. Mo Yan represents Aunt's inhumane treatment of some pregnant rural women; and in one scene, Tadpole listens to a young man describe some of the dark and unfair realities concerning the family planning policy in contemporary time: "Now the situation is that those who have money pay the fine to have more than one baby; those who do not have money stealthily give birth to more than one baby, with officials managing to let 'second wife' (a modern version of 'concubine') have the baby" ("现在是"有钱的罚着生," "没钱的偷着生", 当官的让'二奶'生") (228). As China's population is aging and is heavily weighted toward male children, Mo Yan's story is timely in urging readers to think about the national One-child policy and its loopholes. He does so by forefronting women's vulnerability when their bodies and lives are controlled by the state.

How form links with theme

Both writers adopt experimental forms to support the themes of their novels. The contrapuntal qualities of *The Wild Palms* reveal the two modes of dealing with heartbreak: Harry experiences the seamy consequences of illicit love, accepts grief, and finally extracts some meaning of life from his tragic love; the tall convict, after being rejected by his first love, denies the pain of the loss of love by distancing himself from the female world and prefers to stay in the space of all-male confinement to escape any possible female control. Faulkner's alternating arrangement of the "The Wild Palms" and "The Old Man" narratives intensifies the sense of "bewilderment and outright dissatisfaction" (Moldenhauer 305) in some readers, just as it did its first readers in 1939. This can be seen from its complex publication history: "Signet Books, after having published 'Old Man' and 'Wild Palms' in separate volumes, issued them between one set of covers, but without alternation of chapters, in 1954. Modern Library has ... reprinted 'Old Man' with 'Spotted Horses' and 'The Bear' in one volume. And Malcolm Cowley shared the majority opinion when in his introductory notes to *The Portable Faulkner*, which contains 'Old Man' as an independent selection, he wrote that this story is more effective than 'Wild Palms'" (Moldenhauer 305).

Conrad Aiken "raised his voice in the wilderness when he admired the book's 'fugue-like alternation of viewpoint'" (Aiken 653), and Edmond Volpe avers that the separation of the two narratives "destroys a novel of remarkable depth and startling ingenuity" (213). I agree with them and add that bold innovation in the narrative technique pushes readers' active participation with the narrative, characters, themes, and topics. The interlocking sections of Harry fighting against society and the tall convict fighting against nature complement each other thematically. Themes such as alienation, love, memory, captivity, and freedom are intensified by its central topic of abortion. Frog also employs narrative strategies that require much from readers. Mo Yan uses a combination of epistolary, fictional, and dramatic forms to express his concern with the conflicts between state politics and traditional fertility culture, emphasizing the characters' sense of guilt and the outlets for redemption. The five letters Tadpole writes to a Japanese writer whose father committed crimes as a commander in the 1937-45 Sino-Japanese War serve as guides to the theme of guilt and its redemption. In between the five letters is the legendary life story of Aunt, narrated in combination with some magic realistic elements, most notably her encounter with numerous frogs after her retirement party. On the surface, the ending of the story with a dramatic play being staged is the finished literary product of the narrator, who claims in his first letter that he would write a drama about Aunt. The drama, however, works intertextually. In the play, Aunt is depicted as a conspirator grabbing a baby from a surrogate mother, Chen Mei, for the sake of Little Lion and Tadpole. As such, it highlights the heated matter of surrogacy.

The national and the personal, the macro and micro, are thus intertwined. Aunt's and Little Lion's infertility are symbolic as are Aunt's insomnia and fear of frogs. Both Little Lion and Aunt are barren women. Readers learn of Aunt's infertility from Tadpole's point of view when Aunt is busy chasing down the pregnant Wang Dan:

> It suddenly occurred to me that Aunt is now forty-seven years old. Her youth has long passed and she is now walking on the course of middle age, but her face shows the desolate look of an old woman, revealing the fact that she has experienced the vicissitudes of life. It reminds me of my mother's words who has said the following more than once: What is a woman born for? A woman comes to the world to have babies ... A woman who cannot give birth to a baby experiences the most painful pains; a woman who cannot give birth to a baby is not a complete woman. Moreover, if a woman doesn't give birth to a baby, she will become cold-hearted and will grow old quickly. Mother's words are meant to speak to Aunt, but she never speaks these words in the face of Aunt. Does Aunt's growing older have anything to do with having no children?

我猛然想到，姑姑已经四十七岁了，她的青春岁月早已结束，现在，她正在中年的路上行走，但她的饱经沧桑的脸上，已经显出老者的凄凉。我想起母亲不止一次地说过，女人生来是干什么的？女人归根结底是为了生孩子而来 [...] 一个女人不生孩子是最大的痛苦，一个女人不生孩子算不上一个完整的女人，而且，女人不生孩子，心就变硬了，女人不生孩子，老得格外快。母亲的话是针对姑姑而说，但母亲从来没有当着姑姑的面说过。姑姑的老，是不是真的与没生孩子有关？(173)

Tadpole's mother, a traditional Chinese woman, holds that women's true and natural function is to procreate. She therefore interprets Aunt as unnatural because she devotes her life to the cause of family planning, remains childless after she marries in her fifties, and mistreats pregnant women who violate the family planning policy. Aunt's insomnia and fear of frogs function as additional consequences to the infertility of both Little Lion and Aunt, symbolizing the punishment for their inhumane, heavy-handed enforcement of the national policy. The possibility for atonement comes only through Aunt's marriage to the folk artist Hao Dashou, who is capable of creating vivid clay babies, and their combined efforts in creating the clay babies modeled on the babies Aunt aborted.

The titles of both novels serve the themes significantly. Faulkner's novel was originally titled *If I Forget Thee, Jerusalem*, erased until only recently because of Malcolm Cowley's bowdlerization in *The Portable Faulkner* (1946), which published only "The Old Man" (the 1995 Vintage international edition published the two short stories in alternating ways but still adopted *The Wild Palms* as the title of the whole novel, with the original title appearing in brackets on the cover). Faulkner's original title alludes to the Bible's Psalm 137: "By the rivers of Babylon, there we sat down, yea, we wept, when we remembered Zion. We hanged our harps upon the willows in the midst thereof. For there they that carried us away captive required of us a song; and they that wasted us required of us mirth, saying, Sing us one of the songs of Zion. How shall we sing the Lord's song in a strange land? If I forgot thee, O Jerusalem, let my right hand forget her cunning. If I do not remember thee, let my tongue cleave to the roof of my mouth; if I prefer not Jerusalem above my chief joy" (137.1-6). This rich Psalm expresses the agony of imprisonment in a strange land, with the personal ventriloquizing and amplifying a corporate lament. Jerusalem is a symbol of the freedom that the Jewish captives in Babylon lost but one day might regain (King 506). As a way of responding to life's brutalities, the psalmist reminds captives not to abandon any hope of future freedom by remembering what has been lost. The allusion's focus on freedom and captivity is revealed in the attempted escapes and fated imprisonment of Harry and the tall convict. The line "let my tongue cleave to the roof of my mouth" lends itself to considerations of the authorial drive to voice important matters, as does Faulkner in his novel. Faulkner does indeed use the novel to search for "various possibilities of emancipation from the various prisons of modernism and late modernist culture" (Hannon 134).

Charlotte has no model to imitate, except a culturally inherited idea of passionate love. Deceived by that idea, she ends up with a botched abortion, which for Faulkner is one of the sins drawn from late modernist culture. So too the tall convict is an uncritical consumer of pulp fictions (the very products of the likes of Harry, who works as a pulp writer for a time). He follows the wrong models in such fictions and ends up in prison for a train robbery. Harry, who decides to live with an individual rather than corporate grief over Charlotte's death, also chooses to end up in prison, maintaining the memory of her life and love: "*If I become not then all of remembering will cease to be.—Yes* he thought *Between grief and nothing I will take grief*" (273). Like the captives in Babylon, maintaining the memory of Charlotte is a way of redemption for Harry after Charlotte's death, which is to say after great loss. Mo Yan's title also serves his work: frog (蛙) is a homophone of children (娃), and with a strong power of survival after transforming from tadpoles, the frog is the symbol of life and fertility in Chinese culture. Frogs are related to human beings in the sense that in their original forms, tadpoles and sperm, are similar. Thus the title "Frog" indicates Mo Yan's concern for reproduction and life, particularly his great reverence for life. The title alerts readers to the equally meaningful naming of characters. Most of the characters are named after a specific organ of the body, owing, according to the novel, to the local belief that "petty, vulgar names secure the long life of the named" ("贱名者长生" [5]). It is the combination of different organs that forms a complete life. Mo Yan's story indicates that no one is justified in killing anyone—himself, herself, any other person—no matter the purported reason, since it is a sin that is impossible to be redeemed. Notably, the narrator Tadpole's name provides a persistent reminder of the fragility and brevity of life.

Many debates on abortion focus on the rights of the fetus and women. *The Wild Palms* and Frog, however, demonstrate that society and culture are integral to reproductive rights. The debate of abortion inevitably involves not only ordinary people's attitudes toward pregnancy and motherhood but also national policies and social mores. Although both Faulkner and Mo Yan depict tragic consequences for abortion, they reflect on the social issues concerning reproduction on the basis of different social contexts. Faulkner's discussion of abortion is tightly related to the issues of love, female desire, and personal choice, deeply affected by but not confined to the social framework of marriage. Mo Yan's view on abortion is closely tied to the impact of state intervention. Therefore he discusses abortion in wedlock. Dealing with the same subject matter of abortion, Faulkner asks readers to think about the dire consequences of excessive romantic love, whereas Mo Yan moves them to experience the discomfiting tensions that result from state intrusion on human reproduction. While Faulkner warns readers of the potential risks of falling into the trap of pure passion, Mo Yan appeals for a respect for life. Both do so by highlighting the repercussions on women, men, and reproductive practitioners, whether authorized or not. Both strive, especially through their use of innovative forms, to engage readers as well. Although written about seventy years apart, *The Wild Palms* and Frog represent reproductive issues sensitively and courageously as important and complex matters within societies still lacking a full range of social services such as safe and reliable contraception, protection from sexual and sterilization abuse, sex education, health care, and prenatal care.

Works Cited

Aiken, Conrad. "William Faulkner: The Novel as Form." *Atlantic Monthly* 164 (1939): 650-54.

Capo, B. W. "Can This Be Saved? Birth Control and Marriage in Modern American Literature." *Modern Language Studies* 34.1-2 (2004): 28-41.

Dobbs, Cynthia. "Flood: The Excesses of Geography, Gender, and Capitalism in Faulkner's *If I Forget Thee, Jerusalem*." *American Literature* 73.4 (2001): 811-35.

Eldred, Janet Carey. "Faulkner's Still Life: Art and Abortion in *The Wild Palms*." *The Faulkner Journal* 4.1-2 (1988-1989): 139-58.

Faulkner, William. *The Wild Palms*. 1939. New York: Vintage International, 1995.

King, Vincent Allan. "The Wages of Pulp: The Use and Abuse of Fiction in William Faulkner's *The Wild Palms*." *The Mississippi Quarterly* 51.3 (1998): 503-25.

Galharn, Carl. "Faulkner's Faith: Roots from *The Wild Palms*." *Twentieth Century Literature* 1.3 (1955): 139-60.

Gwin, Minrose C. *The Feminine and Faulkner: Reading (Beyond) Sexual Difference*. Knoxville: U of Tennessee P, 1990.

Hannon, Charles. "Signification, Simulation and Containment in *If I Forget Thee, Jerusalem*." *The Faulkner Journal* 7.1-2 (1991): 133-50.

Harrington, Garry. *Faulkner's Fables of Creativity: The Non-Yoknapatawpha Novels*. Athens: U of Georgia P, 1990.

Inge, M. Thomas. "Mo Yan and William Faulkner: Influences and Confluences." *The Faulkner Journal* 6.1 (1990): 15-24.

Lemke, Thomas. *Biopolitics: An Advanced Introduction*. New York: New York UP, 2011.

Moldenhauer, Joseph J. "Unity of Theme and Structure in The Wild Palms." *William Faulkner: Three Decades of Criticism*. Ed. Frederick J. Hoffman and Olga W. Vickery. East Lansing: Michigan State UP, 1960. 305-22.

Mo Yan (莫言). 蛙 (Frog). Shanghai: Shanghai Literature and Art P, 2012.

Mo Yan (莫言). "说说福克纳老头" ("Say Something about the Old Folk Faulkner"). 会唱歌的墙 (The Wall That Can Sing). By Mo Yan. Beijing: The Writer's P, 2012. 192-94.

Pitay, François. "Forgetting Jerusalem: An Ironical Chart for *The Wild Palms*." *Intertextuality in Faulkner*. Ed. Michael Gresset and Noel Park. Jackson: U of Mississippi P, 1982. 114-27.

Volpe, Edmond L. *A Reader's Guide to William Faulkner: The Novels*. Syracuse: Syracuse UP, 2003.

Author's profile

Lanlan Du teaches English-language literature at Shanghai Jiao Tong University. Her interests in scholarship include queer theory, feminist literary criticism, and comparative literature. In addition to articles in Chinese on the work of Judith Butler and the co-edited volume 美国黑人女性文学 (with Dexiu Weng, 2000) (Afro-American Women Writers), her publications in English include "Women's Writing in the Atlas of World Literature: A Case Study of J. K. Rowling" (*Neohelicon: acta comparationis litterarum universarum* [2011]).

Rural Chineseness, Mo Yan's Work, and World Literature

Chengzhou He

Abstract

In "Rural Chineseness, Mo Yan's Work, and World Literature" Chengzhou He discusses performative acts that Mo Yan employs to create a unique imaginative world of rural China and how Mo Yan's literary works of rural China serve as a means to supplement, resist, revise, or subvert the official discourse of Chinese modernity. The characteristic rural location, the Northeast Township in Gaomi County, a fictionalized place based on Mo Yan's own hometown, is not merely a place, a background of literary writing, but rather a representation of a narrative style, an emotional experience, and an aesthetic. Mo Yan's writings offer not only a personal, local, and unofficial account of an eventful life in twentieth-century China but more importantly his reflections on and criticism of unfolding reality.

The 1990s enacted a "performative turn" in cultural and literary studies wherein the paradigm of culture and literature as text transformed into the concept of culture and literature as event and action. Theories of cultural performativity provide vitality to discussions about literature as cultural components. In his "Culture and Performance in the Circum-Atlantic World," Joseph Roach suggests that the category of literature itself be expanded beyond its traditional sense of a collection of texts to instead encompass a wide range of cultural activities, including oral storytelling, song, mime, ritual, and other such enterprises (45). The theory of performativity originates in the "speech-act theory" of J. L. Austin, whose *How to Do Things with Words*, based on his 1955 William James Lectures at Harvard University, remains a seminal text. Austin distinguishes two categories of utterances: constative utterances and performative utterances. The latter are not true or false but rather perform the action they refer to. An example Austin gives is that of a wedding ceremony: the priest asks, "Do you take this woman to be your lawful wedded wife?" The response "I do" performs the act. The speaker's relationship to the woman is changed by means of the response. But Austin also points out that such a performative utterance may be "infelicitous" or unhappy, if the circumstances are not satisfactory to make the action happen, for example, if the wedding ceremony takes place on stage or in fiction. Therefore, Austin excludes literature from his theory of performative utterances.

Jacques Derrida and others critiqued Austin's "prejudice" against the so-called "non-serious performatives" in literature. In "Philosophy and Literature: The Fortunes of the Performative," Jonathan Culler encourages scholars of literature to remain open to the various interpretations of the performative and to seek opportunities to read literature and performativity against and in cooperation with each other: "I think that rather than try to restrict or simplify the performative's domain by choosing one strand of reflection as the correct one, we ought to accentuate and to pursue the differences between them—so as to increase our chances of grasping the different levels and modes in which events occur; and I take this to be a project requiring the cooperation—albeit the inevitably contentious cooperation—of philosophy and literature, the thinking of philosophy and of literary theory" (518). To understand performativity, two key connotations of its root word "perform" are especially useful. To perform connotes in equal measure to do and to act; that is, one performs a task or performs for an audience. The concept of performativity keeps both of these senses of performance firmly in view (Wagner 1203). A third term, "performanz," refers to the effects of any social/cultural action. Literary performanz may refer to how literary events influence participants by shaping their emotions, constructing identities, and creating imaginative spaces. Performativity is the characteristics of an object, for instance a literary text or an event, such as a literary recital. These characteristics are apparent in a performance when the object or event is framed, presented, highlighted, or displayed.

To say that Mo Yan performs rural Chineseness, then, means that he both performs a rural literary identity for his audience and readers and builds a literary identity of rural Chineseness in his writings. I argue that the rural Chineseness that Mo Yan has performed in his texts and in literary events functions as a counterdiscourse to resist, revise, and supplement, if not subvert, the dominant grand discourse of modern China in a reflective or corrective manner. Further, I argue that Mo Yan's rural Chineseness is performed on different, interrelated levels: on the textual level through such devices as nativist narratives of storytelling and local opera under the label of an imaginative landscape called the Northeast Gaomi Township in Shandong Province and on the cultural level through the author's performances, such as in the Nobel Prize in Literature award ceremony of 10 December 2012, with his speeches and interviews consolidating his image as an author of and from rural China.

"A storyteller" from and about rural China

Immediately after the announcement on 11 October 2012 that Mo Yan was the recipient of the Nobel Prize in Literature and again following the Nobel Prize ceremonies in December in Stockholm, there was a rush of articles on and interviews with Mo

Yan across China and the globe in various media. In contrast with the warm reception and praise of Mo Yan's Nobel Prize by Chinese readers and media, the international media engaged in a heated debate over Mo Yan, his literature, and his political views. Most of the negative criticism is not so much literary as political. The criticism is targeted in particular at Mo Yan's position as vice president of the government-run Chinese Writers Association and his participation in an event of copying Mao Zedong's 1942 speech on literature and arts in Yan'an. In June 2012 some Chinese authors joined in a state-sponsored project to hand-copy Mao Zedong's 1942 "Talks at the Yan'an Forum on Literature and Art" in commemoration of its seventieth anniversary. In "Does This Writer Deserve the Prize?" Perry Link questions Mo Yan's conscious compromises with the regime, although with some reluctance. And he suggests that this is "the price of writing inside the system" (<http://www.nybooks.com/articles/archives/2012/dec/06/mo-yan-nobel-prize/>). Herta Müller, the 2009 Nobel Prize in Literature laureate, goes so far to say that the choice of Mo Yan by the Nobel Committee is "a slap in the face for all those working for democracy and human rights" (Müller qtd. in Flood <http://www.theguardian.com/books/2012/nov/26/mo-yan-nobel-herta-muller>). While Torbjörn Lodén speaks highly of Mo Yan's literary achievements, calling him "a lavish storyteller with roots in century-old oral tradition," he nevertheless expresses doubt over the decision of the Swedish Academy to give the prize to "an author who is so obedient to the regime that he participates in the praise of Mao's Yan'an Speech" (<http://www.dn.se/kultur-noje/kulturdebatt/mo-yans-hyllning-till-mao-forvanar/>; unless indicated otherwise, all translations are mine). Others such as Charles Laughlin and Göran Sommardal defended Mo Yan and launched a critique of the criticisms of Mo Yan. The former poses the rhetorical question, "am I to understand from Mo Yan's critics that unless Chinese writers and artists are more 'politically courageous' and invite imprisonment and exile—or worse—by speaking out directly against their government and political system, their lifetime of artistic labors and achievements will never be worthy of international recognition in the form of a Nobel Prize in Literature?" (<https://www.chinafile.com/what-mo-yans-detractors-get-wrong>).

I outline this debate not to join it but rather to examine Mo Yan's subsequent defense of his political views and thus address the comingling of politics and aesthetics in the performance of Mo Yan's literature, especially how he reflects on modern and contemporary Chinese history and society and the mainstream representations of them in both his speeches and his texts. First and foremost, Mo Yan has often presented himself and also been presented as a storyteller of and from rural China. The title of Mo Yan's "Nobel Lecture: Storytellers" is a far cry from the grand and provocative title of Harold Pinter's "Nobel Lecture: Art, Truth, and Politics" (<http://www.nobelprize.org/nobel_prizes/literature/laureates/2005/pinter-lecture-e.html>). Mo Yan indeed told stories in the speech, including those about his mother and his childhood. As an attendee in Stockholm at the invitation of the Swedish Academy, I found especially touching the story of his mother who died of hunger, disease, and hard work: "After my mother died, in the midst of almost crippling grief, I decided to write a novel for her. *Big Breasts and Wide Hips* is that novel. Once my plan took shape, I was burning with such emotion that I completed a draft of half a million words in only eighty-three days" (<http://www.nobelprize.org/nobel_prizes/literature/laureates/2012/yan-lecture_en.html>). He also shared that his childhood as a cattle and sheep herder after primary school provided rich material for his writings. He said that he learned through listening to "tales of the supernatural, historical romances, and strange and captivating stories, all tied to the natural environment and clan histories. What I should do was simplicity itself: write my own stories in my own way. My way was that of the marketplace storyteller, with which I was so familiar, the way my grandfather and my grandmother and other village old-timers told stories" (<http://www.nobelprize.org/nobel_prizes/literature/laureates/2012/yan-lecture_en.html>). Mo Yan's stories in the speech, as in his fiction, are mostly about his family and hometown.

These stories of his rural Chinese upbringing are clearly related to his criticisms. As introduction to the stories of his Nobel Lecture, he addresses the negative criticisms wielded at him and his literature, specifically in terms of performance:

> The announcement of my Nobel Prize has led to controversy. At first I thought I was the target of the disputes, but over time I've come to realize that the real target was a person who had nothing to do with me. Like someone watching a play in a theater, I observed the *performances* around me. I saw the winner of the prize both garlanded with flowers and besieged by stone-throwers and mudslingers. I was afraid he would succumb to the assault, but he emerged from the garlands of flowers and the stones, a smile on his face; he wiped away mud and grime, stood calmly off to the side, and said to the crowd: "For a writer, the best way to speak is by writing. You will find everything I need to say in my works. Speech is carried off by the wind; the written word can never be obliterated. I would like you to find the patience to read my books. I cannot force you to do that, and even if you do, I do not expect your opinion of me to change. No writer has yet appeared, anywhere in the world, who is liked by all his readers; that is especially true during times like these." Even though I would prefer to say nothing, since it is something I must do on this occasion, let me just say this: I am a storyteller, so I am going to tell you some stories. (<http://www.nobelprize.org/nobel_prizes/literature/laureates/2012/yan-lecture_en.html>).

Mo Yan's performance of rural Chineseness and storytelling in his speech may be interpreted as his response to the subset of his "readers," his critics. As he points out, he is first of all a writer who tells stories. What he has written is based on his own experiences, especially from his life in his hometown.

In his prepared speech at the Nobel banquet, Mo Yan calls himself "a farm boy from Gaomi's Northeast Township in far-away China" and he ends with thanks to "my older relatives and compatriots at home in Gaomi, Shandong, China. I was, am and always will be one of you. I also thank the fertile soil that gave birth to me and nurtured me. It is often said that a person is shaped by the place where he grows up. I am a storyteller, who has found nourishment in your humid soil. Everything that I have done, I have done to thank you!" ("Banquet" <http://www.nobelprize.org/nobel_prizes/literature/laureates/2012/yan-speech.html>). Mo Yan's repeated self-portrayal as "a storyteller of and from rural China" for his readers and audiences is deliberate, and it is deliberate for audiences of ever larger concentric circles: his immediate critics, the audience at the banquet, and the posterity of readers who will read his speech. "A storyteller from rural China" is also the image that Mo Yan presented himself to his large local and international audiences at the Aula of Stockholm University on the day before the banquet. There he recited in Chinese his short story "The Wolf" and an excerpt from the beginning of *Life and Death are Wearing Me Out*. Following each of his recitals, a Swedish actor performed them again in Swedish. Both stories are characterized by animal fable, nativist language, and rural Chinese life. After the recitals, a local journalist interviewed Mo Yan before the audience. The following are from the notes I took: "In rural culture there are historical figures, legends, events, and even myths and ghost stories such as a wolf or a rooster turning into a human. The folk elements and oral tradition figure strongly in my books, as they are part of my experiences at that time." When asked about his views on literature and politics, Mo Yan answered, "Any reader is entitled to ask a writer questions about his views of politics. I am not a politician, but my novels are about politics. The major task of a novelist is to create characters, who then express what the author thinks." Mo Yan once again requested his readers and critics to judge his political attitudes based not on what he has said and done in public but on what is written in his oeuvre. Anyone who has read carefully Mo Yan's writings cannot fail to notice how critical he is socially and politically about China and the human condition.

What Mo Yan said and did before, during, and after the Nobel Prize ceremonies suggests three aspects about his performance: first, he is an author from the countryside; second, literature is about politics; and third, he is a writer who does not speak out his views and thoughts verbally or in live social performance but conveys them with his pen.

The nativist narrative in Mo Yan's novels

In terms of the "Chinese" or nativist aspects of storytelling and narrative, Mo Yan is indebted to P'u Sung-Ling (1640-1715) and his 1680 聊斋志异 (*Strange Tales from a Chinese Studio*). In his article "学习浦松林" ("Learning from P'u Sung-Ling"), Mo Yan tells a story about how P'u might have collected resources for his stories sitting under a big willow tree by a main road at his village; he prepared tea and a smoking pipe for the passersby, who were then requested to tell stories of any kind in return: "Thus, numerous unreliable and fabricated stories became resources of the book *Strange Stories from a Chinese Studio*" (1). In those stories, the boundary between reality and the odd or fantastic is often blurred, and the characters include magical foxes, ghosts, scholars, court officials, and so on. *Strange Stories from a Chinese Studio* has been one of the most popular books in China among both old and young, and there have been numerous adaptations across different media in modern times. P'u's hometown is not far from Mo Yan's and both were nurtured by the rich folk tradition of their native cultures in which people express their wishes and fears, their joy and sadness.

In *Life and Death Are Wearing Me Out* and Mo Yan's other novels and stories, there is a blurring of the boundaries between humans, ghosts, and beasts. *Life and Death Are Wearing Me Out* is about a deceased man called Ximen Nao, who is reincarnated in the human world six times in animal and human forms: a donkey, an ox, a pig, a dog, a monkey, and a millennium baby. At the beginning of the story, Nao is executed by the local revolutionaries even though he did nothing to harm the community except for being a landlord. Performing as narrator, as well as the first bestial reincarnation, Ximen Donkey reveals to readers that he had been a hardworking and kindhearted landlord and should not have been killed. He once saved a dying child, who later became his tenant, and he treated him well. Thus, as a donkey, he avers, "For that alone, you people should not have shot me with your musket. And, on that point, Lord Yama, you should not have sent me back as a donkey! Everyone says that saving a life is better than building a seven-story pagoda, and I, Ximen Nao, sure as hell saved a life. Me, Ximen Nao, and not just one life. During the famine one spring I sold twenty bushels of sorghum at a low price and exempted my tenant farmers from paying rent. That kept many people alive" (12).

Mo Yan's rural experiences also included religious traditions he learned through listening and observing. As can be noted by the reincarnations of Ximen Nao as animals, *Life and Death Are Wearing Me Out* is influenced by the Buddhist ideas about the afterlife. In his Nobel Lecture, Mo Yan told another story, this one about how he got his inspiration for writing this novel from a Buddhist painting: "But it wasn't until the year 2005, when I viewed the Buddhist mural The Six Stages of Samsara on a temple wall that I knew exactly how to go about telling his story" (<http://www.nobelprize.org/nobel_prizes/literature/laureates/2012/yan-lecture_en.html>). "The Six Stages of Samsara" is complicated and it contains strange figures such as a snake body with a horse head and a human body with a dragon head. The images illustrate the basic beliefs of Buddhism on the necessity of suffering, the idea of *karma* or supernatural cause and effect, and so on with the overall message being to do good things during one's lifetime in order to be treated well in future metamorphoses in the afterlife.

In nativist narratives, nature and animals are usually mythologized. During an interview shortly before the Nobel award banquet, Mo Yan spoke about the influence of his childhood life in the countryside on himself and his writings: "firstly,

I was able to establish an intimate relationship with nature. A child growing up in school and a child growing up in the field have different relationships to nature, different feelings for animals and plants. The others were surrounded by other kids and teachers every day. But I was surrounded by sheep, cattle, plants, grass and trees every day. The feelings I had towards nature were so delicate and sentimental. For a long time, I thought animals and plants could communicate with humans. And I felt that they understood what I said. This kind of experience is unique and valuable" (<http://www.nobelprize.org/nobel_prizes/literature/laureates/2012/yan-interview-text_en.html?print=1>). This "intimate relationship" is characteristic of what is called the "magical or hallucinatory realism" in Mo Yan's oeuvre, reminiscent of but distinct from such works as *One Hundred Years of Solitude* by Gabriel García Márquez. Mo Yan has explained time and again that he has read only a little bit of *One Hundred Years of Solitude* and *The Sound and Fury* by William Faulkner and thus he was not familiar with the works' details. Rather, he was interested in how these authors wrote creatively about reality and then drew inspirations from the stories in his hometown's rural culture and in the Chinese tradition of storytelling, such as in *Strange Stories from a Chinese Studio*.

Another feature of Mo Yan's narrative is the mixture of local opera with his storytelling. Before television sets became affordable in the Chinese countryside in the 1980s, local opera was a popular form of entertainment and education. In China, there are hundreds of local operas, such as 越剧 (*yue* opera) in Zhejiang province and Shanghai, 淮剧 (*huai* opera) in northern Jiangsu province, and so on. In Mo Yan's hometown of Gaomi, 茂腔 (*maoqiang*) opera is popular. It has a history of more than two hundred years and a repertoire of more than one hundred plays. There are many *maoqiang* opera houses in Gaomi and its neighboring regions. In his "Reading with Ears," Mo Yan defines going to *maoqiang* opera performances as part of his early education—he completed the fifth grade only—and praises opera as "the open school" for rural people (212). In many of Mo Yan's novels, local opera is an intertext that interacts with the main stories, *Sandalwood Death* being the prime example. The beginnings of some chapters in the novel contain a passage of *maoqiang* opera that is suggestive of what is going to happen in the story's plot. Those passages are written in poetic language for the sake of singing. Additionally, some of the main characters are actors of local *maoqiang* opera, and the protagonist of the novel, Sun Bin, is a well-known actor of *maoqiang* opera. His role in the *maoqiang* play mixes with what he is doing in life. His ideas of heroism, for example, are influenced by the heroic characters he plays in the local opera. In Chapter 13, the people who participate in the peasants' rebellion wear the costumes of the local opera. The blending of performance levels takes on a serious level in Chapters 17 and 18 with the executions enacted as if they were scenes of local opera, and the crowds of local people gathering to watch a spectacle: with "Sun Bin, up on the Ascension Platform" the narrator had assumed that "the wail was an expression of torment over seeing the

Maoqiang Patriarch endure such suffering. Once again, I realized my mistake, for the mournful cry was actually a call for the musicians to prepare their instruments, an opening note" (388).

Mo Yan involves multiple levels of performativity especially with the character Zhao Jia. Zhao performs his role as one of the executioners like a great performance for which he will have to get prepared in order to promote his reputation as a high-rank executioner. It is for the occasion of killing Sun Bin that he invents the cruel and bizarre method of execution called "the sandalwood death." What is more, the victims are willing to accept or are forced to accept the kind of role they are expected to play in this show of death. To satisfy the excited onlookers, the victims recite some often-quoted words or even sing a familiar song before the execution. It is made explicit in the novel that *Sandalwood Death* is also a play and the characters in the novel are also actors. The back cover of the novel thus notes that "this is truly a nationalized novel, really from the nativist circles and devoted to the grassroots." This mixture of fiction and traditional opera is one of the author's strategies to revive the tradition of the classical Chinese novel: "To be sure, this return was not without its modifications. *Sandalwood Death* and the novels that followed are inheritors of the Chinese classical novel tradition but enhanced by Western literary techniques. What is known as innovative fiction is, for the most part, a result of this mixture, which is not limited to domestic traditions with foreign techniques, but can include mixing fiction with art from other realms. *Sandalwood Death*, for instance, mixes fiction with local opera, while some of my early works were partly nurtured by fine art, music, even acrobatics" ("Nobel Lecture" <http://www.nobelprize.org/nobel_prizes/literature/laureates/2012/yan-lecture_en.html>). This kind of blending is essential to modern Chinese literature inclined to learn from both classical Chinese and nonnative, mostly Western, literatures. This is the new literary Chineseness I am contending Mo Yan is etching out. A blending of fiction and Chinese opera can also be found in the novel *Farewell My Concubine* by Lilian Lee, which was made into the internationally successful film of the same name directed by Chen Kaige.

The performativity of Mo Yan's works includes his inscription of a fictional Mo Yan in his fictionalized hometown of the Northeast Gaomi Township. The following example from his 1992 novel *The Republic of Wine* is characteristically self-mocking and satirical:

> As he lay in the relative comfort of a hard-sleeper cot—relative to a hard-seater, that is—the puffy, balding, beady-eyed, twisted-mouthed, middle-aged writer Mo Yan wasn't sleepy at all ... I know there are many similarities between me and this Mo Yan, but many contradictions as well. I'm a hermit crab, and Mo Yan is the shell I'm occupying ... There are times when I feel that this Mo Yan is a heavy burden, but I can't seem to cast it off, just as a hermit crab cannot rid itself of its shell. I can be free of it in the darkness, at least for a while. I see it softly filling up the narrow middle berth, its large head tossing and turning on the tiny pillow; long years as a writer

have formed bone spurs on its vertebrae, turning the neck stiff and cold, sore and tingly, until just moving it is a real chore. This Mo Yan disgusts me, that's the truth. (331)

The appearances of the character Mo Yan in other works by the author Mo Yan, such as *Life and Death Are Wearing Me Out* and 蛙 (Frog), produce multiple effects, which is illustrative of what was referred to earlier as performanz. They suggest that the author's experience of a split between fiction and reality and his enjoyment of the freedom are narrated in the imaginary worlds of his creation. Of special note is that Mo Yan the character does not accord with what Mo Yan the author has done or spoken in public. Paradoxically, Mo Yan the character thus mimes Mo Yan the author's wiliness in his response to the criticisms about his political attitudes. Northeast Gaomi Township as an emblem of rural Chineseness is performed in his texts and in his public performance. At the beginning of his Nobel Lecture, Mo Yan indicates such: "Through the mediums of television and the Internet, I imagine that everyone here has at least a nodding acquaintance with far-off Northeast Gaomi Township" (<http://www.nobelprize.org/nobel_prizes/literature/laureates/2012/yan-lecture_en.html>). Mo Yan mentions Gaomi eight times in his lecture, and at the end he says that "I hope to make tiny Northeast Gaomi Township a microcosm of China, even of the whole world." Since the Northeast Gaomi Township made its first appearance in his 1984 short story "Autumn Floods," it has become his own land on which he has built his home and with which contemporary readers around the globe formulate their concepts of rural China.

By presenting rich and diverse pictures of people's lives in his hometown, Mo Yan consolidates his nativist identity and position as a writer and distances himself from the official orthodox discourse of history, although he now resides in its political center, Beijing. His literature of rural China provides an alternative discourse of modern China, and this serves for a better understanding of the relationship between aesthetics and politics in his fiction.

Rural Chineseness as an alternative discourse

Rural Chineseness is intrinsic to Mo Yan's literary image performed through his texts and across media. The discourse of rural Chineseness in Mo Yan's writings challenges, or rather subverts, the dominant grand narrative of Chinese history and politics. Under the name of ruralness, Mo Yan avoids being overpoliticized by his interpreters and critiques simultaneously the social and political reality in modern China. *Red Sorghum* and *Big Breasts and Wide Hips* provide an alternative view of revolution and social progress. *Red Sorghum* does not follow the usual official pattern of narrating a story of how Chinese people fought against the Japanese invaders during the war period (1937-45). David Der-wei Wang and Michael Berry rightly note that "as the story develops, family history and national history gradually merge, climaxing with 'My Granddad and My Grandma's' annihilation of the Japanese in a guerrilla attack. In this respect, Mo Yan appears to be paying tribute to works of revolutionary historical fiction. But on closer examination, we realize that not only does his revolutionary history fail to deliver the promise of ultimate meaning, but it actually reveals a historical degeneration in which each generation fails to live up to the preceding one" (490). In most Chinese stories about the war against Japan, the protagonists are either Chinese Communist Party members or their supporters, nationalistic and fighting in the name of defending the nation and liberating the people. On the other hand, in *Red Sorghum* Grandpa leads an attack on the Japanese purely out of revenge for the Japanese soldiers killing many villagers. The brave act passed on orally to and inspiring Mo Yan is part of a rural history that supplements, if not deconstructs, the official narrative of history.

Big Breasts and Wide Hips constitutes a further challenge to the progressive narrative and patriarchal ideology that are dominant in the official discourse: "The reason why I think *Big Breasts and Wide Hips* is a great Chinese novel is that it represents the beauty and poetry of the traditional society in the countryside. To put it simply, this novel can be read as a fictional narration of the process in which the traditional society of Chinese countryside was invaded and destroyed. Under the impact of the complicity of the external politics and power, the people and the nativist world that the mother represents were subject to severe harm and damage in both physical and spiritual senses" (Zhang, Qinghua 3). Covering the different eras of twentieth-century China from the Boxer Rebellion of 1900 to the market economy in the 1990s, the novel portrays the gradual breakdown of traditional rural life in China through a family story. The impotency of Jin Tong, the "Golden Boy" son of a Swedish father and Chinese mother, is metaphorical in that it is used to "examine the viability of the model of intimate integration" (Cai 123) between East and West and its impact on just one component of the Chinese nation, rural China.

Mo Yan's novel Frog is an incisive commentary on the family planning (计划生育) or One-child policy as experienced in his hometown. Like *Big Breasts and Wide Hips*, it has been viewed as "a great Chinese novel"; it is the winner of the prestigious national prize, the Eighth Mao Dun Literature Prize of 2011. The One-child policy has been of great import to China in the last quarter of the twentieth century and will continue to exert a huge impact on almost every aspect of Chinese life and society. In most parts of China, especially in cities, it has been strictly implemented with violators severely punished. Mo Yan says, "getting to know the issue of Chinese paternal planning does not mean that one is able to understand China. However, if one is ignorant of the Chinese paternal planning, it is impossible for him to form a sensible understanding of China" ("Listening" 342). Recently, the policy has again become controversial in China as it confronts an aging society. In Frog, Mo Yan adopts an ethical perspective of the grassroots in the countryside characterized by an attitude of regret and forgiveness for the lives that have been lost in response to the national policy. The theme of atonement is mainly expressed on three levels. First, the atonement of the character "my Aunt," who started her medical career as a "barefoot doctor" and a nurse midwife in the countryside. Later, she becomes an administrator who carries out the family planning policy, ensuring that "illegitimately" pregnant women—married women who did not get permission from the local government to give birth—in her township get abortions. Because of her role, the locals give her the nickname "living lord of hell." In the countryside, some extreme actions used to be taken to ensure birth control among the peasants, as the novel chronicles in great detail. After her retirement, Aunt begins to repent for taking away the lives of so many unborn babies.

The narrator's atonement comprises the second ethical commentary. Tadpole's agreement to the abortion of his pregnant wife, Wang Renmei, causes her death. As a member of the People's Liberation Army, Tadpole chooses to abide by the government's family planning policy in order to retain opportunities for promotion in the military. Later, he feels responsible for the death of his first wife and their unborn baby. It is explicitly mentioned in the novel that the author wants to fulfill his wish for atonement through his writing. However, it did not provide the consolation he had wished for, but rather even more guilt. Atonement, however, is performed in Frog in a collective sense in the countryside. Two native craftsmen devote themselves to making earthen figures of babies. Near the end of the novel, Aunt worships the earthen babies, full of rich and specific details of the dead unborn babies: "Aunt puts the earthen baby in her hands into an empty square, and then she withdraws one step. After having ignited three sticks of incense, she kneels down in front of the small altar in the middle of the room. Putting her palms together, she murmurs incessantly" (270). Clearly, such nativist narrative is a response, resistance, or even subversion of the grand narratives of the One-child policy. This local atonement for a national policy performs an understated yet bold atonement at an international level and by extension a fully human one. Mo Yan structures the novel to broaden the theme of atonement with the story being told through long letters to a Japanese friend whose father had been an officer in the Japanese army that invaded China and had been stationed in the region. The atonement of a Japanese man for the harm and damage to the Chinese people caused by his father and the Japanese army thus generalizes the theme of atonement.

It must be noted that, from time to time, Mo Yan addresses political issues directly in his writings such as in *The Garlic Ballads* and *The Republic of Wine*. But more often Mo Yan writes in a metaphorical manner to resist or complement the grand discourse of history and revolution. Literature cannot avoid politics, but it can distance itself from and transcend politics through various literary techniques, such as satire and form. Mo Yan used the rare opportunity of his Nobel Lecture to outline his perception on the relationship between aesthetics and politics: "My greatest challenges come with writing novels that deal with social realities, such as *The Garlic Ballads*, not because I'm afraid of being openly critical of the darker aspects of society, but because heated emotions and anger allow politics to suppress literature and transform a novel into reportage of a social event. As a member of society, a novelist is entitled to his own stance and viewpoint; but when he is writing he must take a humanistic stance, and write accordingly. Only then can literature not just originate in events, but transcend them, not just show concern for politics but be greater than politics" (<http://www.nobelprize.org/nobel_prizes/literature/laureates/2012/yan-lecture_en.html>).

For Mo Yan, then, rural Chineseness is his method to raise questions on the grand narratives of history and politics in China and beyond. For his critics, Mo Yan's performance of rural Chineseness offers a new perspective to read his literature. Others have joined in on performing Mo Yan and his image of rural Chineseness for domestic and international audiences, specifically the film industry. For example, in 1987 Yimou Zhang, a well-known fifth-generation Chinese film director, directed the film 红高粱 (*Red Sorghum*), and Jianqi Huo's 2003 film 暖 (*Nuan*) is an adaptation of Mo Yan's 1985 白狗秋千架 (White Dog and the Swing).

In conclusion, we are invited at the beginning of the twenty-first century to join Mo Yan in the performance of rural Chineseness to inquire into the creation and reformation of Chineseness. Chineseness should no longer be mythologized, orientalized, and approached as unified and unchanging. Instead of being looked at only from the outside, Chineseness along with its conflicts and agencies are to be interrogated, critiqued, and analyzed from inside China and from all perspectives. Through performing a unique rural Chineseness, Mo Yan, instead of what his penname suggests of "being silent," speaks eloquently and forcefully on various political and social issues in his literary works. In that sense, Mo Yan's penname itself is part of his performance as a storyteller.

Works Cited

Austin, J. L. *How to Do Things with Words*. Ed. J. O. Urmson and Marina Sbisà. Cambridge: Harvard UP, 1975 [1955, 1962].
Cai, Rong. "Problematizing the Foreign Other: Mother, Father, and the Bastard in Mo Yan's *Big Breasts and Wide Hips*." *Modern China* 29.1 (2003): 108-37.
Chou, Yu Sie Rundkvist. "Mo Yan: Interview." *nobelprize.org* (2013): <http://www.nobelprize.org/nobel_prizes/literature/laureates/2012/yan-interview-text_en.html?print=1>.
Culler, Jonathan. "Philosophy and Literature: The Fortunes of the Performative." *Poetics Today* 21.3 (2000): 503-19.
Derrida, Jacques. *Limited INC*. Trans. Samuel Weber and Jeffrey Mehlman. Evanston: Northwestern UP, 1988.
Farewell My Concubine (霸王别姬). Dir. Kaige Chen (陈凯歌). Hong Kong: Tomson Film, 1993.
Flood, Alison. "Mo Yan's Nobel Nod a 'Catastrophe,' Says Fellow Laureate Herta Müller." *theguardian.com* (26 November 2012): <http://www.theguardian.com/books/2012/nov/26/mo-yan-nobel-herta-muller>.

Laughlin, Charles. "What Mo Yan's Detractors Get Wrong." *chinafile.com* (11 December 2012): <https://www.chinafile.com/what-mo-yans-detractors-get-wrong>.

Li, Bihua (李碧华). 霸王别姬 (*Farewell My Concubine*). Beijing: People's Literature P, 1993.

Link, Perry. "Does This Writer Deserve the Prize?" *nybooks.com* (6 December 2012): <http://www.nybooks.com/articles/archives/2012/dec/06/mo-yan-nobel-prize/>.

Lodén, Torbjörn. "Mo Yans hyllning till Mao förvanår" ("Mo Yan's Praise of Mao is a Surprise"). *dn.se* (10 December 2012): <http://www.dn.se/kultur-noje/kultur debatt/mo-yans-hyllning-till-mao-forvanar/>.

Mao, Zedong (毛泽东). 在延安文艺座谈会上的讲话 (Talks at the Yan'an Forum on Literature and Art). 毛泽东选集 (Selected Works of Mao Zedong). Beijing: People's P, 1991. Vol. 3.

Mo Yan (莫言). "秋水" ("Autumn Floods"). 白狗秋千架 (White Dog and the Swing). Shanghai: Shanghai Literature and Art P, 2012. 186-98.

Mo Yan. "Banquet Speech." *nobelprize.org* (10 December 2012): <http://www.nobelprize.org/nobel_prizes/literature/laureates/2012/yan-speech.html>.

Mo Yan. *Big Breasts and Wide Hips*. Trans. Howard Goldblatt. New York: Arcade, 2004.

Mo Yan (莫言). 蛙 (Frog). Shanghai: Shanghai Literature and Art P, 2012.

Mo Yan. *The Garlic Ballads*. Trans. Howard Goldblatt. New York: Viking, 1995.

Mo Yan. *Life and Death are Wearing Me Out*. Trans. Howard Goldblatt. New York: Arcade, 2008.

Mo Yan (莫言). 学习蒲松龄 (Learning from P'u Sung-Ling). Beijing: Zhongguo Qingnian Chubanshe, 2012.

Mo Yan (莫言). "听取蛙声一片:代后记" ("Listening to Frogs: Postscript"). 蛙 (Frog). Shanghai: Shanghai Literature and Art P, 2012. 341-43.

Mo Yan. "Nobel Lecture: Storytellers." Trans. Howard Goldblatt. *nobelprize.org* (2012): <http://www.nobelprize.org/nobel_prizes/literature/laureates/2012/yan-lecture_en.html>.

Mo Yan (莫言). "用耳朵阅读" ("Reading with Ears"). 见证莫言 (Witnessing Mo Yan). Ed. Wuchang Tan (谭五昌). Guilin: Lijiang P, 2012. 210-13.

Mo Yan. *The Republic of Wine: A Novel*. Trans. Howard Goldblatt. New York: Arcade, 2011.

Mo Yan. *Sandalwood Death: A Novel*. Trans. Howard Goldblatt. Oklahoma: U of Oklahoma P, 2012.

Nuan (暖). Dir. Jianqi Huo (霍建起). Beijing: Beijing Jinhai Fangzhou Cultural Development, 2003.

Pinter, Harold. "Nobel Lecture: Art, Truth, and Politics." *nobelprize.org* (2005): <http://www.nobelprize.org/nobel_prizes/literature/laureates/2005/pinter-lecture-e.html>.

P'u, Sung-Ling. *Strange Stories from a Chinese Studio*. 1680. Trans. A. Giles Herbert. Honolulu: UP of the Pacific, 2003.

Red Sorghum (红高粱). Dir. Yomou Zhang (张艺谋). Xi'an: Xi'an Film, 1987.

Roach, Joseph. "Culture and Performance in the Circum-Atlantic World." *Performativity and Performance*. Ed. Andrew Parker and Eve Sedgwick Kosofsky. London: Routledge, 1995. 45-63.

Wagner, Matthew. "Performativity and Cultural Studies." *The Encyclopedia of Literature and Cultural Theory*. Ed. Michael Ryan. Malden: Blackwell, 2011. 1203-06.

Wang, David Der-wei, and Michael Berry. "The Literary World of Mo Yan." *World Literature Today* 74.3 (2000): 487-94.

Zhang, Qinghua (张清华). "诺奖之于莫言,莫言之于当代中国文学" ("Nobel Prize to Mo Yan and Mo Yan to Contemporary Chinese Literature"). *Wenyi Zhengming* 12 (2012): 1-3.

Author's profile

Chengzhou He teaches English literature and drama at Nanjing University. In addition to numerous articles in Chinese and English, his book publications include the single-authored *Henrik Ibsen and Modern Chinese Drama* (2004) and 对话北欧经典:易卜生、斯特林堡与哈姆生 (The Scandinavian Canon: Ibsen, Strindberg and Hamsun, 2009), and the edited volumes *Representation of the Other* (2009), 性别、理论与文化 (Gender, Theory and Culture, 2011) and 全球化与跨文化戏剧 (Globalization and Intercultural Theater, 2012).

Part Two
Trunk

The Realpolitik of Mo Yan's Fiction

Sabina Knight

Abstract

In "The Realpolitik of Mo Yan's Fiction" Sabina Knight analyzes Mo Yan's texts in the context of China's politics and censorship. Since winning the 2012 Nobel Prize in Literature, Mo Yan has become a scapegoat for the sins of the regime in which he must survive. Such judgments neglect much that can be learned from his work. By operating in a "gray zone," Mo Yan voices subtle political criticisms which would risk reprisal if presented overtly. Knight posits that the key to understanding his texts is to seek out the underlying meaning in his probing of individual resilience in the face of the relentless forces of instinct, sexuality, and history. Knight examines Mo Yan's careful maneuvering to chronicle China's twentieth-century pain and the individual strength of its citizens to exorcise traumatic historical memories and restore ties of societal unity.

Twenty years ago, on my first day in a PhD program, my mentor Joseph Lau gave me a stack of ten novels. When I expressed doubts about fitting in this leisure reading on top of my coursework, he held up Mo Yan's 酒國 (*The Republic of Wine*) and shook the book at me: "This writer is going to win the Nobel Prize," he said. Such was the impact of Mo Yan's writing on those familiar with it long before he won the Nobel in 2012. Yet, since the award Mo Yan has become a scapegoat for the sins of the regime in which he must survive. Mo Yan's literary range and philosophical depth have received little attention in the recent flurry of press coverage, which has concentrated on his apparent acquiescence to the Chinese government's repression of dissidents. Secure in the comfort of Western freedoms, many writers have lambasted Mo Yan for his public statements and silences (see Goldblatt; He). Few writers have noted that Western authors seldom are judged on their politics or that writers in China have reasons for working within, as well as outside of the system.

Mo Yan now operates under heightened scrutiny. Indeed, the honor was embraced triumphantly by Beijing as the long-awaited global acknowledgment of China's return, not only as an economic powerhouse but as a cultural leader. Mo Yan's was the first Nobel Prize in Literature ever awarded to a Chinese citizen (the 2000 Nobel Prize winner Gao Xingjian had taken French citizenship by the time he won the Prize). Its belatedness was much discussed in light of China's rich literary heritage and cultural renaissance of recent decades. Literature is a fundamental part of what Chinese officials call their country's "national rejuvenation."

Mo Yan's literary legacy offers a rare window into this larger cultural-political mission, and to judge him by his public actions neglects much that can be learned from his work. Mo Yan won the Nobel Prize for his writing, not for political engagement. In the study at hand, I offer a perspective on his politics based not on a few symbolic acts but on a close reading of his literary works. "For a writer," Mo Yan said in his Nobel lecture, "the best way to speak is by writing. You will find everything I need to say in my works" (<http://www.nobelprize.org/nobel_prizes/literature/laureates/2012/yan-lecture_en.html>). His works offer keen insights into truth telling, the role of the writer, history's horrors, destiny, and human will. They also reflect Mo Yan's uses of tradition and modernism, his portrayals of sensuality, aggression, and violence, and his views on individual conscience. Thanks to the efforts of Howard Goldblatt (whose translations I quote in the following discussion), English-language readers can appreciate Mo Yan's powerful fiction.

Controversy over Mo Yan's prize highlights the difficult position of writers in today's China. His speeches and interviews may offer an understanding of his choices, but his fiction offers his most penetrating comments on writing, truth telling, and accommodation to government censorship. In his 1989 short story "Abandoned Child," a bus driver recounts how he was once disciplined for telling the truth. When serving in the army, the driver crashed a jeep into a tree after looking in the rearview mirror to find the deputy chief of staff feeling up the commander's wife. Ordered to file a report, the driver did not spare the truth: "I lost my bearings when I saw the deputy chief of staff feel the woman up, and crashed the jeep. It was all my fault" (158). But his political instructor swore at him, whacked him on the head, and ordered him to redo the report. Asked by the narrator if he did so, the driver replies, "No fuckin' way! He wrote it for me, and I copied it" (158).

The story suggests that being forced to copy other people's words is not the same as choosing what to write. This distinction may lie behind Mo Yan's decision in the summer of 2012 to join other prominent writers in hand-copying Mao Zedong's 1942 "Talks at the Yan'an Forum on Literature and Art" for a commemorative edition. Critics understandably assumed the copying endorsed Mao's exhortation that literature must serve the people and the revolution. That text set the stage for three and a half decades of literary and artistic repression. Mo Yan fueled the fire of this criticism by seeming to defend "necessary" censorship at a December 2012 press conference in Stockholm. Clearly, Mo Yan is no naïf in the Chinese Communist Party's (CCP) reign of thought control. Born Guan Moye (管謨業), he chose his pen name—Mo Yan (莫言, Don't Talk)—to honor his mother's caution against talking too much and in sardonic recognition of his failure to heed her warning. Yet I have been struck by his quiet and unassuming presence at literary conferences in Beijing, where he offered kind encouragement in private meetings but evinced a shy persona in public.

Adroit in his political judgments, Mo Yan has censored himself enough to flourish in what Jeffrey Wasserstrom calls the "gray zone" (xvi-vii; see also Lim and Wasserstrom). This is a subtly negotiated space where the government suffers heterodoxy as long as writers camouflage their dissent in literary metaphor. Like many writers, Mo Yan voices political criticism that would risk reprisal if presented overtly. But since he presents his critique on the sly, often poking fun at himself as a writer, he is allowed to pursue his truth telling. Still, to many he has erred on the side of caution, and his lack of explicit protest has allowed domestic and foreign critics to paint him as an apologist for authoritarianism.

That Mo Yan walks a fine line between writing social criticism and angering communist censors is attested by his prominence in the government-run Chinese Writers Association (CWA). He has been a member of the CCP since 1978, and he joined the People's Liberation Army (PLA) in 1976. In 1982 he became a CCP cadre, a functionary roughly equivalent to a civil servant, and in 1984 he enrolled in the newly established PLA College of Literature and Arts. Now Vice Chairman of the CWA, Mo Yan enjoys a privileged life as one of China's eighty-three million CCP members (about 6% of the population). Yet he often presents his personal history in studiously naive terms. He says he decided to become a writer when a former college student sent to his village for "reeducation" told of a successful writer who ate succulent pork dumplings three times a day. Those were the days following Mao's 1958-1961 Great Leap Forward, when famine killed an estimated forty-five million Chinese. Mo Yan also claims to write strictly for himself rather than for an audience. However, he accumulated a huge audience after a film adaptation of his novel *Red Sorghum* won the Golden Bear prize for best film at the 1988 Berlin International Film Festival. But Mo Yan's recent public statements have only further enraged critics who have never forgiven him for his actions at the 2009 Frankfurt Book Fair, when he walked out after Chinese dissident writers entered: "Some may want to shout on the street," Mo Yan reasoned in a speech at the fair, "but we should tolerate those who hide in their rooms and use literature to voice their opinions" (Jacobs and Lyall <http://www.nytimes.com/2012/10/12/books/nobel-literature-prize.html?_r=0>).

That is what Mo Yan did in "Abandoned Child," which can be read as a modern morality play. The narrator grapples with the ethical burdens of rescuing an abandoned newborn girl. Not only can his family ill afford to raise the child, but his wife hopes to conceive a son despite China's family planning (计划生育) or One-child policy, which would limit them to their first daughter. But the story also illuminates Mo Yan's ethical framework as a writer, as well as his understanding of literature's role in a modern China grappling with its rejuvenation. After a watchdog bites him in the leg at the government compound, the narrator is grateful rather than angry: "Most likely the bite was intended for me to reach a sudden awakening through pain ... I was startled into awareness. Thank you, dog, you with the pointy snout and a face drenched in artistic colors!" (174). When the township head asks whether keeping a watchdog might rupture the government's "flesh-and-blood ties with the people," the narrator points to his injured leg and says such an injury doesn't rupture ties but "molds them" (175). The story thus alludes to Mo Yan's own role as the writer of fiction limning China's twentieth-century chronicle of national pain. His authorial intent may be to awaken readers into awareness, to exorcise traumatic historical memories, and to restore ties of societal unity.

The idea that art molds ties between the government and its citizens frames Mo Yan's place in the current political context. For millennia, rulers in China have understood literary culture to be foundational to political power, and China's survival through three thousand years may have depended as much on its literary traditions as on political history (see Knight, *Chinese* 3). Ancient history books chronicling the achievements of dynasties promoted faith that the universe was ordered and moral, and this faith bolstered belief in each ruling regime's role in carrying out the mandate of heaven. From the Han dynasty (206 BCE-220 CE) until the dawn of the twentieth century, the government was administered by an entire class of literati, scholar-officials trained in classical Confucian texts. Literary culture—which included history and philosophy—was the root of government and civil practice. Scholar-officials both organized history to legitimate ruling regimes and remonstrated not only with artful subtlety but also with loyalty. Similarly, those of Mo Yan's generation believed they were the vanguard of a world-changing revolution. Mo Yan has described this deep faith as one of his reasons for becoming a writer: "It was a time of intense political passions, when starving citizens tightened their belts and followed the Party in its Communist experiment. We may have been famished at the time, but we considered ourselves to be the luckiest people in the world. Two-thirds of the world's people, we believed, were living in dire misery, and it was our sacred duty to rescue them from the sea of suffering in which they were drowning" ("Preface" vii).

The writer's sacred duty had to be carried out within rigid constraints when Mo Yan began writing in the late 1970s. During the Mao Zedong era (roughly from Mao's 1942 "Talks at the Yan'an Forum" to his death in 1976), social realist fiction demanded portrayals of heroic workers, soldiers, and peasants overcoming corrupt landlords and capitalists. In contrast to such black-and-white portrayals, Mo Yan writes fantastical realism, sometimes grotesque, often full of black humor, and sometimes in a style the Swedish Academy praised as "hallucinatory realism" ("The Nobel Prize" <http://www.nobelprize.org/nobel_prizes/literature/laureates/2012/>). By using the artistic liberties of magic realism to challenge the political status quo, Mo Yan and many fellow avant-garde writers continue the tradition of European surrealists and Latin American writers such as Gabriel García Márquez.

Mo Yan is best known for his historical novels depicting the brutal Japanese invasion that preceded World War II. In these works, he joins other post-Mao writers to exhume China's collective traumatic memories. His 1987 紅高粱家族 (*Red Sorghum*) consists of five novellas in which the narrator imagines his grandparents' experiences as the Japanese invade their village. Full of graphic violence, rape, and even a butcher skinning a prisoner alive, the novel chronicles horrors commonly viewed in China as the epitome of twentieth-century cruelties. This historical setting—safely before the culmination of the Chinese Revolution in 1949—adroitly sidesteps the Party's sensitivities and thus flies underneath the censors' radar. But perceptive readers may find that such novels also evoke the horrors that Chinese citizens inflicted on one another during the Cultural Revolution of 1966-1976.

The 2001 檀香刑 (*Sandalwood Death*) could elicit a similar interpretation. But, whereas the butcher in *Red Sorghum* is forced by the Japanese, here Mo Yan depicts a willing Chinese executioner, which perhaps explains his use of a setting even more removed in time. The torture of the protagonist, an opera singer turned rebel during the Boxer Rebellion (1898-1901), may be the most horrific scene I have ever read. The executioner skewers the prisoner alive with a sandalwood shaft, then feeds him ginseng soup to forestall his death and prolong his torture until the opening of the German-constructed railroad.

Writing in the "gray zone" entails much more political risk in works set in the Mao Zedong period and contemporary times. As far back as the 1988 天堂蒜之歌 (*The Garlic Ballads*), Mo Yan depicted a 1987 peasant riot against official corruption and malfeasance in the transition to a market economy. Mo Yan wrote *The Republic of Wine* in 1992, in the years just following the 4 June 1989 Tiananmen Square Incident, so one can read as allegory the plot about its detective investigating a rumor that local officials were eating human babies. His 1996 豐乳肥臀 (*Big Breasts and Wide Hips*) met with such harsh criticism over its depiction of merciless communist revolutionaries that Mo Yan's superiors prevailed upon him to write a letter asking the publisher to discontinue it. In his 2009 prize-winning novel 蛙 (Frog), Mo Yan's account of a village obstetrician exposes the corruption and cruelty of officials enforcing the One-child policy.

Although less acclaimed than *Red Sorghum* and *Big Breasts and Wide Hips*, Mo Yan's real masterpiece of historical fiction is the more explicitly critical 2006 生死疲勞 (*Life and Death Are Wearing Me Out*). The novel begins in purgatory in 1950, where the landowner Ximen Nao has suffered two years of torture before his execution by communist militiamen in the chaos of the revolution. Ximen argues that his decency should win him a reprieve, and the lord of the underworld grants him a series of reincarnations, first as a donkey, then as an ox, a pig, a dog, a monkey, and finally as a big-headed human child. This tragicomic parody of the Buddhist six realms is but one of several narrative devices Mo Yan employs to convey the complexity of history. Through his animal reincarnations, Ximen observes the land-reform movement, the Cultural Revolution, and the headlong embrace of market capitalism in the 1990s. Much of the modern Chinese history chronicled in *Life and Death* is also the history Mo Yan has witnessed. "Big-head," the wise survivor of so many campaigns and so much death, has seen history's horrors, seen death itself, and survived. He has the power of memory but is no more empowered than a child.

Salvation nonetheless lies in preserving the memories. By recounting events from the perspective of animals, Mo Yan can voice criticism that might be too risky coming from a human mouth. In his first reincarnation, for example, Ximen Donkey narrates a memory of communist cadres torturing his widow and concubines to extract the whereabouts of the family's gold, silver, and jewelry. Aware that the women don't know, Ximen Nao the man rushed forth to reveal the hiding place, despite his cynical expectation that the cadres will pocket the treasure for themselves. When Ximen Donkey later hears village officials again pressing his widow for information, the narration explicitly voices the fluidity between Ximen Donkey's mind and that of his earlier self: "At this moment, Ximen Nao and the donkey were one and the same. I was Ximen Nao, Ximen Nao was now a donkey, I was Ximen Donkey" (50). Mo Yan's adroit interweaving of narrators performs a transformation whereby Ximen Nao's successive incarnations move past revenge toward forgiving and even aiding the townspeople. When, later, as Ximen Pig, he sacrifices himself to save children drowning in icy water, his selflessness illustrates the novel's Buddhist underpinnings without detracting from its historical testimony.

The novel uses black humor to convey the horrors of the murderous Cultural Revolution. Mo Yan casts doubt on the success of the CCP's campaign of forced land collectivization when the robust Ximen Ox enables a lone independent farmer with only a wooden plow to outstrip the Commune with its multiple teams of oxen pulling steel plows. During the winter described in the next chapter, the Commune's impoverished peasants are hungry. Yet the Party feeds them propaganda rather than food. The passage turns fantastical after a Red Guard propaganda team arrives in the village on a Soviet truck rigged with four ear-splitting loudspeakers: "The loudspeakers blared so loud a farmer's wife had a miscarriage, a pig ran headlong into a wall and knocked itself out, a whole roost of laying hens took to the air, and local dogs barked themselves hoarse" (157). The raucous propaganda stuns a flock of wild geese that drops from the sky on top of the gathered villagers. Impoverished and starving, the villagers tear apart each bird: "The bird's wings were torn off, its legs wound up in someone else's hands, its head and neck were torn from its body and held high in the air, dripping blood ... Chaos turned to tangled fighting and from there to violent battles. The final tally: seventeen people were trampled to death, an unknown number suffered injury" (158). This fantastical microcosm conveys the hysteria and public murder of innocents during the Cultural Revolution.

The power of Mo Yan's works lies not in his chronicling of events but in his probing stories of individual resilience in the face of relentless forces of instinct, sexuality, and history. The inexorability of these pressures may recall the determinism of Tolstoy. Yet even as Mo Yan's characters succumb to these forces, they also make genuine choices in deciding their lives. The tenacity of human will expresses a vital life force that powers Mo Yan's narrative arcs.

This celebration of human will is hard-won in the face of such strong historical trajectories. Mo Yan came of age during the high tide of socialist theory and socialist-realist literature that emphasized utopian visions of collective revolution. Perhaps in response, Mo Yan's works ask whether responsibility for calamities lies within individuals or in forces beyond their control. As Mo Yan bravely gives his characters responsibility for their individual moral dilemmas and actions, the moral frameworks of his narratives not only depart from socialist certainties but also challenge many liberal and feminist pieties. He depicts instinct and lust, for example, both as frequently destructive and as potentially liberating. Mo Yan described this "humanistic stance" in his Nobel Lecture: "I know that nebulous terrain exists in the hearts and minds of every person, terrain that cannot be adequately characterized in simple terms of right and wrong or good and bad" (<http://www.nobelprize.org/nobel_prizes/literature/laureates/2012/yan-lecture_en.html>). In treating fate, lust, and history in ways which defy easy moralizing, Mo Yan's works question official morality. This questioning may be as significant as his critical portrayals of traumatic history. Against official history with its presumption of unitary truth, his insistence on moral ambiguity challenges authoritarian government. The self-questioning of his narratives is profoundly subversive in a country whose legal system convicts 99% of those prosecuted and where more than fifty thousand censors "harmonize" the internet.

In Mo Yan's own favorite story, the 1985 "白狗鞦韆架" ("White Dog and the Swing"), the now middle-aged male narrator guiltily describes an accident that disfigured a childhood friend and altered the course of her life. When he returns years later, she assuages his guilt by telling him that everything was the work of fate. Yet in a brave refusal of further resignation, the now-married mother of mute triplets pleads with the narrator to conceive a child with her: "It's the perfect time in my cycle … I want a child who can talk … If you agree, you'll save me. If you don't agree, you'll destroy me. There are a thousand reasons and ten thousand excuses. Please don't give me reasons and excuses" (69, translation mine; see also Knight, *Heart* 208). The story ends as the narrator faces this momentous decision. The narrator's great empathy for his friend drives home the frightening freedom made possible by powerful emotions. A mother yearns for a child who can talk; a man yearns to repay a debt.

In *Red Sorghum*, the characters determine their lives by the narrator's grandfather's rape of his grandmother in the sorghum field, his murder of her leprous husband, and her taking over of her deceased husband's distillery. The male characters frequently offer fatalistic explanations for these acts, as when the narrator's grandfather first touches the grandmother's foot and feels a premonition "illuminating the path his life would take" (46). The narrator supports this notion of a destined path:

"I've always believed that marriages are made in heaven and that people fated to be together are connected by an invisible thread" (46). In contrast to the male characters' focus on instinct and fate, his grandmother asserts her own agency, even as she lies dying. On her way to deliver food to her husband and his ragtag Chinese militia, she has been fatally shot by the invading Japanese soldiers: "Grandma lies there soaking up the crisp warmth of the sorghum field ... 'My Heaven ... you gave me a lover, you gave me a son ... you gave me thirty years of life as robust as red sorghum ... don't take it back now. Forgive me, let me go! Have I sinned? Would it have been right to share my pillow with a leper and produce a misshapen, putrid monster to contaminate this beautiful world? What is chastity then? What is the correct path? What is goodness? What is evil? You never told me, so I had to decide on my own ... It was my body, and I used it as I thought fitting" (72).

Mo Yan's emphasis on individual will treads on even more sensitive political territory in his works depicting the excesses of the Mao Zedong era. By acknowledging his characters' own desires and choices, Mo Yan refuses to excuse individuals for the violence and cruelty demanded by the Party's political movements. *Life and Death Are Wearing Me Out* presents stark portrayals of individuals who stand against both political fanaticism and social pressure. Blue Face stubbornly farms his tiny plot of soil as an independent farmer, refusing the Party's pressure to join collectivization. Out of loyalty to his master, Ximen Ox chooses to endure a vicious beating at the hands of the Commune leaders. As Blue Face's son, Jiefang, later recalls, "My tears started to flow as soon as they began beating you. I wailed, I begged, I wanted to throw myself on top of you to share your suffering, but my arms were pinned to my sides by the mob that had gathered to watch the spectacle" (212). He goes on: "You submitted meekly to their cruelty, and that they found perplexing. So many ancient ethical standards and supernatural legends stirred in their hearts and minds. Is this an ox or some sort of god? Maybe it's a Buddha who has borne all this suffering to lead people who have gone astray to enlightenment. People are not to tyrannize other people, or oxen; they must not force other people, or oxen, to do things they do not want to do" (213).

The horror ends when Jiefang watches a Red Guard—Ximen's own son Jinlong—burn Ximen Ox alive: "Oh, no, Ximen Ox, oh, no, Ximen Ox, who would rather die than stand up and pull a plow for the People's Commune" (214). Mo Yan also has Jiefang explicitly note that such individual sacrifice is not in vain: "Ximen Ox died on my dad's land. What he did went a long way toward clearing the minds of people who had become confused and disoriented during the Cultural Revolution. Ah, Ximen Ox, you became the stuff of legend, a mythical being" (215).

Jiefang's emotional commitments make him the most fully evolved character in the novel. After leaving the farming village and becoming a CCP official but trapped in a loveless arranged marriage, Jiefang shows uncommon independence of will in pursuing love with another woman. Although he knows that his refusal to hide his affair as other officials hide theirs will cost him his position and social status, he chooses to live openly with his lover, a choice that his teenage son and friends admire.

As his writing has evolved over the years, Mo Yan has developed a distinctive narrative control. Many of his works unsettle readers by switching among narrators and going back and forth in time. The often-unannounced intercutting of points of view is sometimes so startling as to feel vertiginous, and the use of metafictional narrative layers often heightens the reader's awareness of his or her own role alongside the author in constructing the fictional world. During the 1980s, after the rise of Deng Xiaoping, Mo Yan and other writers followed the reform-era exhortation to "walk toward the world," and much has been written about the influence of William Faulkner and Gabriel García Márquez, writers for whom Mo Yan has expressed admiration. His fictional worlds have also been compared to the dark absurdity of Kafka and the grand historical vision of Tolstoy.

Yet Mo Yan's unique narrative style is deeply rooted in Chinese literary traditions. His fantastical passages follow in the tradition of "records of the strange," a medieval form of "unofficial history" that documented tales of ghosts, fox fairies who take on human form, animals as moral exemplars, and other uncanny phenomena. In the epic sweep of his longest novels, Mo Yan also follows the six-hundred-year-old tradition of Chinese "novels-in-chapters" such as *Journey to the West* and *Dream of the Red Chamber*. *Life and Death Are Wearing Me Out* pays homage to this form by beginning each of its fifty-eight chapters with a couplet that hints at the chapter's content.

The combination of traditional Chinese and modernist elements makes Mo Yan's narratives among the most multilayered in world literature. Throughout *Life and Death*, seemingly realistic scenes are interrupted by obvious flights of fancy, such as when Ximen Pig sees Mao Zedong sitting on the moon, or when dogs gather to party and drink bottles of beer. Yet Mo Yan's narrative playfulness goes far beyond surreal plot elements. He suggests the slipperiness of a single knowable truth through his radical storytelling techniques: tales within tales, flashbacks and flash-forwards, dream sequences, and self-mocking quasi autobiography. The novel alternates among a dizzying cast of narrators that includes the five animals, two principal narrators, and the fictional character "Mo Yan." The main narrators turn out to be Blue Face's son Jiefang and the five-year-old "Big-head," who remembers his earlier incarnations as a landowner, a donkey, an ox, a pig, a dog, and a monkey. Although Ximen Nao was middle-aged when executed, by the time he comes back to life as Big-head, he is a wizened old man who has lived through the twentieth century. Embodied as a five-year-old, he has the mind of a mature adult and the memory of his six earlier incarnations. In the narrative present of 2005, the two narrators converse as the fifty-five-year-old Jiefang recalls his youth as a farmer's son beside the series of loyal farm animals he ultimately recognizes as one soul's reincarnations.

Mo Yan reveals the date of the narrative present about a quarter of the way through the novel by having Jiefang tell Big-head, "I can't let you keep calling me 'Grandpa' ... if we go back forty years, that is, the year 1965, during that turbulent spring, our relationship was one of a fifteen-year-old youth and a young ox ... I gazed into the ox's eyes and saw a look of mischief, of naïveté, and of unruliness" (117). Once this narrative framing becomes clear, readers understand that many passages from the animals' points of view are actually Big-head's memories of his animal incarnations as he speaks to Jiefang. The animals thus possess animal instincts and abilities as well as human knowledge, feelings, and thoughts. Ximen Pig even quotes from classical Chinese literature, muses on Ingmar Bergman's films, and shows intense interest in current events.

As the novel approaches its climax, "Mo Yan" the fictionalized author breaks the fourth wall, addresses the reader directly, and introduces himself as the final narrator. In his youth, this quasi-autobiographical character is frequently made the butt of ridicule, but as a young man he gains a position of modest respectability as a writer and is thus able to help Jiefang during his period of disgrace. Nonetheless, the many mocking references to "Mo Yan" add a wry internal commentary on the novel's accounts. Perhaps warning readers not to believe anyone who claims to present the truth, Ximen Pig cautions against taking "Mo Yan" too seriously: "According to Mo Yan, as the leaders of the Ximen Village Production Brigade were bemoaning their anticipated fate, feeling utterly helpless, he entered the scene with a plan. But it would be a mistake to take him at his word, since his stories are filled with foggy details and speculation, and should be used for reference only" (294).

Whereas Mo Yan's metafictional techniques produce psychological distance, the vivid sensuality of his writing creates a gripping sense of immediacy. But only rarely does Mo Yan employ sensual description in the service of human pleasure. Pleasure is often passed over with a euphemism or an ellipsis. Mo Yan's animals experience far more ecstasy in eating and in sex than do humans.

As with his recurrent scenes of defecation and urination, Mo Yan often treats sexuality as an irresistible, bestial force of nature. Yet sexuality can also offer a path to redemption. Jiefang cannot resist his passion and loses his worldly station as a result. But Mo Yan also foregrounds passion's redemptive power, as when making love speeds Jiefang's recovery after thugs hired by his wife beat him viciously. And in the end, the wife who refused to grant him a divorce forgives the lovers on her deathbed, and Jiefang reconciles with his family once he is able to marry his lover.

More than a painter of pleasure, Mo Yan is a master of the sensuality of pain. The flaying alive and skewering of prisoners and the beating and burning of Ximen Ox are just a few of numerous scenes of graphic violence in Mo Yan's works. The description of the ox's beating will bring a reader to tears, but Mo Yan's narrators at other times seem to exult in the sound of whips striking bodies, the vivid red of dripping blood, and the stench of burning flesh.

Why is there so much suffering in Mo Yan's works? In his many indelible scenes of pain, Mo Yan confronts history and ideology as these forces mark human bodies. By making his characters' bodily experiences the parchment on which he records his chronicles, he avoids direct criticism while still testifying to history's horrors. In *Big Breasts and Wide Hips*, when a Party VIP sentences to immediate death the young children of a Nationalist officer framed for rape, the scene makes a mockery of violence sanctioned in the name of revolution: "On the surface, we'll be executing two children. And yet it's not children we'll be executing, but a reactionary, backward social system" (293).

Might Mo Yan put his characters in profoundly harrowing circumstances in the hope that their suffering might offer a healing catharsis? His sensuality—both of pain and of pleasure—may be key to Mo Yan's underlying faith in redemption. The sensuality of suffering reminds one of Christian penitents who find ecstasy in pain. He may even present the visceral shock of pain to awaken the empathy that could build a better future. Even as we wince at the savagery, we might thank Mo Yan, as the narrator of "Abandoned Child" thanked the watchdog that bit him for his "sudden awakening through pain" (174). In grappling with human aggression, Mo Yan invites readers to confront the dark depths of the human psyche. Under the duress of that darkness, in a world of extreme greed and corruption, his most sympathetic characters also vindicate the human spirit through their passion for life and their abiding devotion to others. The life force that runs through Mo Yan's fiction powers destruction, but it also powers what the narrator of *Red Sorghum* calls "the iron law of love" ("爱情的铁钢规律") (337, translation mine).

I now return to the critics who condemn what they see as Mo Yan's acquiescence to his government's repression. Much of the recent press coverage relies on a binary classification of progovernment versus dissident writers. But astute readers recognize his veiled yet clear political critiques. As Steven Moore wrote in a 2008 review in the *Washington Post*, "Over the last 20 years, Mo Yan has been writing brutally vibrant stories about rural life in China that flout official Party ideology and celebrate individualism over conformity. (How he has escaped imprisonment—or worse—I don't know)" (<http://www.washingtonpost.com/wp-dyn/content/article/2008/05/22/AR2008052203515.html>).

Mo Yan is neither an apologist for the government nor a reflexive dissident. "A great novel," he avers, "has no need to roll around like a coddled pet nor to howl with the pack like a hyena. It has to be like a whale, roaming alone and breathing resonantly and deeply in the depths of the sea" ("To Defend"). He believes in individual conscience even as he takes seriously the contradictions within individuals. His characters don't generally exhibit the uncorrupted core of individual selfhood common in U.S. fiction. Yet the characters who might qualify as heroes evince an almost libertarian allegiance to personal freedom.

One such character is Blue Face, the sole remaining independent farmer in *Life and Death Are Wearing Me Out*. A thorn in the side of the Commune, Blue Face demands respect for his independence in a passage that might convey Mo Yan's personal statement of apolitical tolerance: "No, independent farming means doing it alone. I don't need anybody else. I have nothing against the Communist Party and I definitely have nothing against Chairman Mao. I'm not opposed to the People's Commune or to collectivization. I just want to be left alone to work for myself. Crows everywhere in the world are black. Why can't there be at least one white one? That's me, a white crow!" (305).

Just as Mo Yan's metanarrative techniques repeatedly challenge the existence of any unitary truth—whether voiced by the government or by dissidents—it might be wise to accept him as a nuanced, even contradictory, but ultimately principled and heartfelt writer.

Note

This article is a revised version of Knight, Sabina, "Mo Yan's Delicate Balancing Act," *The National Interest* (March-April 2013): 69-80. Permission to republish to Purdue University.

Works Cited

Goldblatt, Howard. "A Mutually Rewarding yet Uneasy and Sometimes Fragile Relationship between Author and Translator." *Mo Yan in Context: Nobel Laureate and Global Storyteller*. Ed. Angelica Duran and Yuhan Huang. West Lafayette: Purdue UP, 2014. 23–36.

He, Chengzhou. "Rural Chineseness, Mo Yan, and World Literature." *Mo Yan in Context: Nobel Laureate and Global Storyteller*. Ed. Angelica Duran and Yuhan Huang. West Lafayette: Purdue UP, 2014. 77–90.

Jacobs, Andrew, and Sarah Lyall. "After Fury Over 2010 Peace Prize, China Embraces Nobel Selection." *nytimes.com* (11 October 2012): <http://www.nytimes.com/2012/10/12/books/nobel-literature-prize.html?_r=0>.

Knight, Sabina. *Chinese Literature: A Very Short Introduction*. New York: Oxford UP, 2012.

Knight, Sabina. *The Heart of Time: Moral Agency in Twentieth-Century Chinese Fiction*. Cambridge: Harvard UP, 2006.

Lim, Louisa, and Jeffrey Wasserstrom. "The Gray Zone How Chinese Writers Elude Censors." *nytimes.com* (15 June 2012): <http://www.nytimes.com/2012/06/17/books/review/how-chinese-writers-elude-censors.html>.

Mao, Zedong. "Talks at the Yan'an Forum on Literature and Art." *Selected Works of Mao Tse-Tung*. By Mao Zedung. Beijing: Foreign Languages P, 1965. Vol 3, 69-98.

Mo Yan. "Abandoned Child." *Shifu, You'll Do Anything for a Laugh*. By Mo Yan. Trans. Howard Goldblatt. New York: Arcade, 2001. 155-89.

Mo Yan (莫言). 丰乳肥臀 (*Big Breasts and Wide Hips*). Beijing: Zuojia chubanshe, 1996.

Mo Yan. *Big Breasts and Wide Hips*. Trans. Howard Goldblatt. New York: Arcade, 2004.

Mo Yan (莫言). 蛙 (Frog). Shanghai: Shanghai wenyi chubanshe, 2009.

Mo Yan (莫言). 天堂蒜薹之歌 (*The Garlic Ballads*). Beijing: Zuojia chubanshe, 1988.

Mo Yan. *The Garlic Ballads*. Trans. Howard Goldblatt. New York: Viking, 1995.

Mo Yan (莫言). 生死疲劳 (*Life and Death Are Wearing Me Out*). Beijing: Zuojia chubanshe, 2006.
Mo Yan. *Life and Death Are Wearing Me Out*. Trans. Howard Goldblatt. New York: Arcade, 2008.
Mo Yan. "Nobel Lecture: Storytellers." Trans. Howard Goldblatt. *nobelprize.org* (2012): <http://www.nobelprize.org/nobel_prizes/literature/laureates/2012/yan-lecture_en.html>.
Mo Yan. "Preface." *Shifu, You'll Do Anything for a Laugh*. Trans. Howard Goldblatt. New York: Arcade, 2001. vii-xix.
Mo Yan (莫言). 红高粱家族 (Red Sorghum Family). Beijing: Jiefangjun wenyi chubanshe, 1987.
Mo Yan. *Red Sorghum: A Novel of China*. Trans. Howard Goldblatt. New York: Viking, 1993.
Mo Yan (莫言). 酒國 (*The Republic of Wine*). Taipei: Hongfan shudian, 1992.
Mo Yan. *The Republic of Wine*. Trans. Howard Goldblatt. New York: Arcade, 2000.
Mo Yan (莫言). 檀香刑 (Sandalwood Death). Shanghai: Zuojia chubanshe, 2001.
Mo Yan. *Sandalwood Death*. Trans. Howard Goldblatt. Norman: U of Oklahoma P, 2013.
Mo Yan. "捍卫长篇小说的尊严" ("To Defend the Dignity of Novels"). *Dangdai zuojia pinglun* 1 (2006): 24-28.
Mo Yan (莫言). "白狗秋千架." 1985. ("White Dog and the Swing"). 金发婴儿 (The Golden-haired Baby). Wuhan: Changjiang wenyi chubanshe, 1993. 50-69.
Moore, Steven. "Animal Farm." Rev. of *Life and Death Are Wearing Me Out*. *washingtonpost.com* (25 May 2008): <http://www.washingtonpost.com/wp-dyn/content/article/2008/05/22/AR2008052203515.html>.
"The Nobel Prize in Literature 2012." *nobelprize.org* (2012): <http://www.nobelprize.org/nobel_prizes/literature/laureates/2012/>.
Wasserstrom, Jeffrey N. *China in the 21st Century: What Everyone Needs to Know*. Oxford: Oxford UP, 2013.

Author's profile

Sabina Knight teaches Chinese literature and comparative literature at Smith College. In addition to numerous articles, Knight's book publications include *The Heart of Time: Moral Agency in Twentieth-Century Chinese Fiction* (2006) and *Chinese Literature: A Very Short Introduction* (2012).

Mo Yan's *Life and Death Are Wearing Me Out* in a Cultural and Visual Context

Yuhan Huang

Abstract

In "Mo Yan's *Life and Death Are Wearing Me Out* in a Cultural and Visual Context" Yuhan Huang explores visual representations in Mo Yan's novel *Life and Death Are Wearing Me Out* in the context of the Cultural Revolution and its posters. In the novel, the Cultural Revolution is featured in the story of Ximen Ox, Ximen Nao's second reincarnation. Huang's study of the novel's descriptions and propaganda posters shows the ways in which propaganda has been carried out through visual experience and sheds light on the novel's seemingly idiosyncratic narrative and metaphors. This juxtaposition of the contemporary verbal presentation and the era's posters provides an alternative access to understanding a time and space that has become distant to contemporary readers and viewers.

The Cultural Revolution in China (1966–76) is one of the most catastrophic political upheavals of the twentieth century. Much writing and research has been done on this period, most of which is focused on the political and social dimensions of the movement (See, e.g., MacFarquhar; MacFarquhar and Schoenhals). It has also inspired Chinese writers to record the traumatic experiences and personal histories of this period, including Feng Jicai's (冯骥才) 一百个人的十年 (*Ten Years of Madness*) and also to engage in narrating the era retrospectively: in the study at hand I discuss Mo Yan's (莫言) novel *Life and Death are Wearing Me Out* (生死疲劳), a fictional account of the fifty-year experience of a family in Mao Zedong's and post-Mao's China. The novel's protagonist, Ximen Nao, is a landlord in Gaomi county of Shandong Province who in the upheaval of the 1947 land-reform movement is executed for being a "master of exploitation" (24). It is at this point the novel takes a turn to the fantastical. Nao appeals to Lord Yama in the court of the underworld and is later sent back to life as a donkey in 1950. In a creative rendition of completing the six circles of life, death, and rebirth in Buddhism, he is then reincarnated into four other animals, an ox, a pig, a dog, and a monkey, before he is finally reincarnated as a "millennium boy" (58). The creative structural frame serves as a literary vehicle to represent the parallel political movements in China. The Cultural Revolution is featured in the story of Ximen Ox. To readers who are unfamiliar with the social and historical context, the story can seem wildly imaginative and its metaphors mythic. When one reads Mo Yan's novel in its historical context, however, the depth and weight of the novel's fantastic retelling gain greater relevance.

Part of that fuller picture involves the visual experience of the people in the Cultural Revolution, which remains only minimally explored. What did people see in the Cultural Revolution? What color was it? What was the role of artists and what did they believe in? One way to answer these questions is to look at the propaganda posters produced in mass and distributed in the period. Posters, as one of the commonly employed methods for propaganda in Cultural Revolution, has been the subject of study for Stefan Landsberger, Harriet Evans, Kirk Denton, and Francesca Dal Lago, who pioneered the preservation and rediscovery of these important memorabilia from the period. The art of the Cultural Revolution posters is unique within Chinese art history, rupturing the long tradition of ink painting and characterized by its highly political function. As a tool for propaganda, the "graphic voice" of Mao Zedong reached an enormous, and not always literate, audience (see, e.g., Powell). A close study of the visual experience of the Cultural Revolution alongside a close reading of Mo Yan's novel *Life and Death are Wearing Me Out* nuances readers' understanding of both sets of art. Together and individually, the novel and posters provide insights about the shaping of interpretation through representation and about instantiations of looking.

Two key questions govern my exploration of the mechanisms of looking exploited in these works of art: how does ideology influence people's perception of art and conversely how does art serve the purpose of ideology through its self-representation? To provide a contextualization, I examine a particular kind of poster, the "metaposter." W. J. T. Mitchell defines metapictures as "pictures about pictures—that is, pictures that refer to themselves or to other pictures, pictures that are used to show what a picture is" ("Image" 35). "Metaposter," coined from Mitchell's term metapicture, was a popular practice during the Cultural Revolution that depicts the looking or the making of propaganda posters. *Life and Death* inscribes this popular practice in its instances of putting up propaganda and looking at them. This shows the ways that propaganda has been carried out through visual experience and also sheds light on the novel's seemingly idiosyncratic narrative and metaphors. The juxtaposition of verbal presentation and the era's visual presentation provides an alternative access to the understanding of a time and space that has become distant to contemporary readers.

During the Cultural Revolution, the market parade was one of the most iconic public venues for political rallying against counterrevolutionaries. In these events, propaganda teams comprised of Red Guards gave speeches and "counterrevolutionaries" were humiliated and tortured in public. One often reads in the literature about the Cultural Revolution tales of trauma, blood, and tears such as Feng Jicai's *Ten Years of Madness*, which includes the experience of a woman with beautiful hair being shaved in public. Mo Yan's novel depicts a livelier and more humorous yet no less painful version (for Mo Yan's use of humor to assuage pain, see Huang and Duran). Led by its owner Lan Lian, Ximen Ox is taken to a parade. Both the master and the beast endure the humiliation with obedience until a red flag is blown onto Ximen Ox and the ox runs terror-stricken: "If a pair of knives had been attached to them, you could have decimated the crowd and routed the survivors ... Take that red banner off his head! Someone yelled... In running for cover, the people formed tight clusters. Old women were crying, children were bawling." In stopping the turmoil, the butcher Zu Jiujie sears off one of the ox's horns. The enraged ox charges at the fat butcher and "bur[ies] his good horn in Zu Jiujie's plump belly" (176-78). The deceptively simple incident carries mythical elements that call up the visual image of a political rally in the Cultural Revolution, especially with the blowing red banner. Lan Lian's son Lan Jiefang recounts the incident, and describes the feeling of looking at the sun while covering one's head with a red flag as follows: "bright red, like a vast ocean, as if the sun were immersed in an ocean of blood" (176). Propaganda posters were predominately red during the era as was the nation metaphorically. It was a common practice in political rallies such as market parades for people to have either a red flag or a poster in their hands, making the scene a "red ocean."

The phrase 红海洋 (Red Ocean) was used to describe the propaganda movement to "redden" ("赤化") China starting in 1966. Streets, bus stops, walls of schools, factories, shops, hospitals, and even public toilets were painted red. In an age when the sun and Chairman Mao were equated with each other, the color red symbolized the utmost goodness, a progressive and revolutionary color. Following red is the color yellow or gold derived from the rays of the sun. Yellow propaganda slogans were thus added to the red walls. It was a common practice to draw sunflowers around slogans to symbolize the loyal supporters of Chairman Mao, the "sun." Given the time setting of the scene, the context of Red Ocean represents the new world that is yet to come. However, instead of representing peace and prosperity, the madness of the impromptu bullfight represents the irrationality and disorder of the age. The visual imagery of the brief scene rewrites the history of wounds and sadness into a carnivalesque vision.

Similarly, naming in *Life and Death* is visually suggestive and helps to illustrate the ideology of redness at the time. The surnames of Mo Yan's characters reflect a fascinating color scheme that offers metaphorical significance to the novel. The "good" colors of red and yellow fit into the names of politically progressive characters while blue and white ones are assigned to the "counterrevolutionary" characters. The color red is not a common surname in the Chinese language; however, the surname 洪 (Hong) is a homophone for red in Chinese. The name of the head of the village and people's commune, the most progressive communist in the novel, is Hong

Taiyue. The name of the leader of the Ximen Village Militia and commander of the production brigade who executes Ximen Nao at the beginning of the novel is 黄瞳 (Huang Tong), literally "yellow pupils." 蓝脸 (Lan Lian), literally "blue face" owing to the visible blue birth mark on his face, resists joining the people's commune and remains the only independent farmer in the county. Except for the protagonist Ximen Nao, he is one of the most narrated characters in the novel. Mo Yan has acknowledged that the real life basis for this archetypal figure of the ostracized individual is a man who lived in his home-village ("Reading with Ears" 307). Unlike Lan, who manages to live through the Cultural Revolution, the independent farmer dies before the era ends when independent farming became the norm again. Lan's stubbornness seems unwise for a man with his class identity: as an orphan and a poor farmer, Lan could have benefited from a more progressive political attitude. However, as signaled by his blue name and face, his character refuses to be "reddened." Similarly, Ximen Nao's wife whose surname 白 (Bai) literally means "white" is a figure who endures discrimination and suffering because of her status as a landlord's wife.

The ideology of redness is further explored in a wild incident between Lan Lian and his stepson Jinlong. With other young villagers, Jinlong organizes a village branch of the Red Guard, and the group paints their headquarters, including the apricot tree, bright red. When Lan voices disapproval of their action, Jinlong instructs his followers to brush a thick coat of red paint on his step-father's face, justifying that "the whole nation is red, leaving no spot untouched" (163). Jinlong carries out the reddening beyond common sense. It is outrageous, which Mo Yan emphasizes through a representation that flies in the face of the long-cherished tradition of filial duty in China. Political correctness becomes the very rationale to persecute anyone who voices difference. Moreover, Jinlong not only inflicts physical punishment on his step-father by having his face painted red (he is left hurt and unable to see), he also erases the boundaries between private and public, individual and collective. A man's face is equated with a public wall, the possession of the nation more than of the individual. In another instance of absurdity, the dispute is followed by a series of complications with relatives trying to reprimand the son and to help the father.

If the Red Ocean movement reveals a national fetish for redness, brushing red paint over a man's face suggests the insanity of such a craze on the personal level. Propaganda becomes a literary weapon to wipe out those who do not conform. It is not uncommon for propaganda posters of the Cultural Revolution to represent pens and brushes as weapons. In a poster appearing in Feng's collected stories of the Cultural Revolution, a giant hand holds a piece of chalk and writes over a small figure, showing how art should be used as a forceful power to revolutionize the country and people. Further, pens and brushes are often held in the hands of progressive figures in propaganda posters. The cover of 革命大批判文集 (Excerpts of Revolutionary Criticism), a collection of essays intended to educate and provide guidance to the artists of the era, features such an image of three revolutionaries. One is in military uniform with a red star on his cap. He serves as the flag bearer to the other two young people. The man at the back holds high up in his hand Mao's *The Little Red Book*, the most immensely circulated text during the period (see Yang on the cultural meaning and pervasiveness of the booklet). A woman stands in the foreground with a red brush in her right hand and maintains a resolute gesture pointing to the left. *The Little Red Book* and brush replace the more conventional spears and guns as weapons to enforce the ideological power of the Cultural Revolution. The "cultural" in the "Cultural Revolution" denoted by no means "civilized."

Besides depicting artistic tools, painting was a recurrent subject matter in the propaganda posters. It represented a specific form of art intended to contribute to the cultural renovation of society. This is where Mitchell's definition of metapicture is useful: a metapicture can be categorized in three forms. First, a metapicture often includes another picture inside, producing an inner image or an image within an image. Second, a metapicture can also depict the making of an image within a half-finished inner image, redirecting our attention to the production aspects of imaging. We are moved to ask, for example, who, how, and why an artist is making the particular work. And third, a metapicture can also be free from the frame-structure of the inner image as it makes use of visual plays, for example in the Jastrow duck-rabbit image in which the same image can be read accurately in completely different meaningful ways. This third aspect comments on the mechanism of seeing and its physical and social conventions. It encourages viewers to consider and reconsider the ways of looking: how to look and what to look at.

Pictures about the making of pictures can signify a great deal about what images mean and how they are understood in their particular social context. An anonymous poster from the 1970s depicts a worker-artist painting a propaganda mural on a village wall (see figure 1). The poster is accompanied by a large character caption reading "Art comes from the life of struggle, and working people are the masters." The attractive worker-artist occupies the center space. His left arm is held in front of his chest with the palette in his left hand. His right arm extends across the poster to the very left of the frame to a strong hand that holds a brush. His straightened and stiffened right arm looks rather unnatural for a painter at work, yet the gesture acquires a politically progressive expression through its resemblance to a soldier marching ahead. The sense of resolution and dedication to his work in the artist's face coordinates with his painting of people working during the harvest. The image of this worker-artist clearly resembles those of many war-themed posters. It conveys to viewers how poster artists view the practice of painting and situate themselves in society.

As politicized as poster art is, it is a widely held misbelief that poster artists during the Cultural Revolution period cared little about the artistic merits of their work. Poster art served primarily as a popular form of propaganda, but it also evolved into a serious artistic genre in Chinese art history. It became a common practice during the Cultural Revolution for poster artists to combine several kinds of painting techniques, including oil painting, printmaking, woodcut, as well as Chinese traditional painting. Their aesthetics was intertwined with their political beliefs, and the employment of painting was invested with equal importance to the activities of military heroes. The collectivity of the authorship of poster art is of signal importance to its aesthetics and politics. As a whole, poster artists are anonymous rather than individually recognized. Most posters from the Cultural Revolution are unsigned to emphasize the collective nature of artistic creation: art should not be created for individual recognition but for serving and educating the masses.

With artistic talent viewed as a convenient tool to carry out ideological instruction, the public bulletin board became another venue for political struggle, as Mo Yan reflects in *Life and Death*. In one scene, Jinlong makes use of the bulletin board to satirize Lan and his blue-faced son Jiefang as the only independent household, separate from the people's commune. Jinlong creates a "visual feast" with images of tractors, sunflowers, and commune members plowing the field, in contrast to the independent household members, skinny and unhappy: bright colors of red and yellow contrast against sullen colors of blue and white. Villagers gather to appreciate the painting and read its subtitles, denouncing collectively the socially unfit, "the village's obstinate independent farmer Lan Lian and his family, who works on his land with a single ox and plow, the ox with its head lowered, the farmer looking crestfallen, a solitary figure looking like a plucked chicken, his ox like a stray dog, miserable and anxious, having coming to a dead end" (149). Jinlong's work does not really accurately depict the true situation, in which the blue-faced family is in high spirits and their ox young and vigorous. While the young Lan protests his dissatisfaction with the political message, the father articulates an aesthetic evaluation: "That boy has talent. Whatever he draws looks real" (149). This scene shows that with this genre of art, it is more important to look real rather than to be real to achieve its political purpose. Although the bulletin board serves as the center for public opinion and aims to provide one unified voice for the masses to understand and learn from, Lan shows another level of interpretation.

One of the most famous images of Chairman Mao in the Cultural Revolution is Liu Chunhua's 1967 oil painting 毛主席去安源 (Chairman Mao Goes to Anyuan) (see figure 2). It is one of the few instances in which the artist is acknowledged, yet with a twist. In the haste to publish the painting, the artist's name 刘成华 "Liu Chenghua" was recorded mistakenly as 刘春华 "Liu Chunhua" and became known as such thereafter. To this day, the painting itself is more known than the artist and few people know the artist's real name. The negligence of authorship is the result of the collective belief that art is not personal but political. Chairman Mao Goes to Anyuan depicts Mao as a young man on his way to the city of Anyuan to lead a miners' strike. Since its exhibition and publication in 人民画报 (China Pictorial) in 1968, its reception has been overwhelming. More than nine hundred million copies of the painting-turned-poster have been sold (see Ma, Tao 31). Sculptures, badges, stamps, and tapestries of the image have also been regularly manufactured. As the original painting traveled across China to be exhibited, it was honored in the way that Chairman Mao's own presence would have been: it was flown to each city on a special airplane and welcomed by greeting crowds. The image became symbolic and iconic, fulfilling the artist's aims: "Every move of the Chairman's figure embodies the great thought of Mao Zedong. When portraying his gesture, I strive to give significance to every small detail: his head is held high and slightly turned, the gesture of which conveys his revolutionary spirit, dauntless before danger and violence and courageous in struggle, earning victory with his revolutionary spirit" (Liu, Chunhua 34). In the artist's statement, little is written about the actual technique and style of painting and more effort is taken on justifying the painting's intended political effect.

Another example is the 1967 painting 毛泽东思想光辉照亮安源工人革命运动 (Mao Zedong's Thought Illuminates the Anyuan Worker's Movement), a painting created for an exhibition. It was part of a campaign to discredit Liu Shaoqi (刘少奇), Vice Chairman at the time and a politician Chairman Mao distrusted. Before Liu fell out of favor, the Museum of the Chinese Revolution featuring Liu was commissioned and the artist Yimin Hou made the well-reviewed painting 刘少奇和安源矿工 (Liu Shaoqi and the Anyuan Coal Miners) in 1961. In the painting, Liu is in the center of the composition prominently displayed as a determined leader. The later version of the similar theme, Chairman Mao Goes to Anyuan, sought to redefine the iconography of China's revolutionary history by replacing Liu with Mao as the primary organizer of the important 1922 coal miners' strike (see Andrews 338). The political struggle is thus reflected in a curious way of image making.

Mao's famous Anyuan image makes a cameo appearance in *Life and Death* as the decoration of a marriage gift to Jinlong and his wife Huang Huzhu, daughter of Huang Tong (the name literally means "yellow pupils"). It is "a framed mirror with the dedication in red 'Congratulations to Lan Jinlong and Huang Huzhu in becoming a revolutionary couple' in one corner. The mirror was decorated with a drawing of Chairman Mao in a long gown, bundle in hand, as he encouraged miners to rebel in the city of Anyuan" (299). The scene depicts that during the Cultural Revolution propaganda art filled not only the public sphere but also the private one through decorations and posters. It was an honor for households to do so. Mo Yan's modern verbal reference echoes many visual references to the iconic image of Chairman Mao Goes to Anyuan. One example is 千里野营炼红心 (To Go on a Thousand "li" March to Temper a Red Heart), which features a revolutionary who holds the image of Mao leading a revolutionary march (see figure 3). The title of this poster itself requires some interpretation. "Li" is the traditional Chinese measurement for the length of five-hundred meters. A "red heart" takes up the ideology of red to indicate sincerity and loyalty to Mao. The title of the poster thus depicts a long journey or march that shows and enhances the people's loyalty. The image depicts a group of Mao supporters marching to Beijing to pledge allegiance to him. The group carries the painting of the young Mao in front like a religious icon in a ritualistic procession. The image of Mao thus not only serves as a political instrument but also preserves a sense of ritual or activities of reverence usually reserved for religious or sovereign figures. Such veneration is not unfamiliar in Chinese cultural history. In *Sandalwood Death*, Mo Yan describes the retired head executioner for the Qing court returning from the capital to his rural hometown with two imperial gifts: a chair that the Qing emperor had once sat on and a string of prayer beads from the Empress Dowager. With these two imperial objects, Zhao assumes authority. Although he lives in modest dwellings, he requires anyone who sees these objects to pay tribute. The local magistrate, although unwilling and indignant, is forced to kowtow to them: "I could not fall to my knees fast enough, as I again performed the three bows and nine kowtows to that swine [executioner Zhao] and his chair and prayer beads" (79). The image of Mao has been venerated in similar manner. However, its enforcement is not based on law as it was during the Qing era but rather on political advocacy and enforced socialization, and thus the image becomes political idolatry. By showing how the earlier poster is looked at and how it is supposed to be understood, the metaposter teaches the masses to read the embedded message in the poster and to believe what it says. It is in this way that the image worshipping of the Cultural Revolution corresponds and conforms to ideological belief. Mitchell defines "the image as the site of a special power that must either be contained or exploited; the image, in short, as an idol or fetish" ("Image" 151). The image as an idol and the image as a fetish indicate two kinds of images, complementary in form and function. The image as an idol works like a shadow projected in darkness. It is the image behind a specific concept projected in the way that *camera obscura* operates and produces images. The image as a fetish is more material and tangible, imprinting itself on people's consciousness by provoking obsessive behaviors. By combining both images, the poster art of the Cultural Revolution became a powerful tool: it projected a specific ideological belief and it served as an object of worship.

    Another prevalent form of metaposter adopts the scheme of metapicture by showing how the viewer observes and interacts with the image. The viewer serves as an exemplary model for the poster's viewers to emulate, and thus looking becomes a didactic experience. Some posters frame the poster with the moment of teaching. An anonymous poster from the 1970s, 主课 (The Main Lesson) shows a teacher lecturing to a group of students in front of a painting. The image depicts the famous Chinese rebel leader Hong Xiuquan (1814-64), who revolted against the government of the Qing Dynasty (1644-1911). The teacher gestures to the image, calling attention to its interior audience, the students, and to its exterior audience, us, as viewers of the poster. The students listen with eager attention, with one taking notes of what the teacher says. All of the students in the poster wear red scarves (the red scarf is the token for League of Young Pioneers [LYP], a youth organization led by communist party. Children aged six to fourteen are selected to join LYP based on their merits and are often deemed as role models for all other students). During the Cultural Revolution, the LYP acted as Little Red Guards, younger counterparts of the Red Guards who implemented the Cultural Revolution. Thus the red scarf indicates exemplary status, as well as moral and political allegiance to the communist party. By showing these red-scarfed students, the poster invites its viewers to read the lecturing as the passing on of the revolutionary spirit. The red scarves of course make their appearance in Mo Yan's texts including *Life and Death* and 蛙 (Frog).

The Main Lesson also solicits approval and identification from its exterior viewers. The caption of the interior image makes sure that viewers know what the main lesson is about so that they can learn from it, as do the exemplary students. The viewers' viewpoint is located behind that of the students who sit on the ground as if the external viewers would stand in the second row of the class. In this way, the poster encompasses viewers as insiders in the poster who listen to the lecture on painting. While situated technically as outsiders to the poster, external viewers are nonetheless invited to sympathize with the process of learning and the lesson itself. As viewers see the younger generation's eagerness to learn about the revolutionary past, the poster provides viewers with an optimistic political view. Being both the insider and outsider of the poster adds one more layer to the lesson conveyed. By showing how much one can learn from the painting politically, the poster comments on the desirable way to appreciate an image.

In addition to the making and looking in the visual component of posters, verbal text is another important aspect of the posters. Both the interior audience and the exterior audience can read the inscribed verbal message simultaneously. Chen Minsheng's 1974 poster 妇女能顶半边天 (Women Hold up Half of the Sky) features a propaganda billboard with activity happening around it (see figure 4). In front of the billboard, a group of women stands and reads, discussing the poster and the texts plastered around it. The poster on the billboard depicts a woman delivering a public speech with a large slogan beside it: "Smash a thousand years of shackles; women can hold up half of the sky." Other slogans read "The doctrine of Mencius and Confucius is a doctrine of exploitation of women" and "Thoroughly criticize Confucius's false theory of women's subjugation." The texts accompanying the image on the billboard construct a narrative that sustains the feminist discussions by the interior viewers depicted in the poster. At the same time, the texts on the billboard also provide the caption for the exterior viewership and inform viewers, specifically the reading viewers and the non-reading auditors, of the message. It is in this way texts function as at once visual components and semantic elements of the image.

In "Allegory and Iconography in Socialist Realist Paintings," Wolfgang Holz introduces the concept of "dream theatre," with which he articulates the mechanisms of metaposters. By mirroring the viewers inside the image, the posters affect their viewers and manipulate viewers' processes of perception, and this "enlarges the viewer's psyche by introducing him or her into different realities of consciousness while simultaneously turning the act of viewing itself into a visual ritual" (77). Indeed, the way people exploit meaning and moral teachings from images during the Cultural Revolution is similar to a ritualistic visual practice. Poster art is to be looked at, to be read, as well as to be worshipped.

The Cultural Revolution brought catastrophic destruction to Chinese society, leaving traumatic memories not only to those who were persecuted but also to the persecutors: "No matter whether it is those who struck, smashed, and robbed or those who were struck, smashed, and robbed, both were victims. The former were clouded over in the heart having done vicious deeds and the latter were fated to suffer physically and some even to lose their lives" (Ma, Shitu 2). It takes more than an official and impersonal history to understand and ease the social and political trauma wrought by the Cultural Revolution even now. The aesthetic of the artistic genre of Socialist Realism of the era restricted artists from liberal and diversified expression. In this study, I aim at showing some of the creativity and artistry that poster artists of the period developed despite and because of those restrictions. By giving due dignity to those artists and their audiences, we can join Mo Yan in coming to a better understanding of the period and its art.

Mo Yan's *Life and Death* is vivid and personal, filled with imaginative yet historically grounded details of individuals' lives. Attentive to the ultimate incompatibility of the political and the artistic, Liu Zaifu applauded Mo Yan as a "forerunner of life" for writing against the Socialist Realist tradition and defined Mo Yan as someone who "would not accept the monopoly of ideological influence in history writing … returning to the writing of life and individual" (3; unless indicated otherwise, all translations are mine). Liu does not overstate the sense of rewriting history in *Life and Death*. In a serendipitous instantiation of the ease with which historical and literary elements can be erased, I conclude with a passage that evinces Liu's assessment and that is omitted in Howard Goldblatt's translation of *Life and Death Are Wearing Me Out*, and that through its tree imagery serendipitously deepens our understanding of the power of the root-seeking movement of which Mo Yan's works are a major flowering. When Lan recounts his childhood memory of the death of Ximen Ox, he expresses the responsibility to retell what he has witnessed, just as it is the responsibility of all individuals to do: "Ximen Ox, I cannot bear to describe the brutality he has done to you. You have lived four more lives after the ox, traveling between life and death. Many details may have slipped your memory, yet every moment of that day stuck in my mind. If the whole day were a tree with many branches and twigs, I remember not only its boughs, but also each shoot and leaf it bore. Ximen Ox, listen to what I have to tell, because these are the things that happened, and what happened is history. It is my responsibility to retell the history to those participants who have forgotten it" ("西门牛啊，我不忍心对你描述他施加到你身上的暴行，你已经

在牛世之后又轮回了四次，阴阳界里穿梭往来，许多细节也许都已经忘记，但那日的情景我牢记不忘，假如那日的整个过程是一株枝繁叶茂的大树，我不但记得住这株树的主要枝杈，连每一根细枝，连每一片树叶都没有忘记。西门牛，你听我说，我必须说，因为这是发生过的事情，发生过的事情就是历史，复述历史给遗忘了细节的当事者听，是我的责任") (186).

The righteous death of the ox marks the end of the Cultural Revolution. The cruelty of persecution and the stubbornness of the silent resistance depicted in the ox's death are not alien to those who experienced the movement. Ximen Ox's death is thus not only an account of a specific ox in a specific town but also a social and political statement about the experience of a beleaguered generation. Together, Mo Yan's art can go "a long way toward clearing the minds of people who had become confused and disoriented during the Cultural Revolution" (*Life and Death* 215). Similarly, when reflecting on the art of the Cultural Revolution, it is important to bear in mind that the poster artists of the era were also influenced by their visual and cultural context. They strove to picture the bright, beautiful, and hopeful future of China unaware that the same hopes would later be smashed by a cruel reality and that their work would be, by and large, dismissed. The posters of the Cultural Revolution, now relics, bear witness to a time and space and to what people once believed about painting and art. Perhaps, as does Mo Yan, we can approach old and new art as worthwhile reflections upon the society it constituted and study the power and frailty of such images.

Figure 1. 斗争生活出艺术，劳动人民是主人 (Art Comes from the Life of Struggle, and Working People are the Masters), 1970s. From the personal e-library of Yuhan Huang per the Chinese Posters Foundation, Amsterdam.

Figure 2. The oil painting-turned poster 毛主席去安源 (Chairman Mao Goes to Anyuan), 1968. From the personal e-library of Yuhan Huang per the Chinese Posters Foundation, Amsterdam.

Figure 3. 千里野营炼红心 (To Go on a Thousand "li" March to Temper a Red Heart), 1971. From the personal e-library of Yuhan Huang per the Chinese Posters Foundation, Amsterdam.

Figure 4. Cheng Minsheng, 妇女能顶半边天 (Women Hold up Half of the Sky), 1974. From the personal e-library of Yuhan Huang per The University of Westminster Chinese Poster Collection.

Works Cited

Andrews, Julia Frances. *Painters and Politics in the People's Republic of China, 1949-1979*. Berkeley: U of California P, 1994.

Dal Lago, Francesca. "Activating Images: The Ideological Use of Metapictures and Visualized Metatexts in the Iconography of the Cultural Revolution." *Modern Chinese Literature and Culture* 21.2 (2009): 167-97.

Denton, Kirk A. "Visual Memory and the Construction of a Revolutionary Past: Paintings from the Museum of the Chinese Revolution." *Modern Chinese Literature and Culture* 12.2 (2000): 203-35.

Evans, Harriet, and Stephanie Donald. *Picturing Power in the People's Republic of China: Posters of the Cultural Revolution*. Lanham: Rowman & Littlefield, 1999.

Excerpts of Revolutionary Criticism: On Literature and Art (革命大批判文集:文学艺术卷). Beijing: Renmin P, 1970.

Feng, Jicai (冯骥才). 一百个人的十年 (*Ten Years of Madness*). Nanjing: Jiangsu wenyi chubanshe, 1995.

Feng, Jicai. *Ten Years of Madness: Oral Histories of China's Cultural Revolution*. San Francisco: China Books and Periodicals Inc., 1996.

Holz, Wolfgang. "Allegory and Iconography in Socialist Realist Painting." *Art of the Soviets: Painting, Sculpture, and Architecture in a One-Party State, 1917-1992*. Ed. Matthew Cullerne Bown and Brandon Taylor. Manchester: Manchester UP, 1993. 73-86.

Huang, Alexa, and Angelica Duran. "Mo Yan's Work and the Politics of Humor." *Mo Yan in Context: Nobel Laureate and Global Storyteller*. Ed. Angelica Duran and Yuhan Huang. West Lafayette: Purdue UP, 2014. 153–64.

Landsberger, Stefan. *Chinese Propaganda Posters: From Revolution to Modernization*. Armonk: Sharpe, 1995.

Liu, Chunhua (刘春华). "毛主席去安源" ("Chairman Mao Goes to Anyuan"). *China Pictorial* 9 (1968): n.p.

Liu, Chunhua (刘春华). "歌颂伟大领袖毛主席是我们最大的幸福" ("Singing the Praises of Our Great Leader is Our Greatest Happiness"). *Zhongguo wenxue* 9 (1968): 32-40.

Liu, Zaifu (刘再复). 莫言了不起 (The Great Mo Yan). Hongkong: Xianggang zhonghe chuban youxian gongsi, 2013.

Ma, Shitu (马识途). 沧桑十年: 共和国内乱的年代, *1966-1976* (Ten Years of Vicissitudes: Ten Years of Disruption in the P.R. of China, 1966-1976). Beijing: Zhonggong zhongyang dangxiao chubanshe, 2006.

Ma, Tao (马涛). "油画'毛主席去安源'的幕后风波" ("Behind Scene Stories on the Oil Painting *Chairman Mao Goes to Anyuan*"). *Archive World* 5 (2009): 31-6.

MacFarquhar, Roderick. *The Origins of the Cultural Revolution*. Oxford: Oxford UP, 1974.

MacFarquhar, Roderick, and Michael Schoenhals. *Mao's Last Revolution*. Cambridge: Harvard UP, 2006.

Mitchell, W. J. T. "Image and Ideology." *Iconology: Image, Text, Ideology*. By W. J. T. Mitchell. Chicago: U of Chicago P, 1987. 151-208.

Mitchell, W. J. T. "Metapictures." *Picture Theory: Essays on Verbal and Visual Representation*. By W. J. T. Mitchell. Chicago: U of Chicago P, 1994. 35-82.

Mo Yan (莫言). 蛙 (Frog). Shanghai: Shanghai Literature and Art P, 2012.

Mo Yan (莫言). 生死疲劳 (*Life and Death are Wearing Me Out*). Shanghai: Shanghai wenyi chubanshe, 2012.

Mo Yan. *Life and Death are Wearing Me Out*. Trans. Howard Goldblatt. New York: Arcade, 2008.

Mo Yan (莫言). 用耳朵阅读 (Reading with Ears). Beijing: Zuojia chubanshe, 2012.

Mo Yan. *Sandalwood Death*. Trans. Howard Goldblatt. Norman: U of Oklahoma P, 2012.

Powell, Patricia, and Shitao Huo. *Mao's Graphic Voice: Pictorial Posters from the Cultural Revolution*. Madison: Elvehjem Museum of Art, 1996.

Yang, Fenggang. "Soul Searching in Contemporary Chinese Literature and Society." *Mo Yan in Context: Nobel Laureate and Global Storyteller*. Ed. Angelica Duran and Yuhan Huang. West Lafayette: Purdue UP, 2014. 215–20.

Author's profile

Yuhan Huang is working toward her PhD in comparative literature at Purdue University with a dissertation project on literature and art during the Chinese Cultural Revolution. Her interests in scholarship include documentary film and photography, word and image, and art history.

Mo Yan's *The Garlic Ballads* and *Life and Death Are Wearing Me Out* in the Context of Religious and Chinese Literary Conventions

Chi-ying Alice Wang

Abstract

In "Mo Yan's *The Garlic Ballads* and *Life and Death Are Wearing Me Out* in the Context of Religious and Chinese Literary Conventions" Chi-ying Alice Wang discusses Mo Yan's novels in the context of religion and traditional Chinese literature. Like many of Mo Yan's works, these two novels are set in his home county of Gaomi in the Shandong Province, where the first local literary works appear in the form of eleven songs grouped under the sectional title "Airs of Qi" in the earliest collection of Chinese poetry, *The Book of Songs*. Echoing this ancient tradition, folk songs and ditties play a vital role in the two novels as they set the tone of sarcasm and sorrow, the latter because the characters find themselves trapped in 天堂 – simultaneously the word for heaven, the name of the county where *The Garlic Ballads* is set, and the county's hellish reincarnation – which sets up the framework for *Life and Death Are Wearing Me Out*. While ghosts and demons appear and disappear in these novels, there is no reference to God. From the context of the three-thousand-year-old tradition emerges the political monopolization over the Chinese concept of a supreme God.

"Why not *The Garlic Ballads*?" answered Peter Englund, Permanent Secretary of the Swedish Academy, responding to the question "which book should I start with if I want to get to know [Mo Yan's] work?" Englund emphasized the relevance of *The Garlic Ballads* being based on a true incident in the 1980s: "it is not merely history, but contemporary. " ("Nobel Prize" <http://www.nobelprize.org/mediaplayer/index.php?id=1834≥). Mo Yan, however, named *Life and Death Are Wearing Me Out* in response to a similar question druing an interview conducted by the Nobel Prize committee after the announcement of the 2012 Nobel Prize in Literature, stating that it "comprehensively represents my writing style and the exploration I make in the art

of fiction writing" (Mo Yan "Interview" <http://www.nobelprize.org/nobel_prizes/literature/laureates/2012/yan-telephone.html>). My focus is on these two representative novels in the context of religious and Chinese literary traditions to reveal the deeper roots and broader scope of Mo Yan's works.

Mo Yan's novels are characterized by the setting of his native home of the Gaomi Township of the Shandong Province, social criticism, the style of magic or hallucinatory realism, unbridled imagination often self-reflectively called attention to, and striking language. His novels also possess well-crafted narrative frameworks and an ostensive realism founded on not simply magic or hallucinatory references but also, as this study shows, on allusions to religions. In other interviews, Mo Yan claims to be an antitheist and denies involvement in Buddhist study, as the title of *Life and Death Are Wearing Me Out*, a quotation from a Buddhist sutra, would suggest (see "Interview: Mo Yan on *Life and Death*"). Indeed, the fact that he is not a Buddhist demonstrates how foundational China's rich Buddhist heritage infuses the culture as a whole and that it is not limited to its practitioners but rather emphasized by the fact that the supernatural motifs in these two novels are too prevailing to be dismissed as mere literary symbolism without significance on the level of spirituality. Englund calls the term "magic realism" being applied to Mo Yan's works "belittling" because Mo Yan's work is "quite unique with supernatural going into reality" ("Nobel Prize" <http://www.nobelprize.org/mediaplayer/index.php?id=1834>). The supernatural motifs and numerous allusions in Mo Yan's novels are built on the cultural common ground of religious locution and conventions shared by the author and his readers regardless of their religious beliefs. From this point of view, allusions to religion can be appreciated as the employment by a secular writer, and by extension his readers, to give a dimension to his narration of the mundane world. To draw out this claim, I analyze the narrative framework, allusions to religion, and dialectic relation between literary devices and religious references in Mo Yan's *The Garlic Ballads* and *Life and Death Are Wearing Me Out*.

Scholars of modern Chinese literature including David Der-wei Wang and Michael Berry have analyzed carefully Mo Yan's indebtedness to modern Chinese writers since the May Fourth Movement in 1919. These complement Mainland Chinese writers from the 1950s to 1970s whom Mo Yan has mentioned as his literary mentors and whose works comprise points of departure in his writing. However, we can investigate Mo Yan's literary lineage much further back to the onset of Chinese history when folk songs were first collected and compiled with court odes and temple hymns to form the first anthology of Chinese poetry, *The Book of Songs* (eleventh to eighth century BCE). As David Damrosch points out, "world literature is multi-temporal as well as multicultural... All too often, students of imperialism, colonialism, nationalism, and globalization do indeed define their projects in such a way as to restrict their investigations to just the last five hundred years of human history, or the last one hundred years, or even the last few years" (17). As a result, this kind of research is fated to "reproduce one of the least appealing characteristics of modern American—and global commercial—culture: its insistent presentism that erases the past as a serious factor, leaving at best a few nostalgic postmodern references, the historical equivalent of the 'local color' tipped in to distinguish the lobby of the Jakarta Hilton from that of its Cancún counterpart" (Damrosch 17). This is especially the case with *The Book of Songs*, recognized as "the most powerful spring-head for Chinese verse" and by extension highly pertinent in all other forms of Chinese literature (Wells 165).

What Mo Yan and other Chinese writers inherit is far more than what they learn from their immediate mentors or writers whom they study "in the last five hundred years." What they all share is the immense body of the Chinese culture since it was first recorded and transmitted, so strongly in fact, as the Introduction to this volume notes, that his works are part of the *root* or *root-seeking* literature in China (see Duran and Huang). Such cultural ties with the distant past are especially pertinent in Mo Yan's case as his works are rooted in the very land on which the first states of Qi and Lu were established. These ancient and powerful voices in the form of songs, ditties, odes, and hymns have been recorded since the early Zhou Dynasty (1046-256 BCE). Last but not least in this line of singing children, illiterate bards, aristocratic poets, and proletarian writers who relay the stories of their homeland, Mo Yan tunes in to these voices and makes them a vital part of his narrative strategy.

Narrative framework

Mo Yan calls *Life and Death* a landmark among all his novels set in his hometown of Gaomi because it distinguishes itself from his earlier works in its formal structure, language, and narrative perspectives ("Mo Yan Talks"). Mo Yan considers new literary forms as the only territory left for writers of his generation to explore and display their talents. In *Life and Death* and *The Garlic Ballads*, Mo Yan employs his storytelling talents by merging various narrative perspectives and applying them with sophisticated stream of consciousness into conventional forms of Chinese fiction. His ingenuity and revitalization justly wins the praise of Englund, who calls Mo Yan an "extremely skillful narrator" ("Nobel Prize" <http://www.nobelprize.org/mediaplayer/index.php?id=1834>). In his complex sources of inspiration, Mo Yan acknowledges William Faulkner, Gabriel García Márquez, and reaching a bit further back into his own culture, the Chinese writer Pu Songling (1640-1715), but mostly he agrees with many commentators, scholarly and popular, that the form of *Life and Death* is an homage to traditional Chinese fiction ("Nobel Lecture" <http://www.nobelprize.org/nobel_prizes/literature/laureates/2012/yan-lecture_en.html>).

The homage is indeed pervasive. For example, all fifty-three chapters from Book 1 to 4 open with a title in the form of a couplet, a convention observed by classical Chinese fiction writers until the beginning of the modern era. The title couplet is a poetic device in which individual words at the corresponding positions of the two lines match syntactically and semantically. These couplets provide a thematic clue for the content of the chapter, accentuate the rhythm of fictional narration with poetic rhetoric, and bring in another form of aesthetic pleasure to the reading experience. Mo Yan fully takes this device a step further: in each of the six parts of *Life and Death* he takes a new narrative perspective, that of the newly adopted form of life of the protagonist Ximen Nao, who undergoes the cycle of reincarnation from human to donkey, ox, pig, dog, monkey, and then back to human at the end. This structural design enables the author great freedom in shifting narrative perspectives not merely from person to person but from various persons to a variety of animals, each with its own distinct personality as they relate the story of the village in Gaomi stretching half a century from 1950 to 2000.

Mo Yan utilizes repeatedly this unique narrative device in his treatment of chaotic scenes as he builds up tension, maintains perfect control of the multitude of characters involved, depicts details ranging from the gory to grotesque to farcical, and imbues the mess with extraordinary emotional and psychological complexity. At times, similar scenarios in different parts of the novel narrated from different perspectives intensify the inner coherence, multiply the layers of meaning, and make a fuller account of the episodes. Such is the case in Chapter 5, when the narrator shifts from Ximen Nao's donkey reincarnation back to his human self of the previous life. Ximen Donkey recalls the last scene of confrontation between Ximen Nao and his persecutor Hong Taiyue. Ximen Nao overheard the false accusation his third concubine Wu Qiuxiang made against him, saw the delight in her eyes when she was released, and heard the crying of his frightened young children Jinlong and Baofeng. All the intense emotions accumulated in this scene do not end with the execution of Ximen Nao but are brought to a new climax in the remarkable scene in Chapter 14 when the next reincarnation of Ximen Nao, Ximen Ox, butts his former concubine Wu to the ground while his son Xinmen Jinlong whips him and jumps on his back trying to control him. The narrator of this chapter, Lan Jiefang, the son of Ximen Nao's other concubine Yingchun and his farmhand Lan Lian, comments on the events years later when he addresses the five-year-old boy Lan Qiansui, the last reincarnation of Ximen Nao: "I didn't know you were the reincarnation of Ximen Nao, and was clueless about the complexity of feelings you were experiencing in the presence of Yingchun, Qiuxiang, Jinlong, and Baofeng. A tangled mess, I suppose, when Jinlong hit you, it was a son striking his father, wasn't it? And when I yelled at him, I was cursing your son, isn't that so? Your heart must be full of conflicting emotions. A mess, a real mess, your mind all twisted out of shape, and only you can make any sense of it" (127).

This much-delayed, moving commentary is grounded in ancient Chinese folk religious tradition. Lan Jiefang mentions noticing a missing chunk of Ximen Ox's ear: "Maybe Jinlong had swallowed it. King Wen of the Zhou was forced to eat the flesh of his own son. He spit out several lumps of meat, which turned into rabbits that ran away. By swallowing a piece of your ear, Jinlong was eating his own father's flesh, but he'll never spit it out, and it will turn into waste that he'll expel" (127-28). The episode of King Wen of Zhou being forced to eat the flesh of his own son is elaborated in Xu Zhonglin's seventeenth-century novel 封神演义 (The Legend of Deification), a fictional embellishment of 史记正义 (Shiji Zhengyi), an eighth-century annotation of Sima Qian's 史记 (The Record of History). Mo Yan's allusion to this anecdote underlines the cold, treacherous character of Ximen Jinlong.

In Mo Yan's writing, the multiple-perspective narration is a versatile tool for presenting the complex emotions of his fictional characters. Ximen Nao's own narration of hearing the cry of his son Jinlong during his persecution transmits to readers the intensity of his fatherly love even when he faces utmost humiliation and death. This love stands in dramatic contrast to the betrayal by his son. While Ximen Ox remains silent throughout the scene, readers can sense the explosive anger and despair contained in him with the aggression of his physical tortures. To add insult to injury, the story is now told by Lan Jiefang, whose existence as a result of the union of Ximen Nao's former concubine and farmhand is another betrayal to the protagonist. On top of all these layers of emotions and narrations, Mo Yan adds the final touch of cannibalistic allusion with his application of intertextuality. This is an homage to Lu Xun's (1881-1936) famous claim that the entire Chinese history can be summed up in one word, cannibalism. It is also a point of departure from the official ideology since 1949: whereas cannibalism had officially faded into history, this novel represents it as just as rampant in the new China. Regardless of Mo Yan's disclaimer about religiosity, the religious framework in the form of Buddhist reincarnation not only strings together plots dispersed in several chapters but also provides a dimension of ethics, culture, and spirituality.

The later conventions of Chinese fiction and the modern device of narration resonate with the much older tradition of Chinese literature, limited neither to the genre of fiction nor to the written text. 赋 (*fu* or narration) is considered the first and foremost of the three literary devices—the other two are 比 (*bi* or metaphor) and 兴 (*xing* or stimulation)—characterizing the first anthology of Chinese poetry, *The Book of Songs*. In his 2012 lecture at Peking University "Language and History: New Historical Novels," Mo Yan attributed the vitality of his language to the inspiration he received from the 民间 (the common people), which is exactly the same source that gives rise to and retains the songs from three thousand years ago. At least two legacies of these songs can be identified in Mo Yan's works. First, the simplicity and the immediacy of the ditties of children and the songs of the blind singer in *Life and Death* and *The Garlic Ballads* are direct descendants of these ancient folk songs. Second, the themes of love, marriage, hunting, and social criticism invested in the lyrics bespeak the same spirit of flirtatious lovers, anticipating newlyweds, athletic hunters, and outspoken critics of corruption, immorality, and injustice. The voices of these songs echo each other, then and now, at the two ends of Chinese history.

Each chapter of *The Garlic Ballads* opens with a song of the blind singer Zhang Kou. In the first two chapters, Zhang Kou sings about the fertile land, the clear water in the gurgling river, the juicy garlic sprouts, the handsome young men and women, and the farmers' dream of building new houses with the money they make by selling their garlic. In the songs of Qi, the anonymous ancient singers sing about the rushing water in the River Wen (Poem 105), the teaming fish caught in the fish-trap set by the bridge (Poem 104), and the athletic hunter and the handsome young men (Poems 97, 103, 106). From Chapter 3 on, Zhang Kou's songs begin to carry a satiric overtone as the lives of the garlic peasants take a downward turn. Satire then turns into sharp accusation against corrupted officials (Chapters 8 and 9), followed by encouragement of defiant actions (Chapters 11 and 12). From Chapters 13 to 20, Zhang Kou continues to depict the plight of the people under the persecution of the local officials.

The songs of Qi also allude to the scandals of their leaders, Duke Xiang of Qi, his sister Wenjiang, and her husband Duke Huan of Lu. According to the historical record, Duke Huan of Lu and his wife Wenjiang visited Qi in 684 BCE, fifteen years after their marriage. During their visit, Duke Huan discovered the incestuous relationship between his wife and her brother Duke Xiang of Qi. As a result, Duke Xiang arranged for an assassin to kill Duke Huan. To appease the anger of Lu, Duke Xiang had the assassin executed but continued the incestuous relationship with his sister. This scandal is the subject of several poems in *The Books of Songs*, three of which are included in the songs of Qi. In "Southern Hill" the poet comments in the first stanza: "But the way to Lu is easy and broad, / For this Qi lady on her wedding-day. / Yet once she has made the journey, / Never again must her fancy roam," and in the last stanza, "When one takes a wife, how is it done? / Without a match-maker he cannot get her. / But once he has got her, / No one else must he approach" (Allen and Waley 80). The poet's allusion to the strong taboo against spousal infidelity is explicit.

One may wonder why poems like this would be included in *The Book of Songs*, a text sanctioned by Confucius and canonized as one of the five Chinese classics. When Confucius urges his disciples to study *The Book of Songs*, the master cites "to give expression for complaints" as one of the four major functions of poetry and "serving one's lord" as the way one should employ learning (*Analects* 17.9). In the context of Confucian convention, social criticism is seen as a major function of Chinese literature. This imbedded literary purpose compels Chinese intellectuals in the Confucian tradition to take as their obligation to expose the erroneous, criticize injustice, and speak up for the injustice suffered by ordinary people.

Readers may ask a similar question about Mo Yan's inclusion of the salacious and gory details in his criticism against those in power in his works. Mo Yan and his fellow writers in Mainland China grew up in the anti-Confucian era when Confucianism was criticized and Confucian texts hardly available. Their heroes in Chinese literature were Lu Xun and his fellow writers of the May Fourth generation who criticized the so-called feudal Chinese society in anticipation of a new China. Ironically, this tradition of social criticism and intellectuals' concept of such criticism as their obligation are rooted in the poems in *The Book of Songs* and thereby nourished by Confucius and his followers. In the early twentieth century, when Lu Xun and other writers in the following generation turned against Confucianism, they seemed to forget that this critical spirit was handed down to them by none other than the ones they disparaged. Mo Yan inherits the same critical spirit, but in *The Garlic Ballads* and *Life and Death* he takes his writing a step further and subjects his emotions and political concerns to literary considerations: "My greatest challenges come with writing novels that deal with social realities, such as *The Garlic Ballads*, not because I'm afraid of being openly critical of the darker aspects of society, but because heated emotions and anger allow politics to suppress literature and transform a novel into reportage of a social event. As a member of society, a novelist is entitled to his own stance and viewpoint; but when he is writing he must take a humanistic stance, and write accordingly. Only then can literature not just originate in events, but transcend them, not just show concern for politics but be greater than politics" ("Nobel Lecture" <http://www.nobelprize.org/nobel_prizes/literature/laureates/2012/yan-lecture_en.html>). By "writing novels that deal with social realities," Mo Yan picks up an electronic version of the writing brush handed down from the poets and writers in Chinese history, from the anonymous poets of "Southern Hill" to Lu Xun, to make his own contribution to his time and society. Literary space converges with historical space and transcends historical facts in a higher level of reality.

Mo Yan parts ways with the ancient tradition in the way he delivers his criticism. The songs of Qi are mild in tone and restrained in rhetoric even when the subject matter involves scandalous sexual relationships, violent multimurders, and deceptive cover-ups. In "Wicker Fish-Trap," Wenjiang's wedding escorts are described in similes such as "a trail of clouds," "thick as rain," and "like a river." These serve as elaborate foils of her scandalous behavior, which become just as spectacular as her pompous wedding entourage or the clouds, the rain, and the river in nature, which no one fails to perceive (Poem 104). On the other hand, Mo Yan's criticism is sharp and direct, and his language so striking and unreserved that he gives free rein even to scatological descriptions of the intolerable condition and despicable scenes in prison in *The Garlic Ballads*.

In the name of revolution, the new China since 1949 mounted one political campaign after another until the death of Mao Zedong in 1976. The 温柔敦厚 (gentle and kind) Confucian poetic aesthetics was rejected as dated and weak, vilified as decadent and retrogressive, and roundly condemned. Through these stormy decades, the critical spirit in traditional Chinese literature turned progressive and crudely grassroots, especially in terms of the language of some writers who grew up in this environment. Still, Mo Yan's love for the land is apparent in his depictions of the beauty and power of nature, echoing the voices of his predecessors three thousand years ago. In terms of social criticism, one can also sense the *noblesse oblige* Mo Yan took upon himself as a writer when he completed *The Garlic Ballads*, a novel of nearly half a million characters in forty-three days. These are clearly the legacies he inherited from the collective culture of China shaped by the first work of Chinese literature (on literature and major religions in China, see Mitchell and Duran).

Religious allusions

Amid others, three major sources of supernatural allusions in Mo Yan's *The Garlic Ballads* and *Life and Death* deserve special attention: 1) Chinese conventions, 2) the Buddhist concept of life and death, and 3) references to Christianity. The first source, consisting of the collective body of Chinese political-religious mythology and mystical folktales, by far commands the oldest, most complex, and most prevailing presence in these novels. The second source gives rise to the narrative structure, thematic metaphors, and major symbolism of *Life and Death*. The third, although much less conspicuous, is employed and reveals some universal values to be found in major religions despite their great divergences elsewhere. Biblical references are beginning to be accepted by the Chinese as a part of modern culture (see Yang).

In his Nobel Lecture, Mo Yan told his audience the following about when he was a child: "I was, without a doubt, a theist, believing that all living creatures were endowed with souls. I'd stop and pay my respects to a towering old tree; if I saw a bird, I was sure it could become human any time it wanted; and I suspected every stranger I met of being a transformed beast." This theist inclination does not stem merely from his own imagination but has a common root shared by folks around him: "Wherever I happened to be ... my ears filled with tales of the supernatural, historical romances, and strange and captivating stories, all tied to the natural environment and clan histories, and all of which created a powerful reality in my mind" ("Nobel Lecture" <http://www.nobelprize.org/nobel_prizes/literature/laureates/2012/yan-lecture_en.html>). The adult Mo Yan now considers himself an antitheist, but his childhood perception of the supernatural remains vital and takes on new life in his writing. Only by careful study will one discern the most vigorous contentions displayed on the common ground shared by ancient Chinese convention and Mo Yan's contemporary *The Garlic Ballads*. The most fundamental contentions are neither the riot of the peasants against their oppressive local officials nor the ill-fated lovers against their persecuting selfish family members, but the more deeply rooted dialectic relationship of the state versus religion.

Ever since the first historical dynasties, Chinese political regimes have officiated religious views and practices, just as is the case in ancient Western political states. The most noteworthy supernatural power is certainly the concept of the supreme god. A number of modern scholars, including Wang Guowei, consider the transition between the Shang and the Zhou Dynasties in 1046 BCE as the most significant change in ancient Chinese history, as the Zhou ushered in its own beliefs to complement and gradually replace Shang conventions. One of the most crucial concepts revolves around the idea of God 帝 (*Di*) or 上帝 (High God), worshipped by the Shang. In *Early Chinese Religion*, Robert Eno's study of the etymology of 帝 and theories regarding the identity of God leads to the conclusion of the essential ambiguity of the Shang idea of God. Eno is positive, however, that the Zhou Dynasty comes up with "the innovation of a single supreme deity governing all aspects of the experienced world" (76). The "single supreme deity" in the Zhou concept is not entirely inherited from the *Di* of the Shang. Rather, the Zhou introduces another word, literally sky or heaven (*Tian* or 天) to denote the transcendental dimension complementing the more personal denotation of *Di* as God.

Modern scholars of Chinese philosophy recognize a number of definitions of *Tian* in the early Zhou Dynasty, including "the physical sky, the ruling *Tian*, the fatalistic *Tian*, the naturalistic *Tian*, the ethical principal" (Fung 31), the "first and foremost a metaphysical and religious idea" (Eno, *Confucian* 5), the transcendental *Tian* (see Lao), and "in general, God's Providence ... draped in the cloak of 'August Heaven, God on High'" (Chen 207). With the evolution and expansion of the Chinese language, the meanings and connotations of *Tian* grew exponentially in its forms of idioms. In *The Book of Songs*, *Tian* appears 170 times, including many in idioms containing the term such as 蒼天 (*cangtian*, azure sky or heaven) or azure, 天子 (*Tianzi*, the son of Heaven, also an epithet referring to the king), and 天命 (*Tianming*, mandate of Heaven). In comparison, *Di*, including all its related idioms, appears only forty-three times, barely 25% of the total references of *Tian*. The last kings of Shang adopted the word *Di* to add sublimity to their royal title. The Zhou claimed their victory over the Shang as dictated by the mandate of Heaven, *Tianming*, and the Zhou kings called themselves the sons of Heaven, *Tianzi*. To ensure the support of the people, the founding fathers of the Zhou raised the concept of virtue (德) and underscored its significance by propagating the virtuous characters of the rulers on the one hand and admonishing their royal lineage to cultivate and practice morality on the other. As the notion of *Tian* becomes increasingly theoretical and abstract, the legitimacy of the ruler hangs more heavily on morality.

In modern Chinese, the meanings of *Tian* and its idiomatic terms remain as vital and versatile as ever. The Chinese title of *The Garlic Ballads* is 天堂蒜薹之歌 (The Garlic Ballads of Tiantang). The Chinese idiom 天堂 (*Tiantang*) means Heaven or Paradise. In the novel, it is also the fictional name of the county where the garlic peasants' riot takes place. The ostensive irony of the place name and the hellish conditions are reinforced by the first song of the blind singer Zhang Kou as he praises his county in terms of the *Tiantang* of "the mortal world" (人间天堂) and the distgusting stench of rotting garlic permeating the novel's opening scene. As the story unfolds, the mundane paradise becomes increasingly hellish in the experiences of the protagonists Gao Ma and Gao Yang. The irony extends to the last chapter in the official announcement from the local government that acknowledges the disaster and proclaims the procedure it takes to restore justice. In this announcement, the *Tiantang* county and its adjacent *Cangma* (literally azure horse) county are referred to collectively as 苍天 (*Cangtian*, Azure Sky or Heaven) Municipality. While *Cangma* is derived from the name of the actual county *Cangshan* (苍山, azure mountain) in Shandong where this riot took place historically, the term *Cangtian* has a further connotation. Appearing eight times in *The Book of Songs*, the meanings of the idiom *cangtian* range from the physical sky (Poem 65, Poem 121) to the judging supernatural power to whom people would plea in persecution and suffering: "Oh, Heaven, azure Heaven, / Take note of that proud man, / Take pity upon that toiler!" (Poem 200). Just as the county named *Tiantang* or Paradise in the mundane world is characterized by the odor of corruption, the municipality called *Cangtian* or Azure Heaven is no less ironic. The irony is driven deeper by another usurpation of title: the abusive jailors instruct the prisoners to address them as "government," a term no less awkward than it is satirical in the context of the novel's plot. After all the abuse, the meek Gao Yang (高羊, with its pun on lamb [羔羊] in Chinese) names his only begotten son "law abiding" (守法 or *Shoufa*). The sarcastic absurdity now becomes apparent in light of the Chinese political convention in which, for purposes of self-glorification and legitimacy, the sacred is secularized and the secular deified as the pre-modern monarchs dubbed themselves as *Di* or "Sons of God." In the end, in *The Garlic Ballads* both "Heaven" and "government" are claimed by hypocritical abusive impostors. The upper hand the political power seems to gain over religion turns out to be mockingly empty and deceptive.

The second source of allusions comes from the Buddhist concept of life and death, which inspires Mo Yan's narrative framework and the thematic metaphor of *Life and Death Are Wearing Me Out*. The title of the novel, literally "wearies of life and death," is quoted from the Buddhist sutra 八大人觉经 (Eight Great Realizations) from 中华大藏经 (Chinese Tripitaka 362) translated to Chinese by the Persian Buddhist monk An Shigao who came to China to teach Buddhism in the second century CE. This text sums up the Buddha's basic teaching about the correlation of human desires, sufferings, and relief from the vicious cycle of desires and pain. In the epigraph, Mo Yan quotes the second great realization from the sutra containing the phrase "wearies of life and death," which Howard Goldblatt renders as "The Buddha said: 'transmigration wearies owing to mundane desires. Few desires and inaction bring peace to the mind" (Epigraph). The novel is by no means thereby an evangelical tract of Buddhism. Rather, Mo Yan adopts the Buddhist view of desire and suffering to construct the major structure and themes of the novel. The protagonist Ximen Nao is not the only one caught in this trap. The antagonist characters Hong Taiyue and Ximen Jinlong are blown to pieces in each other's arms in their insatiable pursuit of power and wealth, exemplifying the destructive result of human desires.

Extratextually, Mo Yan has also emphasized the Buddhist foundation of the work. He avers that during a visit to a Buddhist temple he saw a group of images which inspired him to set his novel *Life and Death* in the framework of the six realms of *samsara*. The structure of the Buddhist cycle enables him to present his characters and events of the story through the eyes of a group of animals. Mo Yan chose five animals he knows well from his early experience in the village to animate the consecutive reincarnations of his protagonist Ximen Nao. What distinguishes Mo Yan's literary metaphors from religious allegory is the absence of didactic doctrines. Instead, Mo Yan's personal knowledge of these animals, both physically and psychologically, and his talent as a storyteller brings human consciousness and bestial nature into a dynamic fusion. A case in point is Ximen Donkey's romantic relationship with the female donkey Huahua culminating in their sexual union: "Feelings of great joy erupted, surging over me, and over her. My god!" (58). This overt description of sexual joy is empowered by the personified animals but at odds with the traditional Chinese Buddhist doctrine of abstinence. Ximen Donkey's ecstatic cry "My god!" (我的天哪!), though containing the word *Tian* (Heaven), is such a common Chinese exclamation that it hardly strikes any religious overtone.

Through his consecutive reincarnations, Ximen Nao is given one opportunity after another to face life and death and thus to put an ever widening distance between his current life and that of the executed landlord full of grudges and hatreds. Along this process, the memories of Ximen Nao's life are replaced gradually by the consciousness of the new animals. The purgatorial procedure is not achieved in the underworld but rather completed during multiple lifetimes in the world. Thus religion is employed as a literary device to state the theme that the ultimate triumph of life comes from leaving the old life to time and oblivion. While Mo Yan draws a perfect circle of narration by ending the novel with Lan Qiansui's announcement "My story begins on January 1, 1950" (3, 540), the verbatim echo of the very first sentence of the book, the ingenuity of his design emerges in correlation with the cyclical representation of *samsara* reincarnation, often depicted in the image of the Buddhist wheel. Embedded in the seemingly perfect symbolism, however, is the paradox: the human reincarnation of Lan Qiansui is neither the nirvana proclaimed in Buddhist teaching nor the ultimate solution to human desires and suffering. With the restoration of human existence, has the soul achieved any spiritual advancement or redemption, or is it simply undergoing the same cycle again and again? After all, in spite of the spiritual dimension of the novel, the ultimate concern of the novelist is the stories of life, not the redemption of the soul.

The third source of Mo Yan's allusions is universal religious values held by religions which do not have a long history of contact with China, such as Christianity. Biblical references are neither prominent nor prevailing but rather strategically employed at crucial moments. The first one appears in reference to the love of Lan Jiefang and Pang Chunmiao, the second one is at the death of Lan Lian. The love that displays the greatest mutual commitment in *Life and Death* is that between Lan Jiefang and Pang Chunmiao. Their persistence and sacrifice eventually turn their adulterous relationship into a union forgiven by Lan Jiefang's dying wife and accepted by his father. After they are forced to leave their hometown in humility, they start a new life of cohabitation in another township. At their shabby new residence, everything about life is reduced to the minimum: "We cooked, we ate, and we made love" (475). For lack of extra clothing, they even stay naked, which Lan Jiefang makes light of by saying self-teasingly, "This is the Garden of Eden," a reference to the Book of Genesis (2.8-25), lines omitted in the English translation: "因为我们仓皇出走，根本没带换洗衣服，所以我们大部分时间是赤身裸体。赤身裸体做爱是正常的，但当我们每人捧着一个碗，赤身裸体对坐喝粥时，荒诞和滑稽的感觉就产生了。我自我嘲讽地对春苗说："这里就是伊甸园" (471). Earlier, when Ximen Dog leads Lan Jiefang's son to the dorm of Pang Chunmiao where she and Jiefang had been making love, Lan Jiefang claims, "we'd promised not to open the door even if God came knocking" (470). Here, for the word "God," Mo Yan chooses the Chinese epithet of the Christian term 上帝 (*shangdi*), reminiscent of the episode in Genesis when God seeks out Adam and Eve as the couple hide themselves in shame after they sinned by eating from the prohibited fruit from the Tree of Knowledge of Good and Evil. What compelled Lan Jiefang to open the door was certainly not God but his recognition of the dog's barking, which implied the presence of his son. The greater irony falls on the allusion to the Garden of Eden as the fictional episode subverts the biblical story: Lan Jiefang and Pang Chunmiao were banished into their Garden of Eden after they committed sexual transgression against his marriage. There is no discernible theological connotation behind the biblical allusion. It is clear, however, that Mo Yan is confident his contemporary Chinese readers will pick up the irony behind a verbal allusion that has become part of the common expression shared globally in cultures with a Christian heritage and without.

At the conclusion of Book 4, Lan Lian's epitaph "everything that comes from the earth shall return to it" at once strongly echoes the biblical verse "then shall the dust return to the earth as it was: and the spirit shall return unto God who gave it" (Ecclesiastes 12.7) and sums up his life and another major theme of the novel, the inseparable ties between humans and the land. One wonders what happens to the soul of Lan Lian. In Mo Yan's fictional world, while the physical body returns to the earth, the spirit falls into *samsara* instead of returning to God. There are only wearying incessant cycles of life and death, with no sight of Buddhist nirvana or biblical rest.

Lan Lian, the last independent peasant in the entire Mainland China, represents the last Chinese farmer in the conventional sense who loves the land as much as he loves his life because his livelihood comes from the land, and he owns it. The sacred ties between humans and the land date to the beginnings of Chinese culture. In the Shuo Gua chapter of *The Book of Changes*, Heaven, Earth, and humans are considered the three powers constituting the universe. Chapter 25 of the Daoist classic *Dao De Jing* claims, "therefore Dao is great, Heaven is great, earth is great, / And the king is also great … / Man follows the ways of earth, / Earth follows the ways of Heaven, / Heaven follows the ways of Dao; / Dao follows the ways of itself" (qtd. in DeBary 59). In *Life and Death*, Lan Lian is the one who follows the way of Earth throughout his life until his final return to the earth. His roots in the Earth also give him the unique insight into the reality behind the apparent as he never fails to recognize Ximen Nao in his reincarnations.

Lan Lian's insistence on the ownership of the land contrasts to the values embraced by Hong Taiyue and Ximen Jinlong. Hong Taiyue, a beggar before 1949, never owned any land. Ximien Jinlong was among the first in the family to relinquish ownership of the land in answering the call to join the commune. In the name of revolution, their rejection of land eventually cuts off their ties to their origin, which turns Jinlong into the treacherous son who later eats the flesh of his birth father (the reincarnated ox), lashes him with a whip, and burns him to death in one of the most gruesome scenes of the novel. Jinlong hardly shows any more mercy to his adopted father Lan Lian when he orders his follower to brush red paint on Lan Lian's face or when he threatens to hang him on the tree. One is left wondering if these two instances combine to form another Christian allusion, since they so closely echo the imagery surrounding Jesus Christ, his face reddened from the blood coming from his crown of thorns as literary and visual imagery represents his crucifixion on a cross.

Between Heaven and Hell is the human world, the "Middle Kingdom" where people live and die, love and hate, sustain each other, and struggle against one another. In *The Garlic Ballads*, "Heaven" is a nominal imposture referring to the county where the air under the sky is polluted by rotting garlic symbolizing political corruption and government, as suggested by the self-claimed title of the jailors, is mired in injustice and persecution. In *Life and Death*, God or Buddha is left out, but the Lord Yama and Hell constitute the reality of the fictional world of the novel. While the carefully crafted novel fits itself into a cyclical structure of narration, the corresponding cycle of *samsara* offers no exit from the weariness of life and death. The spiritual significance of the novel lies in Chinese tradition, since the ultimate rest is bestowed to Lan Lian, the one who follows the way of the Earth. In the light of *Dao De Jing*, Lan Lian is in turn following the way of Heaven and The Way (Dao) itself. In the end, he is blessed with the perfect union with nature or self-so (自然). Yang Xiong in the Han Dynasty would regard him as the "true man ... who has never become separated from the Great Oneness" (DeBary 209).

Because of its direct allusion to Buddhism in its epigraph and strong allusion to Buddhist *samsara*, *Life and Death* readily warrants discussions of religious elements, which are as deep as they are varied. *The Garlic Ballads* demonstrates that even when religious elements are not thematized strongly, they are infused in the setting in a China that is in turn infused with a rich religious heritage. If we are both willing and able to apply the tools with which the secular study of religious studies supplies us, many of Mo Yan's works and those of his contemporaries can be better appreciated for their innovations and the discipline of comparative cultural studies can fulfill its promises for fulsome, careful, and sensitive conversation.

Works Cited

Allen, Joseph R., and Arthur Waley. *The Book of Songs: The Ancient Chinese Classic of Poetry*. New York: Grove P, 1996.

Chen, Lai (陈来). 古代宗教与伦理: 儒家思想的根源 (Ancient Religion and Ethics: Sources of Confucian Thought). Beijing: Shenghuo dushu xinzhi sanlian shudian, 1996.

中华大藏经 (Chinese Tripitaka). Beijing: Zhonghua shuju, 2004. 106 Vols.

Confucius. *The Analects*. Ed. D. C. Lau. Harmondsworth: Penguin, 1979.

Damrosch, David. *What Is World Literature?* Princeton: Princeton UP, 2003.

DeBary, William Theodore. *Sources of Chinese Tradition*. New York: Columbia UP, 1960.

Duran, Angelica, and Yuhan Huang, "Introduction." *Mo Yan in Context: Nobel Laureate and Global Storyteller*. Ed. Angelica Duran and Yuhan Huang. West Lafayette: Purdue UP, 2014. 1–19.

Eno, Robert. *The Confucian Creation of Heaven: Philosophy and the Defense of Ritual Mastery*. Albany: State U of New York P, 1990.

Feng, Youlan, and Derk Bodde. *A History of Chinese Philosophy*. Princeton: Princeton UP, 1952.

Holy Bible: King James Version. New York: American Bible Society, 1980.

Lagerwey, John, Marc Kalinowski, and Herbert Franke. *Early Chinese Religion*. Leiden: Brill, 2009.

Lao, Siguang (劳思光). 新编中国哲学史 (New History of Chinese Philosophy). Taipei: Sanmin, 1988.

Mitchell, Donald, and Angelica Duran. "A Textbook Case of Comparative Cultural Studies." *Mo Yan in Context: Nobel Laureate and Global Storyteller*. Ed. Angelica Duran and Yuhan Huang. West Lafayette: Purdue UP, 2014. 195–212.

Mo Yan. *The Garlic Ballads*. Trans. Howard Goldblatt. New York: Arcade, 2012.

Mo Yan (莫言). 天堂蒜薹之歌 (The Garlic Ballads of Tiantang). Beijing: Zuojia chubanshe, 2013 [1988].

Mo Yan (莫言). "专访：莫言谈生死疲劳聊天实录" ("Interview: Mo Yan on *Life and Death Are Wearing Me Out*"). 论莫言生死疲劳 (On Mo Yan's *Life and Death Are Wearing Me Out*). Ed. Xiong Zhiqin (熊志琴). Hong Kong: Tianhe tushu, 2010. 63-85.

Mo Yan (莫言). "莫言北京大学演讲 语言与历史：新历史主义小说" ("Language and History: New Historical Novels"). Beijing: Peking UP, 2009.

Mo Yan (莫言). 生死疲劳 (*Life and Death Are Wearing Me Out*). Beijing: Zuojia chubanshe, 2013.

Mo Yan. *Life and Death are Wearing Me Out*. Trans. Howard Goldblatt. New York: Arcade, 2008.

Mo Yan. "Mo Yan: Interview". *nobelprize.org* (2012): <http://www.nobelprize.org/nobel_prizes/literature/laureates/2012/yan-telephone.html>.

Mo Yan. "Nobel Lecture: Storytellers." Trans. Howard Goldblatt. *nobelprize.org* (2012): <http://www.nobelprize.org/nobel_prizes/literature/laureates/2012/yan-lecture_en.html>.

"The Nobel Prize in Literature 2012: Prize Announcement." *nobelprize.org* (2012): <http://www.nobelprize.org/nobel_prizes/literature/laureates/2012/announcement.htm>.

Sima, Qian (司马迁). 史记 (The Record of History). Beijing: Zhonghua shuju, 1985. 10 Vols.
Wang, David Der-wei, and Michael Berry. "The Literary World of Mo Yan." *World Literature Today* 74.3 (2000): 487-94.
Wells, Henry W. *Traditional Chinese Humor: A Study in Art and Literature*. Bloomington: Indiana UP, 1971.
Xu, Zhonglin许仲琳. 封神演义 (The Legend of Deification). Taipei: Guiguan tushu, 1984. 2 Vols.
Yang, Fenggang. "Soul Searching in Contemporary Chinese Literature and Society." *Mo Yan in Context: Nobel Laureate and Global Storyteller*. Ed. Angelica Duran and Yuhan Huang. West Lafayette: Purdue UP, 2014. 215–20.

Author's profile

Chi-ying Alice Wang teaches Chinese language, literature, and culture at Purdue University. Her interests in scholarship include Chinese literature, culture, and art history. Wang's recent publications in English include "The Teaching of Chinese Culture in an American University," *Perspectives on Chinese Language and Culture* (Ed. Ik-sang Eom, Ya-fen Chen, and Shih-Chang Hsin, 2010).

Religious Elements in Mo Yan's and Yan Lianke's Works

Jinghui Wang

Abstract

In "Religious Elements in Mo Yan's and Yan Lianke's Works" Jinghui Wang discusses how Chinese folk versions of the religious concepts of incarnation and atonement are represented in Mo Yan's *Life and Death Are Wearing Me Out* and Yan Lianke's *Dream of Ding Village*. Wang analyzes the intratextual and extratextual parallels of the novels from the striking textual parallels of their boy narrators, the narrators' physical ailments, the near-contemporaneous historical settings, and their inclusion and sophisticated representations of rural life and their attendant Buddhist and Chinese folk beliefs; to the biographies of the authors. This article then discusses some of the key differences between the authors' aims and styles that may help to account for Yan Lianke's much more limited reception in China and globally.

While direct references to formal religion have been actively avoided in specific cultural arenas such as literature in China for brief periods the long, rich history of Chinese religion has ensured its cultural permanence. The recent Economic Reform (改革开放) or Opening-up Policy has fostered renewed versions of traditional Chinese religions such as Taoism, Confucianism, and Buddhism and of younger religions such as Islam and Christianity in particular (see Mitchell and Duran for a description of this recent religious history). Two recent literary works demonstrate how Chinese folk religions are represented in Chinese literature, articulated neither to evangelize nor mock but rather to reflect and comment: Mo Yan's *Life and Death Are Wearing Me Out* and Yan Lianke's *Dream of Ding Village*. The intratextual and extratextual parallels of these two novels are provocative; they include their boy narrators, the near-contemporaneous historical settings, and their inclusion and sophisticated representations of rural life and their attendant Buddhist and Chinese folk beliefs.

Narration of Buddhist and Chinese folk beliefs

On one of the opening pages (above the list of "Principal Characters") of *Life and Death Are Wearing Me Out* is the epigraph "The Buddha said: Transmigration wearies owing to mundane desires / Few desires and inaction bring peace to the mind" (n.p.), which comes from the second awakening of the eight great awakenings in *The Sutra of Complete Enlightenment*. The epigraph thus sets up the novel's cultural logic located in the basic doctrine of incarnation in Buddhism. The protagonist and main narrator of *Life and Death*, Ximen Nao, starts off as a landowner in Gaomi Township and undergoes reincarnations as a donkey, an ox, a pig, a dog, and a monkey until finally being born again as a human, Millennium Boy. Through the artistic application of incarnation, the novel covers China's rural history of fifty years from roughly 1950 to 2000, starting from the founding of New China and ranging through the Land Reform Movement (1947-52), the Great Leap Forward (1958-60), the Cultural Revolution (1966-76), and the Opening-Up Policy (1978-) until the new millennium. Through the eyes of animals and human beings, readers are given multiple perspectives of the lives of Chinese peasants with their tenacious but suffering spirit.

Dream of Ding Village also adapts spiritual aspects into its literary frame. The novel is narrated by the ghost of a boy and covers a suffering decade in Ding Village. The villagers give up their long practice of going to the Temple of Guangong (the Chinese god of war) to ask for his blessing. They find that Guangong does not bring them wealth but that selling blood does. So they tear down the temple and crowd the blood station only to find themselves punished by a plague of fever ten years later. The funerals of the narrator's uncle and aunt-in-law and also the ghost wedding ceremony held for the narrator illustrate the pervasiveness of the belief in an afterlife in China.

The finesse applied to Chinese religions in these novels may strike some readers as anomalous given the perception outside of China that religious practices remain dormant in China and the claimed nonreligiosity of Chinese people. These novels are two important examples evidencing that it is inaccurate to say that the Chinese have no religion. In the past two thousand years, Chinese people's worldviews have been founded on strong, native Chinese folk traditions shaped by Confucianism, Taoism, and Buddhism. Hans Küng and Julia Ching point out that a prime characteristic of Chinese religion is the coexistence of these three religions and Chinese people's participation in the three religions (225). Chinese folk beliefs are flexible and for over a millennium have developed into hybrids which integrate elements of Confucianism, Taoism, and Buddhism. Originally, the teachings of Confucius were about humanistic ethics and moral conduct: "He dismissed speculation about the supernatural and insisted on the need for personal responsibility in the context of formal relationships between men and women, parents and children, rulers and subjects. In later centuries, Confucianism was adopted as the state orthodoxy and came to dominate official thinking, culture, and education" (Melton and Baumann 237). While in practice the Chinese populace found that this highest ideal of knowledge brought them little chance of daily success, it provided a comprehensive set of explanations about not only life but also the afterlife. Straddling secular ethics and religion, Confucianism is more concerned with how humans should behave when alive and views spirits from an aloof perspective.

This leaves a lacuna for Taoism and Buddhism to fit in, because of their attention to heaven and the afterlife. The Han dynasty (202 BCE-220 CE) saw the rise of Taoism, as well as the arrival of Buddhism from India. Both were adaptable in China: "Buddhism and Taoism were also aspiring to strengthen their respective liturgical and evangelical monopolies. To integrate one another's favored rituals was undoubtedly viewed as the best means to consolidate the status of their clerical organizations and to attract or keep faithful followers by providing them with the most fashionable religious trends, even if this meant borrowing conspicuously from the opposing camp's heritage" (Mollier 19). Buddhism emphasizes the regulations of desire and the importance of inaction, while Taoism accentuates inaction to a higher degree. The foremost Taoist scripture, Lao Tse's *The Tao Te Ching*, provides Tao's consistent philosophical position and penetrating insights into its key term of 无为 *wuwei* (nonaction), namely the paradoxical nonaction that in itself is a sort of action: "Regress and again regress, until coming to not acting. When not acting then there is nothing not done" (101). This advocacy was favored by ancient Chinese emperors, as it helped quiet down possible civilian rebellions. It should be noted that before Buddhism and Taoism, concepts of spirits or gods were only connected to good or bad fortune in the present life without a sense of retribution or rebirth. The fully formed concepts of incarnation or rebirth after physical death and karma were imported with Buddhism and Taoism and quickly became rooted in the worldviews of the Chinese people, although in a hybrid form.

The incarnations represented in *Life and Death* is different from those of traditional Buddhism or Christianity. "Incarnation" in Christianity refers to the action of God coming to Earth in the form of Jesus Christ roughly two-thousand years ago. Incarnation in Buddhism refers to the Sanskrit *samsara*, the eternal cycle of birth, suffering, death, and rebirth. The traditional "Wheel of Dharma" that is often used as the visual symbol of Buddhism captures the six realms ascribed to Buddhist incarnation: the realm of gods or God, Titans or Asura, human, animal, hungry ghosts or Preta, and Hell. The first three realms are outcomes for goodness, thus higher levels of existence than the latter three. These six levels of existence of rebirth are determined by karma, the total effect of a being's actions and conduct during the successive phases of the being's existence. It is through actions of goodness and spiritual practice that one is able to reincarnate into a higher level of existence and finally become free from the Wheel of Dharma.

In *Life and Death*, incarnation does not adhere strictly to Buddhist doctrine. It does not disambiguate different levels of existence among the six different reincarnations of Ximen Nao. Instead, it provides a structure for storytelling, with each of the reincarnations narrating approximately ten years in China after the 1950s. In an interview on the novel, Mo Yan commented on his appropriation of Buddhist terms and made it clear that he intended it to be more of a metaphor: "When I wrote this novel, my real intention was to understand the six-spoked Wheel of Dharma as Time. It provides a person with opportunities in the long river of time. He reincarnates again and again, facing life and death. When one experiences the trial of life and death, he will achieve very different understandings of society and life" (Xiong 74; unless indicated otherwise, all translations are mine).

Similarly, the novel's use of karma is distinct from Buddhist morality. Traditional karma does not work in Ximen Nao's life or afterlife. At the beginning of the novel, Ximen Nao depicts himself as a benevolent and noble landowner: "I am innocent! Me, Ximen Nao; in my thirty years in the land of mortals I loved manual labor and was a good and thrifty family man. I repaired bridges and repaved roads and was charitable to all. The idols in Northeast Gaomi Township temples were restored thanks to my generosity; the poor township people escaped starvation by eating my food. Every kernel of rice in my granary was wetted by the sweat of my brow, every coin in my family's coffers coated with painstaking effort. I grew rich through hard work, I elevated my family by clear thinking and wise decisions. I truly believe I was never guilty of an unconscionable act" (4). If there is some indication in this case that the narrator is insufficiently detached from self-interest or self-awareness to give an accurate self-assessment, there is another example. His adoption of Lan Lian, who was deserted outside the temple, convincingly shows him to be a conscientious person. Yet, he is not rewarded. Instead, he suffers what seems by and large unfair punishment from the new government. First, he is targeted during the Land Reform Movement in 1948 and executed so that his land can be redistributed (7). Then, after his death, he does not enter the realm of gods or humans. Instead, he is sent to Lord Yama's Audience Hall in Hell, where he sees "Lord Yama, underworld judges seated beside him, oleaginous smiles on their faces" (1). Strictly speaking, Lord Yama is not a Buddhist figure: he derives from Taoism. Lord Yama tortures Ximen Nao in an attempt to elicit his admission of guilt. But Ximen Nao argues for his innocence and utters no word of repentance. Though he earns the unspoken respect of many of Yama's underworld attendants for his tenaciousness, he does not satisfy Lord Yama, who grows so sick of him that he orders to have him flung into a vat of boiling oil, "tumbled and turned and sizzled like a fried chicken for about an hour" (1).

Ximen Nao's reincarnation seems inconsistent with karma, since the narrative has provided readers with no explanation of any previous wrongdoings. He is reborn back in his village on Earth as a donkey on 1 January 1950. To Ximen Nao, this is degradation rather than the reward for a person who has worked hard and behaved well. In many of Mo Yan's and other Chinese writers' works, dramatic conflict arises from the nonaction of karma, that is, kind people are not rewarded with good retribution, which partly manifests Mo Yan's "symbolic meaning" or adaptation of Buddhist incarnation. Ximen Nao articulates understandable perplexity: "Is there no justice in heaven or on earth, in the world of men or the realm of spirits? Any sense of conscience? I protest. I am mystified!" (12). In addition to contradicting the essence of Buddhist karma, the novel also shows Mo Yan's contemporary understanding of the six realms of incarnations. He emphasizes the quantity of six, instead of the levels themselves. Indeed, the numerical division has been unfixed in Buddhism, which tends to contravene fixed notions. While Mahayanan Buddhism, predominant in China, enumerates six realms, earlier sources list five realms and some Buddhist traditions cite eight or ten.

In *Life and Death*, nonetheless, during the process of incarnation, the doctrine of karma itself maintains in part in terms of the accumulated moral energy of a person's life determines his or her character, class status, and disposition in the next life. When Ximen Nao is reborn in animal forms, his incarnations still hold his character and remember his past experience. Indeed, near the end of the novel, the narrator calls attention to the latest reincarnation again being male, "a chubby little baby boy" (539). Mo Yan thus uses a karmic characteristic as a literary device, to provide a consistent point of view, despite the occasional adding of other narrators, such as Lan Jiefang, or a character called Mo Yan. Similarly, as much as Ximen Nao is relieved when he is able to return to life as a human on New Year's Eve 2000, fifty years after the death of his previous human body, readers are prepared for the narrative arc to conclude, thus creating a sort of literary release that mirrors the ultimate release to nirvana sought in Buddhism.

Insofar as Ximen Nao's six incarnations are concerned, the main matter is not whether the religious belief is authentic or faithful to the canon but rather the coherence of Mo Yan's narrative. The symbolic significance of Ximen Nao's incarnation is that no matter in what form or where he is reborn, he faces the fate of suffering and painful death. To most characters, both human and nonhuman, life is bitter and short: Ximen Nao dies in his thirties "trussed up like a criminal, marched off to a bridgehead, and shot" (4), two of Ximen Nao's wives hang themselves (363, 507), Ximen Nao's son Jinlong is decimated by Hong Taiyue's human bomb, and they "depart this world together" (489), melancholy Huang Hezuo dies of cancer (507), ambitious Pang Kangmei is sentenced to death due to corruption (479), true-love-seeking Pang Chunmiao is killed in a car accident (516), desperate Lan Kaifang commits suicide (536), innocent Pang Fenghuang dies while delivering a baby (539), penitential Ximen Huan is stabbed to death (527), Ximen Donkey is slaughtered by the starving peasants (102), Ximen Ox is clubbed to death by Ximen Jinlong (206), Ximen Pig dies saving a drowning child (377), and Ximen Monkey is shot dead by Lan Kaifang (528). Mo Yan's work depicts the tragic and brutish ending of each individual on a sorrow-ridden earth. This coordinates well with the foundational Buddhist concept of the first Noble Truth of *dukkha* (suffering of desire). Even when Ximen Nao is reincarnated as the

Millennium Boy Lan Qiansui, he still suffers physically from hemophilia and spiritually from the torture of the memory of the past: "Small in body, he had a remarkably big head, in which near total recall" (539) existed. The suffering on both levels adheres to the Buddhist seamlessness of body and mind, external and internal.

Whereas *Life and Death* integrates most fully Chinese Buddhism, many works of contemporary Chinese literature, such as *Dream of Ding Village*, forefront Chinese folk beliefs. This is not to say that *Life and Death* ignores Chinese folk beliefs. Mo Yan includes many signs of folk beliefs in the novel, such as the Earth God Temple and the God of War Temple in the village where Ximen Nao lives. Additionally, readers will most likely notice Confucian, Taoist, and Buddhist elements in both novels. Like Mo Yan, Yan Lianke centralizes religious elements in giving the narrator a specific physical disability. Mo Yan's big-headed Millennium Boy is "born with a strange bleeding disease that the doctors called hemophilia, for which there was no cure. He would die, sooner rather than later" (539). That death, however, is not narrated in *Life and Death*. Serendipitously enough, Xiaoqiang, the short-lived boy whose death is also associated with blood in *Dream of Ding Village*, seems almost like a continuation of the final narrator of *Life and Death*, even in terms of the setting of a poor village and in the first decade of the twenty-first century. The problems that the fictional Ding villagers face are those faced by many actual Chinese villagers searching for prosperity in 1990s. Ghost Xiaoqiang tells the story of how this small village is decimated by HIV/AIDS as a result of unregulated blood selling. To people in Henan Province, one of the most crowded areas in central China, blood had become a valuable commodity. Yan creates in *Ding Village* a fictional version of the hundreds of villagers induced to sell their blood to government-run blood stations in the mid-1990s. What readers see from this novel is a common scenario actually going on in hundreds of villages in China during that period. *Dream of Ding Village* represents that blood business could be profitable as long there is a stable flow of donors. To secure the supply of donors, the government tries different ways to promote people's eagerness to donate their blood. When Ding villagers are reluctant to sell their blood, the local government organizes them to visit other model blood donation villages where they witness those villagers' happy life: as long as they agree to donate their blood, they get bonuses, such as "vegetables and meat from the local council for free" (28). They gain social status symbols as well: their government-built houses are labeled with different numbers of stars showing their different levels of contribution to the blood supply.

The narrator's father, Ding Hui, rises to the top of the local social rank and makes a big fortune through exploiting the situation, first by organizing villagers to donate blood at blood-plasma collection stations as a Blood Head (10), then by selling coffins during the HIV/AIDS epidemic as a merchant. In order to make more money, he forsakes his morality. He sets up his own private blood collection center with no facilities to screen donors or sterilize collection instruments. He buys and resells blood so as to earn a higher margin. To reduce costs and get more profit, he uses one syringe on four people and stealthily replaces the 700cc blood bags with 500cc ones so as to cheat more blood from donors. The ignorant villagers are so eager to sell their blood in order to become rich quickly that they sell blood more frequently than their bodies can tolerate, seeing no danger of being exposed to dirty syringes and tainted cotton and not caring about being used or cheated. The spread of greed is followed by the spread of a "fever," a term that reflects the local folk's primitive understanding of AIDS. Deepening the emotional impact, even Blood Head's brother, the narrator's uncle, Ding Liang, gets infected and faces early death. There are three generations in this novel: Xiaoqiang the grandson, Ding Hui the father, and Ding Shuiyang the grandfather. They all face Buddhist *dukkha*: Xiaoqiang is poisoned because of his father's greediness, and Ding, believing in karma, kills his son Hui in the hopes of enacting atonement. Xiaoqiang's death through poisoning shows the villagers' limited understanding of karma. Ten years after the craze of blood selling in Ding Village, almost the whole village is wiped out with no responsibility taken or enough reparations paid. Bursting with anger and unable to fight the strong, some villagers take revenge on any weak they can find. They first poison Ding Hui's fowls, then poison Ding Hui's pigs, and finally poison Ding Hui's then-twelve-year-old son Xiaoqiang (9). The response of Dings' neighbor, Xiao Ming's mother, is that "it is karmic" (112).

After his poisoning early on in the novel, Xiaoqiang, a ghost wandering around the village, serves as the narrator. Rather than utilizing the Buddhist concept of immediate reincarnation as with Nao in *Life and Death*, Yan makes use of the traditional Chinese folk belief that after the human body dies, the human soul still exists and observes the living. The Chinese name for "ghost" is 鬼 (*kuei*), which refers to the spirits of humans shortly after death who wander until they are absorbed back into the earth. This folk belief of *kuei* can be traced back to the Shang Dynasty (1500-1100 BCE) and has influenced all of China throughout its two-millennium history. Xiaoqiang's ghost keeps crying to his grandfather for help, and this is partly the reason why Ding Shuiyang finally kills Ding Hui.

Every region in China developed its own particular traditions, practices, and beliefs related to gods, ghosts, and ancestors. All over China, local deities made up a varied pantheon including spirits of local heroes, versions of Taoist and Buddhist deities. Ancestor worship is most common and plays a central role in kinship, lineage, and clan systems. Most households have a small altar where respect is paid to previous generations. Yan represents such an altar in Ding Hui's house (134). Ancestors and deities are expected to answer petitions. If they fail to do so, the supplicant is perfectly entitled to switch allegiance to others, which explains why Ding villagers tear down the God of War Temple. The entire religious system in China is decentralized, unsupervised, and subject to local conditions. Temples in China are often dedicated to several gods, and there is no concept of exclusivity. This kind of religious folk belief is the foundation of Blood Head Ding Hui's otherwise unaccountable action of exhuming the dead body of his son Xiaoqiang for a marriage to a dead girl, Lingzi. In Ding Hui's plain and simple concept, his son could still have a family and live a happier life in the afterlife through the ghost marriage. Lingzi is chosen because "she is the daughter of the county magistrate … She acquired a rare disease and drowned in water, after her father became the county magistrate and started organizing the whole town to sell blood" (260). Ding Hui and other villagers believe that even in death there is still a rigidly divided social hierarchy.

The ghost marriage ceremony between Xiaoqiang and Lingzi is not the only one. Ding Hui arranges thousands of pairs of deceased for ghost marriages. Ironically, although Ding Hui gets monetary benefit for these ghost marriages, he still gets praise from other villagers. An old man in Cai County says, "Director Ding is a good man. He sells coffins at a low price to Shang Yang villagers, solving problems for the dead, and now he arranges marriages for the boys and girls who died single, solving problems for those alive" (247). The reason for this praise of Ding Hui is that those alive believe in the concept of the afterlife, too, and are relieved to learn that their relatives will have company in that afterlife. Religious traditions merge and transform in the novel as they do in actual practice. While there is no Buddhist reincarnation in *Dream of Ding Village*, there is karma, which is closely linked with atonement. The narrator's grandfather, Ding Shuiyang, believes that his grandson Xiaoqiang is poisoned and Ding Liang acquires AIDS as punishments for the deeds of his son, Blood Head Ding Hui. Ding Shuiyang fears the death of his other two grandchildren and the infection of other relatives, so he begs Ding Hui to kowtow in front of each family in Ding Village and then commit suicide in order to atone for his bad actions. This request exemplifies the valuation of the divine over the mundane. After Ding Hui refuses and after he fails to kill Ding Hui with his own hands, Ding Shuiyang himself kneels down and kowtows in front of all villagers as a proxy for his son begging for the villagers' forgiveness (44).

It is worth pausing here to call attention to how deeply Chinese cultural practices are related to Chinese religious practices: kowtowing or bowing deeply and even prostrating oneself is a practice that goes as far back as the Shang Dynasty. This expression of deep respect was used at least since the Han Dynasty in the presence of the emperor as much as in front of religious emblems and items. With the introduction of Confucianism in the fifth century BCE, the practice was extended so that children bowed to parents as a show of respect, but also reconceived philosophically to enable the kowtower to physically and mentally instantiate humility (an early version of behavioral psychology). Thus grandfather Ding Shuiyang takes it upon himself to atone for his elder son's social iniquity. His assumption is, of course, a far cry from a Christian concept of personal sin, but perhaps not too far from the sense of social and familial sin to be found in Jewish and Islamic religions. In atonement for his son's sin, he converts the village elementary school into a nursing home that shelters AIDS patients deserted by their family members. Ding Hui is aware of his sin and knows that Ding villagers hate him, but he says to his father, "So long as you do not want me to die, nobody of Ding Village dares to challenge me" (274). Seeing that his own substitutionary atonement is not enough and he himself has become the only person to end the sin of his son, Ding Shuiyang finally strikes Ding Hui on the head with a baton. Before Ding Shuiyang strikes his son dead, he experiences a hallucination that his grandson is reluctant to leave his tomb, crying: "Grandpa, save me please" (275). The reason for Ding Shuiyang's killing of his son is to save the grandson from all the family ills and to extract the son from the infernal dungeons to which his bad karma has condemned him.

Whether Buddhist, Taoist, or atheist, contemporary Chinese readers understand the doctrines manifested in these acts: the doctrines of karma are widely adopted in Chinese people's daily life. The general Chinese populace may not go to temple for serious learning, but they have integrated many religious practices and enjoy increased freedom to adapt Buddhist and Taoist doctrines. Before the founding of communist China, every village had at least one Buddhist or Taoist temple. Most were built on fertile soil with good *feng shui*. Many who encounter suffering or dissatisfaction in their life go to temples to seek for relief and try doing good deeds as atonement.

Authorial representations of religious beliefs and practices

The cultural significance of *Life and Death* and *Dream of Ding Village* as contemporary Chinese works that include religious concepts and practices cannot be overstated. A great number of Chinese writings involve the depiction of gods, ghosts, or strange images that satisfy the curiosity of humanity about the unknown. *Strange Tales from a Chinese Studio* (聊斋志异) from the Qing Dynasty (1644-1912) is typical of Chinese literature in its combination of folk belief within a social context. There, readers can find vixen spirits, ghosts, scholars, court officials, Taoist exorcists, and beasts with supernatural powers, all to be found in Mo Yan's works, too, of course. To cite just one example, the well-known story "The Painted Skin" (Pu 47-51) narrates the story of scholar Wang who is bewitched by an evil spirit disguised as a pretty girl but ultimately saved by his devoted wife. This story tries to tell readers not to be misled by surface beauty. The May Fourth Movement (五四运动) (1919) with its advocacy of its version of democracy and freedom required modern Chinese literature to develop under the banners of science and reason, denouncing the traditional feudal sense of the spirits of people. It attempted to change the mentality of people's fanatical worshiping of spirits, because spirits were held to be superstitious and against science or reason. As such, "spirits" novels (灵异鬼怪小说) encountered more and greater obstacles with the founding of communist China in 1949. This new era ruled out superstitious beliefs, including well-formed religions, and emphasized the grand narratives of political propaganda. The Social Realist writers of this period narrated rural life that elaborated more on actual struggles between old and new practices than on spirits or ghosts. The most popular works in the 1950s were Shuli Zhao's 1955 三里湾 (San Li Bay), Bo Qu's 1957 林海雪原 (Lin Hai Xue Yuan), and Libo Zhou's 1958 山乡巨变 (Shan Xiang Ju Bian), all of which depict a panorama of rural life in the newly built communist China.

With the advent of the Economic Reform (改革开放) or Opening-up Policy early in 1980s, China opened its door to the world with the aim of learning how to boost its economy. As can be expected, new ideas filtered into literary writing as well. In the mid-1980s, Chinese literature encountered magical realism, especially with the works of Jorge Luis Borges and Gabriel García Márquez. Spirits returned to Chinese narrative in the 1980s and were resurrected in Chinese writers' fictional narrations of everyday life in China. Through adapting trends in foreign literature, Chinese writers explored the historical fragments of national memory by taking spirits novels to a new stage. The Western world is probably most familiar with the nuanced use of this genre through Maxine Hong Kingston's *Woman Warrior*, in which spirits are used in order to represent life metaphorically and to express their present worldly wishes. Chinese literature of the 1980s regenerated once-suppressed traditional folk beliefs in grand narratives with such spirits novels as Pingwa Jia's 1993 废都 (The Deserted City), Zhongshi Chen's 1993 白鹿原 (White Deer Plain), Shaogong Han's 1985 爸爸爸 (Dad), and Mo Yan's *Red Sorghum*. Chinese scholars and critics rightly note that this group of novels receives guidance from both the Chinese classical spirits narrative tradition to "write about the world life metaphorically through ghosts, and express thoughts through spirits" (Wang 5), and from contemporary Western constructs, such as "linking techniques, maze, and void and suspense with no solution" (Nan 56).

On entering the twenty-first century, the best Chinese writers have successfully rid their works of the traditional construct of contrasting the old and new or finding solutions for social problems. Instead, they have innovated their style, content, and even genre to present social problems with no intention of resolving them. Both *Life and Death* and *Dream of Ding Village* provide readers with perspectives on residents in rural areas struggling to find a way out but hopelessly hindered by the despicable, dark, wretched, and pathetic side of human nature. Both employ religion and folk beliefs in supporting roles. Using religious belief, the two writers give tentative accounts of the life of not only the souls after the death of the body but also the earthly rural life of numerous wretched peasants in China.

The biographies of Mo Yan and Yan

In addition to the connections between specific aspects of the two novels are connections in the biographies and historical contexts of Mo Yan and Yan: both were nourished by the Yellow River civilization and its derivative dominating folk beliefs, they share similar historical backgrounds, and they challenge the state in similar, but not the same, ways. These similarities by no means determine their artistic productions, as indeed their different success, reception, and literary output demonstrate. Lying in the central part of the "Middle Kingdom," from which "China" takes its name, the Yellow River is one of China's most significant water sources, stretching over 5400 kilometers, covering nine provinces, and nourishing millions of people. For generations, peasants have depended on the river for their livelihood and have seen the rise and fall of the various dynasties and different regimes. The river itself has generated a rich foundation for Chinese culture and diverse Chinese folk beliefs. It is believed that Chinese civilization is divided into six cultural districts visualized as a giant flower in which the Central Plain is nourished by the Yellow River and forms the center of the giant flower surrounded by the five petals formed by other districts (see Yan 38-50). Contemporary Chinese writers from various regions along the Yellow River have captured the diversity of folk beliefs from their respective areas. Each of China's nine provinces has its own representative contemporary writer, such as Jia from Shaanxi Province, Rui Li from Shanxi Province, Mo Yan from Shandong Province, and Yan from Henan Province. As much as Mo Yan sets many of his works in Gaomi Township of Shandong Province, as he does with *Life and Death*, and Yan sets *Dream of Ding Village* in Ding Village—a small village of eight hundred people—Jia builds his 废都 (Deserted City) in Xi'an of Shaanxi Province, and Li makes the most of the quiet Lüliang Mountains in厚土 (Thick Soil).

The Shandong and Henan provinces are neighboring and are also the last two along the Yellow River before it finally enters the Bohai Sea. This geographical proximity helps to account for the similarity in the folk beliefs reflected in Mo Yan's and Yan's novels. The folk beliefs from these areas are still inflected with Buddhism, although with expected deviance. To investigate the origin of this kind of Buddhism, one should follow the Yellow River tracing back to its cradle, the Qinghai-Tibet Plateau, through which Buddhism makes its way into central China. As the Yellow River flows eastward to the middle area of China, it picks up and integrates local spiritual and cultural thinking, resulting in the rich forms of folk beliefs in the Henan and Shandong provinces. In Mo Yan's hometown Gaomi, every village had at least one Buddhist temple before the founding of communist China. There is a striking similarity between the two authors' childhoods and adult life experiences. Both born in the 1950s (Mo Yan in 1955 and Yan in 1958) and in the countryside, they made their way out of rural life by joining the army, Mo Yan in 1976 and Yan in 1978. During these years, there was no college entrance examination that could bring young peasants the chance to study in colleges and then to work in cities. So joining the army was the only way for powerless rural people to change their fate. They both took the opportunity of serving in the army to further their education and both graduated from the same department of the same college, in the Department of Literature, Arts College of People's Liberation Army, Mo Yan in 1986 and Yan in 1991. Their literary careers also bear a striking resemblance: they both started publishing in the 1980s and their fictions are affected by Western writing techniques. Additionally, both are regarded highly in the Chinese literary world. They have garnered the two major Chinese literary awards: Mo Yan the Mao Dun Prize in 2011 and Yan Lianke the Lu Xun Literary Prize in 1995-1996 and 1997-2000.

Amid these parallels are intersections: the slightly older Mo Yan has sometimes exhibited the duty of an elder brother to Yan. When Yan ran into a legal suit with Shanghai Arts Press about *Dream of Ding Village*, Mo Yan served as a mediator to help the two sides reach a compromise. Mo Yan and Yan are friends both in daily life and in the writing field. They both reside in Beijing now and are members of the Chinese Writers Association. The basis for their intersections may have as much to do with their similar heritage as their bravery in depicting cultural truths which may contravene the will of the state. Both tend to challenge existing social norms including censorship. As Lanlan Du posits, Mo Yan criticizes China's family planning (计划生育), or One-child, policy. Yan criticizes the government for another matter related to health and human services, namely the blood-selling scandal in the Henan Province that led to the outbreak of HIV/AIDS and huge loss of life. Further, both Mo Yan and Yan are audacious in touching political taboos. Thus it is natural to question why Mo Yan's Frog was published and 丁庄梦 (*Dream of Ding Village*) banned when first published in Chinese. One preliminary answer is that Mo Yan is more tactful than Yan in dealing with political taboos. Mo Yan shows how a writer in a socialist country can internalize the censoring function in his writing and subsequently become globally renowned as testified by his Nobel Prize in Literature. For example, in Frog we can read Mo Yan's tact in dealing with censorship (see Chen).

In Frog, Mo Yan describes the abortion provider Aunt with features acceptable to state ideology, such as her hard-working nature and her admission to the communist party in 1955 on the same day that "she delivers the 1000th baby in her midwife career" (112), her break from her former boyfriend after he flies to Taiwan (118), and her not holding a grudge for "being wronged during the Cultural Revolution" (130) but instead claiming that she is "born the communist party's member, dead as party's ghost" (120): she is a faithful population-control policy implementer. The description of these pro-government acts goes uncensored. Mo Yan is also good at employing hallucinatory realism to depict the unspeakable parts of his stories. For example, to develop the plot toward Aunt's final wakening of her conscience, he has the croaks from thousands of frogs shock Aunt into feeling remorse for her previous merciless and cruel acts (169). On the other hand, Yan is more straightforward: it is not simply that he is not as subtle as Mo Yan, however: "Much of the best contemporary writing from the mainland also follows in China's humanist tradition, including Yu Hua's 余华 (1960-) *To Live* 活着 (1992) and *Chronicle of a Blood Merchant* 许三观卖血记 (1995). And whereas Yu's portrait of a desperate father who nearly dies selling his blood offers a subtle critique of market capitalism, Yan Lianke's 阎连科

(1958-) *Dream of Ding Village* 丁庄梦 (2006) directly indicts the government's blood-selling profiteers who unleashed an AIDS epidemic in Henan province. As Yan's characters die 'like falling leaves,' his haunting novel may be a twenty-first version of Camus's *The Plague* (1947)" (Knight 106-07).

In the postscript of his novel, Yan points out that he feels pained for his hometown of the Henan Province and many other poor provinces suffering from the HIV/AIDS epidemic. He finds himself unable to do anything but cry out for the "uncountable HIV/AIDS carriers" with "unprecedented desperation and helplessness" (287). Before publishing the book, he signed a contract with Shanghai Arts Press and claimed that he would donate 50,000 Yuan of his royalties to Xinzhuang Village in Henan Province where he conducted his research for the novel. These actions led to the book's fate of being censored. The fatal factor for the book's being banned is textual: Yan does not adopt any dodging tactics in his style or content, and except for the narrator being a dead boy, *Dream of Ding Village* is a plainly realistic novel. With Xiaoqiang as its omniscient narrator, the novel is like documentary literature describing the problem of AIDS in a Henan village and the irresponsibility of the government. Thus it has faced a different fate from that of Frog.

In conclusion, I posit that Mo Yan and Yan are both great Chinese writers with masterful writing techniques, bountiful human consciousness, and acute sensitivities to China's cultural heritage. As much as *Life and Death* and *Dream of Ding Village* provide us with a panorama of rural life in the China of the recent past, their biographies and historical contexts give us a sense of literary formation and development during the same time period. The complexity of folk beliefs prevailing among Chinese people has a similarly complex analogue in governmental practices related to Chinese literary practices. Besides Mo Yan and Yan, there are many other Chinese writers who address the religious and philosophical practices of incarnation and atonement in the daily life of the present common Chinese populace.

Works Cited

Chen, Thomas. "The Censorship of Mo Yan's天堂蒜薹之歌 (*The Garlic Ballads*)." *Mo Yan in Context: Nobel Laureate and Global Storyteller.* Ed. Angelica Duran and Yuhan Huang. West Lafayette: Purdue UP, 2014. 37–49.

Chen, Zhongshi (陈忠实). 白鹿原 (White Deer Plain). Beijing: Writer's P, 1993.

Du, Lanlan. "Abortion in Faulkner's *The Wild Palms* and Mo Yan's蛙 (Frog)." *Mo Yan in Context: Nobel Laureate and Global Storyteller.* Ed. Angelica Duran and Yuhan Huang. West Lafayette: Purdue UP, 2014. 63–76.

Han, Shaogong (韩少功). 爸爸爸 (Dad). Beijing: Peoples Literature P, 1986.

Jia, Pingwa (贾平凹). 废都啊, 废都 (The Deserted City). Lanzhou: Gansu People's P, 1993.

Knight, Sabina. *Chinese Literature: A Very Short Introduction.* Oxford: Oxford UP, 2011.

Küng, Hans, and Julia Ching. *Christianity and Chinese Religions.* New York: Doubleday, 1989.

Lao, Tse. *The Tao Te Ching.* Trans. Edmund Ryden. Oxford: Oxford UP, 2008.
Li, Rui (李锐). 厚土(Thick Soil). Beijing: Peoples Literature P, 2008.
Melton, J. Gordon, and Martin Baumann, eds. *Religions of the World: A Comprehensive Encyclopedia of Beliefs and Practices.* Santa Barbara: ABC-CLIO, 2002.
Mitchell, Donald, and Angelica Duran. "A Textbook Case of Comparative Cultural Studies." *Mo Yan in Context: Nobel Laureate and Global Storyteller.* Ed. Angelica Duran and Yuhan Huang. West Lafayette: Purdue UP, 2014. 195–212.
Mo Yan (莫言). 蛙 (Frog). Shanghai: Shanghai Literature and Art P, 2012.
Mo Yan. *Life and Death Are Wearing Me Out.* Trans. Howard Goldblatt. New York: Arcade, 2008.
Mo Yan. *Red Sorghum.* Trans. Howard Goldblatt. New York: Penguin Books, 1994.
Mollier, Christine. *Buddhism and Taoism Face to Face.* Honolulu: U of Hawai'i P, 2008.
Nan, Fan (南帆). "叙述的平衡" ("Balance of Narration"). *Nanfang wentan* 4 (2004): 56-57.
P'u, Sung-Ling. *Strange Stories from a Chinese Studio.* 1680. Trans. A. Giles Herbert. Honolulu: UP of the Pacific, 2003.
Qu, Bo (曲波). 林海雪原 (Tracks in the Snowy Forest). Beijing: Writer's P, 1957.
Sutra of Complete Enlightenment, The. Trans. Guo-go Bhikshu. Boston: Shambhala P, 1999.
Wang, David Der-wei (王德威). 现代中国小说十讲 (Ten Lectures on Modern Chinese Fiction). Shanghai: Fudan UP, 2003.
Xiong, Zhiqin (熊志琴), ed. 论莫言生死疲劳: 红楼梦奖 2008 得奖作品专辑 (On Mo Yan's Novel *Life and Death Are Wearing Me Out*: Collective Essays on the Work of the 2008 Hongloumeng Prize). Hongkong: Tiandi tushu youxian gongsi, 2010.
Yan, Lianke (阎连科). 丁庄梦 (Dream of Ding Village). Shanghai: Shanghai Arts P, 2006.
Yan, Lianke. *Dream of Ding Village.* 2006. Trans. Cindy Carter. New York: Grove P, 2011.
Zhao, Shuli (赵树理). 三里湾 (Three Mile Bay). Beijing: Popular Literature P, 1955.
Zhou, Li Bo (周立波). 山乡巨变 (Great Changes of the Mountain Villages). Beijing: Writer's P, 1958.

Author's profile

Jinghui Wang teaches comparative literature at Tsinghua University. Her interests in scholarship include comparative literature, multiculturalism, and postcolonialism. In addition to numerous articles, Wang's book publications include 永远的流散者: 库切评传 (Foreigner Forever: On J. M. Coetzee) (2011).

Mo Yan's Work and the Politics of Literary Humor

Alexa Huang and Angelica Duran

Abstract

In "Mo Yan's Work and the Politics of Literary Humor" Alexa Huang and Angelica Duran present close readings of the diverse type of humor in Mo Yan's short stories and novels. Mo Yan's texts are in deep conversation with the long tradition of humor in Chinese writings, yet are also innovative thus extending that tradition. Huang and Duran attend to the ways in which silence as comic technique and authorial self-construction works in terms of the character Mo Yan in *The Republic of Wine*, *Life and Death Are Wearing Me Out*, *POW!*, and other novels. The study also teases out Mo Yan's use of Chinese humor (幽默, *youmo*), primarily in his novella *Shifu: You'll Do Anything for a Laugh*. They conclude with a discussion of the ribald humor of understatement that Mo Yan utilizes in *The Republic of Wine* and *Big Breasts and Wide Hips* to comment on sexual peccadillos.

One of the most prolific writers in contemporary China, Mo Yan, the 2012 Nobel Prize in Literature Laureate, has been at the center of some of the most significant literary events of his time. His writings are energized by several interconnected themes and styles ranging from magic realism to black humor and from epic historical novel to bawdy fable. The comic visions in the works of Mo Yan are sometimes neglected in the English-speaking world. This owes in part to the difficulty of translating humor across languages and culture. As Jocelyn Chey and Jessica Milner Davis note in their *Humour in Chinese Life and Letters*, "in terms of accessing Chinese humor by non-Chinese literature audiences, the need for translation—particularly of literary jokes and humorous writing—adds a level of difficulty (as well as itself contributing many examples of unintended funniness)" (29). Culturally, Chinese readers may be more on the lookout for comic elements given a literary and cultural tradition in which the serious and comic seek rather than forsake each other. That tradition extends deeply, as Henry W. Wells also notes in his book-length study of Chinese humor: "The Taoists and the sect of Ch'an Buddhists made virtually a religion of humor, performing ceremonial dances about a sacred toad. Even the Confucian scholar-statesmen devised a scheme of values cordial to humor, to say the least" (9). The near invisibility of comic elements may be owing to readerly predisposition toward Chinese literature generally and Mo Yan's works in particular. Chey and Milner Davis note the long-standing critical foundation for the dearth of current critical attention to this topic. They call attention to the fact that, about a century ago, when the U.S. writer and translator Lionel Strachey took on the daunting task of translating and compiling the compendium in fifteen volumes *The World's Wit and Humor*, "he drew distinctions between differing European traditions but did not extend his sampling into Asian languages, beyond Omar Khayyam whose work was well-known in translation" (2).

To this broad inattentiveness to traditional Chinese humor, we can add readerly expectations of serious themes and neglect of comic elements in Mo Yan's contemporary works. His better-known historical novels are known for their serious nature, such as 红高粱家族 (*Red Sorghum*), made even more renowned by Zhang Yimou's award-winning film version, which chronicles the sober history of pain for a rural Chinese village in the turbulent 1930s. Paradoxically, the very seriousness of Mo Yan's driving political and social commentaries in works like this should alert readers to look for comic elements since, as C. T. Hsia has shown in *The Chinese Sense of Humor*, humor in general, and Chinese humor in particular, retaliates against and helps with coping with "the powerful repressive forces of society" (35). Literary humor frames and informs serious subject matters in Mo Yan's stories, and the writer sometimes uses a serious tone to contrast frivolity and human folly.

Mo Yan blends bawdy and humorous modes to construct counternarratives to the grand narrative of the nation-state, similar to other contemporary writers who parody socialist realism. In the 1996 novel *Helden wie wir* (*Heroes Like Us*), the East German writer Thomas Brussig has the novel's first-person narrator ask in a self-reflexive and playful tone: "The story of the [Berlin] Wall's end is the story of my penis, but how to embody such a statement in a book conceived as a Nobel Prize–worthy cross between *David Copperfield* and *The Rise and Fall of the Roman Empire?*" (5). The connection between the Wall and its attendant political extensions to the narrator's penis is absurd, enabling the hilarious commentary on the Cold War. We can look to *The Republic of Wine* and *Life and Death Are Wearing Me Out* for Mo Yan's similar strategy to create a sense of comic absurdity. *The Republic of Wine* is a parody of Chinese food culture written in the reinvented genres of detective and epistolary novels. Toward the end of the novel, on his way to Liquorland on the invitation of Li Yidou, a doctoral student in "liquor studies at the Brewer's College" there, the character Mo Yan reminisces that "back when I was leaving Beijing my bus passed through Tiananmen Square, where ... Sun Yat-sen [commonly referred to as the father of the Republic of China founded in 1911], who stood in the square, and Mao Zedong [leader of the People's Republic of China from its establishment in 1949 until his death in 1976], who hangs from the wall of the Forbidden City, were exchanging silent messages past the five-star flag hanging from a brand-new flagpole" (333). This is but one of numerous examples of Mo Yan's subtle and humorous readings of China's political culture and figures (see Yuhan Huang on the significance of public visual culture in China). At the same time, his sympathetic and passionate pleas for the characters being ridiculed preclude any sense of superiority derived from historical hindsight, as if "we now know better."

Mo Yan's works—whether generically categorized as hallucinatory realism, the fantastic, epic historical novel, or salty fable—are peppered with a variety of types of humor. We chart a selection of such modes of expression in Mo Yan's short stories and novels to show their diversity and interplay as elements that contribute to the depth and charm of his works. That they would play such an integral role should come as no surprise given the penname 管谟业 (Guan Moye) adopted for his prolific and assertive writings: 莫言 (Mo Yan) ("Don't Talk"). This seemingly serious claim to silence or an author's abstinence from speech may be seen as a gesture of self-mockery or self-praise. It is also a critical tool: a tool to speak the unspeakable in writings which reimagine political history and the history of sexuality.

The silence of the writer Mo Yan creates a unique space for the articulate character Mo Yan, a regular in his novels, such as *The Republic of Wine* and *Life and Death Are Wearing Me Out*. The evolution of the character Mo Yan in *Life and Death* attests to the seriousness that is derived from the humorous. The novel revolves around the themes of social injustice, hunger, poverty, and the irrational aspects of the Cultural Revolution. Mo Yan frames these harrowing themes in a facetious version of the Chinese Buddhist notion of reincarnation. The novel's central character, landowner Ximen Nao, negotiates with the king of the underworld and returns to his village reincarnated in turn as a donkey, an ox, a pig, a dog, a monkey, and, finally, a big-headed boy. There is also a character named Mo Yan. Similar to Brussig's *Heroes Like Us*, *Life and Death Are Wearing Me Out* parodies official narratives about the history of the People's Republic of China from 1950 to 2000 through the metaphorical framework of the Buddhist idea of the six paths of reincarnation. It thus revitalizes a long-standing cultural and literary device that goes back to the Chinese classic *Journey to the West* and the Monkey King. At once sophisticated and basic, this "humor has its roots in animal vitality, which when joined with the nature of man, reveals itself in the physical manifestations of smiling and laughing" (Wells 11). Ximen Nao, a landlord executed for his bourgeois sins, goes through a series of reincarnations and along the way interacts with humans, fights with other animals for survival, and observes and comments on Chinese—and human—society as it goes through momentous historical changes.

In Book 1, the character Mo Yan is mentioned only as a writer of the drama *Black Donkey* (30, 39, 74, 102) and short stories (8, 12, 52, 53), which the narrator characterizes as "nonsense, not to be believed" (82). In Book 2, the narrator refers to Mo Yan as one of the "clever, glib students" (117) of Ximen Village who has a talent for making up "limericks" (119), which are particularly ribald rhymes. When the character Mo Yan appears in the early chapters, he is a young "ruffian" (119) and a bit of a whiner (131), for whom the narrator finds little sympathy as when for example "Mo Yan mistakenly picked up [a firecracker] and bang, his lips parted as it tore a hole in his hand. Serves you right!" (206). His characterization begins to change in Book 3. On the first page of that Book, the spirit of Ximen Nao sees among the sad witnesses to the horrific death of his second reincarnation, Ximen Ox, "Mo Yan, smeared with snot and tears" (219). Later, he is portrayed as a kind, middle-aged man: Mo Yan, "who had risen to the position of editorial director of the local newspaper, gave [the forlorn Lian Jiefang] a job as an editor and found work for Pang Chunmiao in the dining hall" (477). Finally, in Book 5, by far the briefest Book (515-40), he takes over to narrate the surprising, sad, and hopeful ending of the novel. Mo Yan's authorial self-inscription, like the rest of his uses of humor, thus does not come off as narcissistic or haphazard. Rather, Mo Yan reinvigorates the neglected tradition of literary humor in contemporary China with comic yet sympathetic portrayals of individuals in a fragmented world of postsocialist marketization (see Chen; McGrath). Both underprivileged individuals and bureaucrats alike find themselves in comic and sometimes absurd situations.

Mo Yan adapts folklorized Buddhist traditions of reincarnation as a frame to extend both the narrative voice and the reach of the social commentary, not limited to China or to a specific era but rather to all humanity and all times. Ximen Donkey paraphrases communist slogans to persuade two black mules to share their food with him: "Don't be so stingy, you bastards, there's enough there for all of us. Why hog it all? We have entered the age of communism, when mine is yours and yours is mine" (92). In another episode, Mao Zedong, who has just passed away, sits on a "solemn and bleak" moon (a reversal of Mao as the crimson sun in communist iconography) while two piglets, Piglet Sixteen (Ximen) with his girlfriend Little Flower on his back, follow him ardently: "We wanted to get closer to the moon so we could see Mao Zedong's face with even greater clarity. But the moon moved with us, the distance remaining constant no matter how hard I paddled ... Schools of red carp, white eels, black-capped soft-shelled turtles, fly up to the moon, an expression of romanticism; but before they reach their goal, the pull of gravity brings them back [to become] meals for waiting foxes and wild boars" (340).

Piglet Sixteen's playfulness and facetiousness should not be confused with the penchant for the frivolity in Zhu Wen's *I Love Dollars* or Wang Shuo's *Please Don't Call Me Human* and *Playing for Thrills*. Whereas the frivolous hooligans in Wang's many bestsellers of the 1990s may represent a departure from a socialist past of idealism and innocence and unabashed embrace of the postsocialist present of shrewdness (see Wang, Jing 261-62; Huang, Yibing 78-79), a number of Mo Yan's characters such as Ding Gou'er in the *Republic of Wine* and Ding Shikou in the novella

Shifu: You'll Do Anything for a Laugh are caught uncomfortably between different modes of existence, between the past and the present. They are thrown overnight into a new world with a different cultural logic, akin to the protagonist Hank Morgan, who is transported back in time to the medieval British court of King Arthur in Mark Twain's burlesque novel *A Connecticut Yankee in King Arthur's Court*.

Mo Yan has attested to the way he has merged China's tradition of humor and his unique use of the self-reflecting character Mo Yan to write novels about the Cultural Revolution. An example of Mo Yan's dark and cold humor in characterizing madness and absurdity is in his use of colloquial language of political sloganism. During the Cultural Revolution, the long-standing, common practice of people greeting each other with the exchange "Have you eaten?—I have" was replaced. Instead, people made use of political slogans, so that if one began, "Chairman Mao," the other was supposed to respond "lives ten thousand years." Mo Yan recounts how a "woman Red Guard encountered the madman in our village, and asked, 'Chairman Mao,' however, the madman answered with fury, 'fuck your mother.' The Red Guard took the madman to the village revolutionary director, who simply replied, 'he is an idiot'" (119). Thus the author Mo Yan's regular comments in various novels and various interviews about the stupidity or madness of the character Mo Yan should be understood as part of this cultural complex.

There is plenty in human nature, independent of politics that can serve as the target of humor. In *POW!*, Mo Yan concentrates the humorous arc on the narrator Luo Xiaotong's obsession with meat. Unlike Bei Dao or Gao Xingjian, who are more vocal and critical of the Chinese government, Mo Yan's critique is often more subtle. Chris Cox rightly observes that *POW!* "doesn't land any blows on the Chinese regime" (<http://www.theguardian.com/books/2013/jan/19/pow-mo-yan-review-fiction>). The backdrop of any comedy is key to the way the quotidian engages with large-scale societal events and trends. Luo's story is grounded in the added dispossessions women face during cultural turmoil, as is the case with Luo's mother in the development of a meat-packing plant, representative of the industrialization China faced in the twentieth century when its population grew substantially and from the perspective of a monk presented in an intimate and most definitively unsacred manner. The monk who listens to the story in *POW!* has animal urges that coordinate interestingly with the animal forms taken on by the narrator of *Life and Death Are Wearing Me Out*. As such, the festival of carnivore delight gives some insights into the initial basis for the vegetarianism that infused into Buddhism after it entered into China and became Chan Buddhism—prior to that, begging Buddhist monks would accept any form of food, including meat. Hector Tobar is insightful in calling narrator Luo "Mo Yan's Candide," since Voltaire's eponymous work also celebrates the connoisseurship that can be developed by those near starvation when every little bite counts (<http://articles.latimes.com/2012/dec/14/entertainment/la-ca-jc-mo-yan-20121216>). And like *Candide*, *POW!* is an acquired taste: Mo Yan achieves and maintains the comic level by juxtaposing the large-scale background and the intimate details of not just camels-as-food but rather camel tongue, not just horse-as-food but also horse testicles, and not just mundane beef but cow anuses.

We can learn much about the complexity of laughter and humor by tracing a few moments of each in *POW!* In the nearly four-hundred-page narration of his obsession with meat and his fractured family life, amid the town's corrupt manipulations of farmers, workers, and the meat market to Wise Monk Lan, narrator Luo mentions but few instances of laughter. Some of his narration, however, clearly shows that he learned from his mother that laughter is used as a social control to confirm social mores. Early on in the novel, he interrupts his story of Aunty Wild Mule, the mistress of his father, Dieh, because he becomes confused by his own sexual desire for her: "I can't tell any more of my story right now. I'm confused. The Wise Monk seems to be able to read my mind, since I didn't say any of this but merely thought it. But he knows. His sardonic laugh brings an end to my lustful thoughts. All right, I'll go on" (29). The laughter of others functions as a deep-seated social control for the narrator, as shown in two other stories. He tells of his mother, Yang Yuzhen, dragging him around town shortly after she learns that Aunty Wild Mule has died and left behind a daughter. In the account, observers witness Yang and Luo "obviously puzzled" (77). Luo slows down his account to describe one observer: "The man on the motorbike turned to look at us. What's so damn interesting about us? I may have hated Mother, but not as much as I hated people who stared. She'd told me that people who laugh at widows and orphans suffer the wrath of Heaven. Which is what happened: He was so busy staring at us that he ran into a poplar tree" (78). In the midst of his nearly two-page-long description of the accident and the man, he describes the driver as "one of my father's drinking buddies. His name was Han, Han *shifu*. Father told me to call him Uncle Han" (78).

In another case, he describes cursing his mother for a painful home-haircut: "Shave my head? She was going to cut it off! 'Help,' I shouted. 'Help … murder … Yang Yuzhen is going to murder me …' I guess my shouts weren't as effective as I thought, because her rage was abruptly replaced by snorts of laughter. 'You little swine, is that the best you can come up with'" (127). His actions in turn cause passing-by children to stand "just beyond the door, giggling and watching the comedy play out in front of them" (90). The story comes back to the matter of laughter as a mechanism of social control as his mother asks, "Aren't you ashamed of crying like that?" (128). Elsewhere, Yang voices her awareness of laughter as an expression of superiority by others and her attempts to avoid being the object of laughter. In discussing a proposed invitation to have the powerful Lao Lan to their house in thanks for a loan, she notes that "if you're going to have him over do it right. He'll laugh if you give him common fare. Don't invite someone if you're afraid of spending money" (127). It is not just Luo who holds the view that laughter is meant to mock or indicate implicitly one's superiority. During a festival, the well-dressed Lao manages to get himself into "a pile of loose ostrich shit and he winds up flat on his back. Noticing that his employees are trying to keep from laughing, he cries 'Think that's funny, do you? ... Go ahead, laugh, why don't you?'" (132). When they do, he threatens to fire them and shoot them.

Detailed images and detailed word usage are Mo Yan's forte in his varied comic touch: his unique sense of humor is defined, among all things, by his use of the term 幽默 (*youmo*), a keyword in the story *Shifu: You'll Do Anything for a Laugh*. *Youmo* has been traditionally used to describe Chinese humor since it first appeared in a 1924 article by Lin Yutang. It literally means "silence" and "tranquility." The word itself dates back to the poetic verse of Qu Yuan (屈原) (340-278 BCE). For Lin, humor is an understated form of expression. Humor is distinct from boisterous laughter and is often at its best when it is discreet. So far, Mo Yan's discretion has indeed been insufficiently grasped by his readers. Contrary to what its title suggests, the novella does not provoke belly-rolling laughter (see Chey and Davis). However, it does capture vividly a series of comic situations in which a fifty-something laid-off factory foreman finds himself. One month away from retirement with pension, Old Ding, a hardworking man with firm ideological investments in an era before market capitalism, is laid off despite the manager's exaggerated reassurance: "You're a veteran worker, a provincial model worker, a *shifu*—master worker—and even if we're down to the last man [in the coming years of financial setbacks], the man will be you" (2). Later on, Ding is moved to tears by similarly vain promises and praises made by the vice mayor (5). Ding is unable or unwilling to distinguish between disingenuous remarks and earnest offers of help, much like the displaced titular character of Cervantes's *Don Quijote*. Yet it is clear immediately that Mo Yan does not follow any of his literary predecessors, even Chinese ones like Lu Xun, in reducing characters to the grim situations they are caught in. Old Ding remains innocent at heart as he adapts to the brave new world, seemingly having just awakened from a dream (5).

Old Ding's innocence is accentuated by the cynical verbal quirk throughout the narrative by his apprentice Lü Xiaohu (Little Hu): "Master, you have a good sense of humor; *shifu*, you'll do anything for a laugh!" Little Hu repeatedly uses "humorous" (*youmo*) to describe Old Ding's antics and moral assumptions, which are increasingly at odds with the new society. Such comments, offered at regular intervals, serve to steer a potentially traumatic personal history toward a comedy of manners filled with Ding's "discursive ineptness" (151). Ding's earnestness toward everything in life and moral conscience does not sit well with Little Hu's life philosophy of laissez-faire. Within the story, *youmo* takes on several meanings, ranging from absurdly incongruous to amusingly odd. Little Hu uses the word *youmo* in friendly nudges to prevent Ding from becoming a laughing stock. Excited by Ding's idea of converting an abandoned bus hulk in the suburb into a lakeside love nest to rent out by the hour to couples (the same way a pay toilet operates), Little Hu urges

Ding to stop worrying about whether it is moral and just do it, for, after all, "what's there for a laid-off worker to be embarrassed about!" (29).

Somewhat of a miniature of the poignancy of the comic with the development of the character Mo Yan in *Life and Death Are Wearing Me Out*, Little Hu's use of *youmo* twice at the end of the story emphasizes the incongruities between the quixotic Ding and the abased world around him. With great determination, Ding drags Little Hu and a policeman to retrieve the bodies of a couple that he believes to have committed suicide in his bus hulk, only to find it empty. Cornered, Ding chooses to indulge in an abject attitude toward the unknown, refusing to believe that the couple may have simply left without his knowledge. He concludes that "it was a pair of spirits." Little Hu responds: "Shifu, you really will do anything for a laugh, won't you?" (58). While he finds Ding's fiasco amusing, he also regards compassionately the split between a confused mind and an incorruptible soul. Therein lies the significance of *youmo*.

As existing scholarship on Chinese comic culture testifies, although *youmo* is derived from the English "humor," it is in fact hard to render precisely in other languages. Howard Goldblatt renders appropriately Little Hu's verbal quirk into English as "Shifu, you'll do anything for a laugh," thereby avoiding the thorny problem of translating *youmo* to English. Little Hu's use of *youmo* does not correspond to usages of the English word "humor," at least not in the sense of boisterous laughter. It seems that doing anything for a laugh is the only way out for Ding as he scrambles to reinvent himself in the face of a social structure that has turned its back on him. For Ding, the hut in the woods embodies both his shame and the pleasure-seeking couples' shame. He feels like a voyeur, but more importantly he imagines that his illicit business exposes his other source of shame: being laid off at an old age. From Little Hu's and the narrator's perspectives, the *youmo* of Ding's situation arises from this conflation of private and public realms. The bus hulk is decked out with "everything couples might need for their trysts," but Ding has to learn to solicit business in the open. In his mind, this liminal space publicly announces the unfortunate turns in his private life (34).

Some types of humor do get lost in translation, like the "linguistic punning humor uniquely connected to the Chinese language *xiehouyu* ... a saying with the latter part suspended ... leaving the hearer to extrapolate the second part and interpret it as a pun for another word or phrase with a different meaning" (Chey and Davis 8). Thus this perambulation of just some key aspects of Mo Yan's humor has striven to be provocative rather than comprehensive, to showcase an element in Mo Yan's literary toolkit that he himself might not have noticed had it not received sufficient attention: in *Life and Death Are Wearing Me Out*, he "doth *protest too much,* methinks" (*Hamlet* 3.2) but not to the tragic ends to which William Shakespeare draws his drama. Even when author Mo Yan represents character Mo Yan as sympathetic, starting in Book 3, he surrounds him with comic elements or puts him in comic situations. A particularly multilayered moment occurs in a long passage in which Ximen Pig describes that his "morning exercises" are interrupted by thee jalopies riding in to the farm, which "bumped and rattled" so much that it looked "like long-tailed monsters" (235). The situational humor—what comprises a pig's morning exercises?!—prepares readers for the sight-gag featuring the drivers and passengers disembarking the technological monstrosities, culminating with Mo Yan's exit: "I saw Lan Jinlong, his hair a mess and his face covered with grime, climb out of the first cab. Then Zhu Hongxin and Dragon Sun climbed out of the second vehicle, and finally, the remaining three Sun brothers and Mo Yan climbed out of the last one. All four faces in this last group were coated with dust, looking like the terra-cotta warriors of the First Emperor" (235).

Mo Yan's technique is focused: he uses only visual and kinesthetic images to lead to a trenchant simile. The simile refers to the famous "Terra Cotta Warriors and Horses," the collection of nearly nine thousand life-size statues dating from the third century BCE. Three finely tuned elements add to the basic sight-gag to create humor. First is the anachronistic reference to the statues by narrator Ximen Pig, who lived decades before the 1974 discovery of the statues: Chinese readers would be well aware of at least the decade of this impressive find. Second is the juxtaposition of this group of local-yocal government officials with the regal figures. Third, and the subtlest, is the replacement of the regal terracotta "horses" by the three jalopies, or "iron horses" as they were called. The second and third elements thus incisively yet subtly depict the resources of China's early twentieth-century officials as clearly and amusingly inferior to those of China's third century. Author Mo Yan's self-deprecating inclusion of character Mo Yan in such a statement minimizes any outrage—perhaps its subtlety may even curtail many readers' recognition of it.

Character Mo Yan, however, is saved from the sexual escapades that comprise so much of Mo Yan's humor. Chinese writings have a long heritage of varied sexual humor, from slapstick to the macabre. Its success is difficult, since it is easy for writers to sway from the pornographic to the disgusting, without any literary pay-off. Sabina Knight is thus helpful in the attention she has given to P'u Songling's 1766 *Strange Tales from a Leisure Studio*, "the pinnacle of classical-language tales." She notes that it is P'u's "erudition" that lays the foundation for his "satirical humor" in his "stories [that] bring out the fluidity of selfhood and sexuality" (70). Two examples show the breadth and depth of Mo Yan's similar skill.

In *The Republic of Wine*, character Mo Yan has engaged with an epistolary relationship with the aspiring writer Li Yidou, but it is not until near the end that he makes an appearance in the action of the main narrative. His entrance recalls the entrance of the main character, forty-eight-year-old Ding Gou'er, to Liquorland. Ding makes a sexual pass at the younger truck driver and later engages in sex with her, in what seems like a setup between her and her husband Diamond Jin. The narrative is very suggestive about this newcomer's sexual daring but constantly pulls back, as in this scene: "Miss Ma picked up the uncorked bottle of liquor and carried it to the bathroom, with Mo Yan close on her heels. The room was still steamy, tendrils of whiteness lending it an air of romance. Miss Ma emptied the bottle into the bathtub, releasing a heavy, rather stimulating cloud of aroma—alcohol, of course. 'There you go, Mo Yan. Jump in.' She smiled as she walked out, and Mo Yan detected a vague sense of romance in that smile. His emotions stirred, he nearly reached out to put his arm around her and plant a kiss on her ruddy cheek. But he clenched his teeth to keep his emotions in check and saw Miss Ma out" (341). The narrator sets up again the possibility of the character Mo Yan engaging in a sexual peccadillo, only to have the rug pulled out. Author Mo Yan well recognizes that the blurring of fiction and reality is too fuzzy to characterize his avatar as promiscuous. Fictionally representing himself as "keep[ing] from doing something he shouldn't" (342), Mo Yan reifies marital fidelity and at the same time he keeps readerly interest going to the very end.

The other instance involves narrator Shangguan Jintong's description in *Big Breasts and Wide Hips* of the banquet following his "Sixth Sister" Shangguan Niandi's wedding: "Niandi, who sat in the chair beside [the groom, Babbit], was wearing a white gown, open at the neck to reveal the top half of her breasts. I nearly drooled … a look of smug contentment showed on her heavily powdered face. Lucky Niandi, how shameless you were. The Bird Fairy's [her eldest sister's] bones weren't even cold before you walked down the aisle with the American!" (230). The quotation is part of an ongoing joke throughout the novel, one of Jintong's numerous and hilarious indications of his obsession with breasts: breasts as food source, however, for a young man who refuses to be weaned until he is seven years old. The juxtaposition between his view of breasts as food source and as sexual object is brought to the fore shortly after, when the good-natured Babbit pats Jintong's "head with one of his big hands. 'Your mother's breasts belong to you, youngster,' he said with a wink. 'But your sister's breasts belong to me' … I drew back [moving away from his big and imposing hand] and glared hatefully at his comical, ugly face" (233).

Goldblatt's translation of the passage reflects the tone of Mo Yan's original ("我躲闪开他的大手，仇视地盯着他的既滑稽又丑陋的脸" [196]) with the right measure of comical connotations. "Comical" (滑稽) in Mo Yan's original indicates a sense of funniness and amusement. Unlike humor, this word is often used in a derogatory way. The "sniping" of the youngster, like an old biddy, resonates with the figure of the gossip; and its resonance is deep. The foundation of gossip is the presumed hard-heartedness on display. But hard-heartedness in this case verges on a needed sense of perseverance amid the devastating toil and pain that the Shangguan sisters have undergone and will continue to undergo. Further, Shangguan Niandi's "shamelessness" is shown as poignant passion in subsequent scenes where she chooses to stand by her man, despite the added danger that doing so brings to her.

Characterized by a keen sense of comedic effect that makes many scenes in his works resemble short theatrical skits, Mo Yan's works deploy various comic modes to construct alternative narratives about China, revising the affective spectrum of the literary experience. We conclude with Luigi Priandello's metaphor for comic contrariness: "Ordinarily, the artist concerns himself only with the body. The humorist concerns himself with body and shadow at the same time and sometimes more with the shadow than the body. He notes all the fine turns of that shadow, how it stretches this much or grows that much fatter, as if to make fun of the body, which all this time does not concern itself with the shadow or its size" (Pirandello qtd. in Holland 25). If characters such as Old Ding are the shadows, their comic proportion and shapes will point us to the source of light.

Note

Portions of this article first appeared in Alex Huang, "Mo Yan as Humorist," *World Literature Today* 83.4 (2009): 32-35. Copyright release to the author.

Works Cited

Brussig, Thomas. *Heroes Like Us*. Trans. John Brownjohn. New York: Farrar, Straus and Giroux, 1996.

Chen, Sihe (陈思和), ed. 中国当代文学史教程 (A Course in the History of Contemporary Chinese Literature). Shanghai: Fudan daxue chubanshe, 1999.

Chey, Jocelyn, and Jessica Milner Davis. *Humour in Chinese Life and Letters: Critical and Traditional Approaches*. Hong Kong: Hong Kong UP, 2011.

Cox, Chris. "*POW!* By Mo Yan: Review." theguardian.com (19 January 2013): <http://www.theguardian.com/books/2013/jan/19/pow-mo-yan-review-fiction>.

Holland, Norman. *Laughing: A Psychology of Humor*. Ithaca: Cornell UP, 1982.

Huang, Yibing. *Contemporary Chinese Literature: From the Cultural Revolution to the Future*. New York: Palgrave Macmillan, 2007.

Huang, Yuhan. "Mo Yan's *Life and Death Are Wearing Me Out* in a Cultural and Visual Context." *Mo Yan in Context: Nobel Laureate and Global Storyteller*. Ed. Angelica Duran and Yuhan Huang. West Lafayette: Purdue UP, 2014. 107–22.

Knight, Sabina. *Chinese Literature: A Very Short Introduction*. Oxford: Oxford UP, 2011.

McGrath, Jason. *Postsocialist Modernity: Chinese Cinema, Literature, and Criticism in the Market Age*. Stanford: Stanford UP, 2008.

Mo Yan. *Big Breasts and Wide Hips*. Trans. Howard Goldblatt. New York: Arcade, 2011.

Mo Yan (莫言). 丰乳肥臀. 上海:上海文艺出版社 (*Life and Death Are Wearing Me Out*). Shanghai: Shanghai wenyi chubanshe, 2012.

Mo Yan. *Life and Death Are Wearing Me Out*. Trans. Howard Goldblatt. New York: Arcade, 2008.

Mo Yan. *The Republic of Wine*. Trans. Howard Goldblatt. New York: Arcade Publishing, 2000.

Mo Yan. *Shifu: You'll Do Anything for a Laugh*. Trans. Howard Goldblatt. New York: Arcade, 2001.

Tobar, Hector. "Mo Yan's *POW!* Packs a Punch, However Veiled." latimes.com (14 December 2012): <http://articles.latimes.com/2012/dec/14/entertainment/la-ca-jc-mo-yan-20121216>.

Wang, Jing. *High Culture Fever: Politics, Aesthetics, and Ideology in Deng's China.* Berkeley: U of California P, 1996.
Wang, Shuo. *Playing for Shrills.* Trans. Howard Goldblatt. New York: Penguin, 1998.
Wang, Shuo. *Please Don't Call Me Human.* Trans. Howard Goldblatt. Boston: Cheng & Tsui, 2003.
Wells, Henry W. *Traditional Chinese Humor: A Study in Art and Literature.* Bloomington: Indiana UP, 1971.
Zhu, Wen. *I Love Dollars and Other Stories of China.* Trans. Julia Lovell. New York: Columbia UP, 2007.

Author's profile

Alexa Huang teaches English literature, East Asian languages and literatures, and international affairs at George Washington University. Her interests in scholarship include Shakespeare, comparative literature, intercultural performance, translation, and globalization studies. In addition to numerous articles, her single-authored book publications include *Chinese Shakespeares* (2009) and *Weltliteratur und Welttheater. Ästhetischer Humanismus in der kulturellen Globalisierung* (2012), and her edited volumes include *Shakespeare in Hollywood, Asia, and Cyberspace* (with Charles S. Ross, 2009) and 新世纪国外中国文学译介与研究文情报告 (with Hongtao Liu, 2013) (Sourcebook of Chinese and Sinophone Literary Studies in North America in the New Millennium).

Author's profile

Angelica Duran teaches English, comparative literature, and religious studies at Purdue University. Her interests in scholarship include comparative literature, disability studies, and Renaissance British literature. In addition to numerous articles and chapters, Duran's single-authored book publications include *The Age of Milton and the Scientific Revolution* (2007) and her edited volumes include *A Concise Companion to Milton* (2007) and *The King James Bible across Borders and Centuries* (2014).

Part Three
Roots

Cosmopolitanism and the Internationalization of Chinese Literature

Ning Wang

Abstract

In "Cosmopolitanism and the Internationalization of Chinese Literature" Ning Wang traces the origin of the practice of cosmopolitanism in China and elsewhere and offers a new construction of this controversial concept from a literary and cultural perspective. Wang argues that in China's recent past to talk about cosmopolitanism from a literary point of view was mostly to identify Chinese literature with Western literature. Wang posits that with the advent of globalization, the rapid development of Chinese economy, and Mo Yan's 2012 Nobel Prize in Literature, the dynamic is becoming mutual and that the success of Mo Yan's work lies mostly in his narration of the fundamental problems Chinese people are confronted with in a broad cosmopolitan context with regard to human concerns at large.

The construction of a theoretical discourse of globalization by Western scholars has accelerated in recent years. As a corollary, cosmopolitanism has once again become a significant theoretic topic: it appears in the works of philosophers and sociologists, and more frequently, it is quoted and discussed by literary and cultural studies scholars. These studies interpret and deal with cosmopolitanism from the perspectives of political philosophy and culture but touch upon literature and culture to varying degrees and for different ends. Starting in the mid-1990s, we find, for example, Martha Nussbaum and Joshua Cohen dealing with the relations between patriotism and cosmopolitanism in general or Tim Brennan dealing with this topic from a perspective of literary and cultural studies. Pheng Cheah's and Bruce Robbins's *Cosmopolitics: Thinking and Feeling beyond the Nation* touches upon the topic by incorporating all three. The recent interest in world literature is naturally associated with the rise of cosmopolitanism in the contemporary era. Since I am a scholar of literature, what I am most interested in is how different literary works represent cosmopolitan ideas in contrast to nationalism. In speaking of world literature, I have previously pointed out that world literature can be defined in different ways, as 1) a canonical body of excellent literature of all countries, regardless of region, 2) a global and cross-cultural perspective and a comparative horizon in the study, evaluation, and criticism of literature in general, and 3) a literary evolution through production, circulation, translation, and critical selection in different languages (see Wang, "World Literature" 5). My discussion of cosmopolitanism is based on this definition of world literature.

Cosmopolitanism revisited

As an interdisciplinary theoretic concept and critical discourse, the roots of cosmopolitanism date back to ancient Greek philosophical thought. The word-roots of cosmopolitanism also come from the Greek: *cosmos* from κόσμος, meaning the universe, and *polis* from πόλις, meaning city. Hence the term means "world city" or "world state." Cosmopolitanism is first of all a political philosophical concept whose ethical color is strong. That is why it is closely related to literature and culture in the current global era. As we know, in the beginning of the twentieth century and especially after World War II, many former colonial countries became independent. Thus nationalism permeated all literary works produced at the time. But now, along with the process of globalization, cultural exchanges have become frequent, and this cannot but influence literary creation. The fundamental meaning of cosmopolitanism is that all human beings, regardless of their ethnic or other affiliations, belong to a big single social community. Cosmopolitanism, therefore, approximates the current construction of the discourse of globalization according to which people all share a fundamental ethic and right transcending individual nations or countries. All theoretical terms, including cosmopolitanism and globalization, are laden with positive and negative associations. All their important dimensions cannot be covered within a limited space, but a few deserve critical attention. According to Craig Calhoun, cosmopolitanism means something different on different occasions: it refers to the world as a totality rather than individual places or communities, and it indicates that those holding this belief feel at home in a diversified community (428). In short, it mainly refers to inclination and endurance in this sense. Additionally, this sort of cosmopolitanism breaks through the boundary of the nation-state stands in opposition to patriotism to some degree and nationalism entirely.

Cosmopolitanism is usually discussed on the philosophical, political, and sociological levels as well as on the cultural and literary levels. The philosophical dimension of cosmopolitanism dates back to the works of Plato and Aristotle, who opposed cosmopolitanism on the basis of the fact that people usually lived in their own city or state and stuck to particular political doctrines. Therefore, they tended to identify with it. When enemies invaded their state, citizens would rise up to defend their homeland. For the ancient Greeks, good citizens should not share too strong an affiliation with those outside of the state. However, we cannot conclude that all ancient philosophers were against cosmopolitanism. Other intellectuals who traveled to other countries possessed and articulated a more universal ethics. The first Western philosopher who did not confine himself to a particular state was Diogenes, whose idea of the "citizen of the world" has remained a principal notion of cosmopolitanism. What many contemporary thinkers pursue is not the interest of a particular nation-state but the universal value and interest of humankind in its entirety including ethics, and thus they are not limited philosophically or, by extension, politically and socially (see, e.g., Appiah). Although modern scholars seldom quote these ancient ideas in their discussion of cosmopolitanism, they echo and develop their ideas. This is particularly the case with Enlightenment philosophers, who fixated on cosmopolitanism. In 1795 Immanuel Kant put forward a sort of cosmopolitan law or right in his article "*Zum ewigen Frieden. Ein philosophischer Entwurf*" ("Perpetual Peace: A Philosophical Sketch"). Although Kant's ideas are still influential in current discussions on cosmopolitanism, some critics find his ideas inconsistent. This complaint is partly owing to the tension of the concept of cosmopolitanism itself. Kant also introduced a "cosmopolitan law," which refers to the domain of a third kind of law—public law—apart from constitutional and international law. In cosmopolitan law, individuals have all rights as citizens of the earth rather than those of a particular country. Kant's "citizen of the earth" here comes from the "citizen of the world" but is more expansive (see Wood 59-76).

While Christopher Columbus's discovery of the Americas in 1492 enabled him to become one of the earliest cosmopolitanists in action, Kant's pioneering ideas of cosmopolitan thought laid a foundation for many of the claims by cosmopolitanists since the nineteenth century. With Columbus's discovery, capitalist expansion, the absorption of weak countries' national industries, and the formation of a new division of international labor laid the groundwork for the actualized process of globalization. I do not mean that the imposition of a specific value system by Columbus and his attendant cultural and state apparatus onto weak countries' national industries legitimates global capitalist expansion: I simply lay out the process. Between the Age of Discovery and the Age of Globalization, Karl Marx and Friedrich Engels described the market capitalist practice of breaking the boundaries of the nation-state and expanding their own forces in their *Communist Manifesto*. In dealing with the consequence of such capital expansion, Marx and Engels look to its parallel intellectual expansion: "And as in material, so also in intellectual production. The intellectual creations of individual nations become common property. National one-sidedness and narrow-mindedness become more and more impossible, and from the numerous national and local literatures, there arises a world literature" (69). As a result, production and consumption are not limited to their own countries but extend into distant countries and even continents. Equally important as an ideological reflection of capitalism, cosmopolitanism covers everything from industrial production to literary and cultural production. From today's point of view, we may well come to the conclusion that the contributions made by Marx and Engels lie in their discovery both of surplus value under the capitalist system and the regulation of globalization in economy and culture. Their descriptions and discussions have become important theoretic resources of twentieth-century political philosophers and literary and cultural scholars in their discussion of the issues of modernity and literary and cultural globalization. A revolutionary aspect of their broad cosmopolitan vision is their inclusion of the proletarians of various countries and their argument that all individuals share fundamental characteristics and common interests. This is a key matter when we turn to Mo Yan, who so closely associates himself as a rural citizen as much as a global citizen. As with the influence of Aristotle's and Plato's cultural context on their cultural theories, so with Marx's and Engels's. Marx himself was a cosmopolite and his Jewish ancestry and later communist belief contributed to his choice to travel and settle everywhere as a citizen of the world conflating diaspora with homeland and work in the interests of humankind. The First International (1864–76) and Second International (1889–1916) Labor Parties founded under the influence of Marxian thought were characterized by his cosmopolitan tendency and political and organizational practice. The Third International, or Comintern (1919–43), established by Vladimir Ilyich Lenin, was dissolved largely because of the rise of nationalism and the independence of different national communist parties.

Upon entering the second half of the twentieth century, the process of economic globalization has also speeded political and cultural globalization. According to Jan Aart Scholte, since the 1960s the use of the term "globalization" has spread throughout languages, professional environments, and academic disciplines. However, globalization as it is understood in recent times is a relatively new term that implies a sort of development, process, tendency, and change. It covers all aspects of economy, politics, and culture. Hence, globalization has contributed to a renewed interest in contemporary academia toward cosmopolitanism. The phenomenon of globalization can be categorized into four aspects: internationalization, liberalization, universalization, and planetarialization. The four aspects overlap substantially since they all refer to the increase of the social relations crossing the boundaries of nation-states at large. Thus many people emphasize several implications of these four notions, although these aspects emphasize matters differently (see Scholte 526–32; see also Bartoloni <http://dx.doi.org/10.7771/1481-4374.2340>). While the advent of globalization has thus provided cosmopolitanism with notions for its rise, cosmopolitanism has in turn provided globalization with a sort of theoretic discourse. Ulrich Beck and Edgar Grande remind us that we should take into account a process connecting the two: global connections are a sort of "cosmopolitanization," and cosmopolitanism is nothing but a feeling and attitude coming from ethic responsibility (5-6). The founding of transnational organizations represents the institutionalization of such a practice. For example, the League of Nations and the United Nations are such international organizations of global governance. Obviously, these international organizations cannot replace the function of the state, let alone the so-called world government. Rather, they function as a sort of utopian governing organization. And this is why critics often attack cosmopolitanism's philosophical and political levels.

We can thus see that cosmopolitanism is not always consistent. Different descriptions of it sometimes cause confusion if different people try to understand it from different angles. Calhoun addresses the multidimensional orientations and contradictions of cosmopolitanism and pertinently points out that in using the concept cosmopolitanism, scholars are often confused and therefore appear inconsistent:

> "Cosmopolitan" is claimed sometimes for a political project: building participatory institutions adequate to contemporary global integration, especially outside the nation-state framework. It is claimed sometimes for an ethical orientation of individuals: the suggestion that each should think and act with strong concern for all humanity. It is claimed sometimes for a stylistic capacity to incorporate diverse influences and sometimes for a psychological capacity to feel at ease amid difference and appreciate diversity. It is used sometimes for all projects that reach beyond the local ... It is used at other times for strongly holistic visions of global totality, like the notion of a community of risk imposed by potential for nuclear or environmental disaster. It is used at still other times to describe not individuals but cities, as for example New York or London, contemporary Delhi or historical Alexandria gain their vitality and character not from the similarities of their residents but from the concrete ways in which they have learned to interact across lines of ethnic, religious, national, linguistic and other identities. (431)

From a political perspective, those against cosmopolitanism hold that, as far as the nation-state is concerned and on which nationalism and patriotism are based, cosmopolitanism does not have such a "world nation" or "world government" above a particular nation and its agency, and that therefore the claim for cosmopolitanism is meaningless. At best, today's new cosmopolitanism transcends the old cosmopolitanism on the ethical level and the limits of Kant's legal cosmopolitanism and becomes a sort of cultural cosmopolitanism.

From cosmopolitanism to world literature(s)

Literary and cultural studies scholars have long been interested in cosmopolitanism given its significant traces in literary works. For example, Douwe Fokkema was a vanguard in applying this topic to world literature. With a perspective drawn from globalization, he transcended the old-fashioned Eurocentric or West-centric versions of cosmopolitanism trying to find a sort of alternative cosmopolitanism in non-Western contexts. His concern in globalization is cultural plurality and diversity. Trained in Sinological and comparative literary study, Fokkema did not absorb the limits of Eurocentrism and West-centrism. Rather, he was able to integrate some of the traditional ideas from Chinese culture related to cosmopolitanism. For instance, the Confucian concept of "brotherhood all over the world" (四海

之内皆兄弟) is an analogue to the pursuit of a human unity as advocated also by cosmopolitanism (Fokkema 1-17). To this Confucian doctrine, Chinese people should view all those coming from afar as friends. His findings are echoed in Sinological globalization circles. Wei-ming Tu and Chung-ying Cheng have enthusiastically promoted the universality of Confucianism in the West (see Cheng; see also Mitchell and Duran for the inherently dynamic nature of religions and religious philosophy). Tu tries to realize equal dialogue between contemporary Neo-Confucianism and Western modernity by reviving a sort of Neo-Confucianism (see Tu), and Cheng puts forward a sort of "world philosophy" parallel with world literature (see also Wang, "Reconstructing").

From my perspective as a Chinese scholar of comparative literature and world literatures who has practiced cosmopolitanism through global scholarly interchange since the 1980s, I would like to offer my own theoretical construction of cosmopolitanism. I have drawn the following ten forms I find to be enabling resources for approaching world literatures, whether foreign or from one's native time and place. That is, cosmopolitanism could be described as 1) something transcending the nationalist form, 2) a pursuit of moral justice, 3) a universal human concern, 4) a cosmopolitan and even diasporic state, 5) something decentralizing and pursuing a pluralistic cultural identity, 6) a pursuit of human happiness and cosmopolitan unity, 7) a political and religious belief, 8) a realization of global governance, 9) an artistic and aesthetic pursuit, and 10) a critical perspective from which to evaluate literary and cultural products. Of course, there could be more constructions of cosmopolitanism from other perspectives: perhaps political scientists or sociologists would put more emphasis on the nation-state. However, my definitions do not contradict the importance of the nation-state but subsume that element to the literary expressions which emerge from the nation-state. Elaborating on some aspects in literary cosmopolitanism with regard to literary creation and criticism should clarify this point.

A number of the aforementioned forms respond to some persistent literary themes of universal significance—such as love, death, and jealousy—themes which scholarly and general readers have for centuries regularly recognized (for how these themes relate to basic plots, see Christopher Booker). These themes find particular embodiment in the works by great writers who represent these themes most vividly and profoundly. For example, in Western literature Shakespeare, Goethe, Tolstoy, Ibsen, Kafka, and other writers whose works have been included in major world literature anthologies have all represented these persistent themes in their works in ways which provoke enduring interest. So their works have become world literature by fulfilling and transcending the limits of national literatures defined both geographically and in terms of era. Considering my ten forms in terms of world literatures may help us advance our understanding of aesthetics, to develop more fully, for example, the work of Roman Ingarden on the societal aspects of aesthetics. Literary criticism must continue to address striking national characteristics: actively, as Shunqing Cao and Miaomiao Wang demonstrate in this volume, as well as inertly in response to reader reception, which of course is dependent on translations into languages available to different sets of readers. Equal attention must continue to be given to more universal characteristics and to the pursuit of a sort of common aesthetics. Fiction, poetry, and drama are genres of all national literatures, although they appear differently in different national literatures—other genres do not. To take Chinese literature as a case in point, 辞 (*ci*), a lyric based on rhythmic and tonal pattern, is unavailable in other languages as is 赋 (*fu*), an intricate literary form combining elements of poetry and prose popular from Han times to the Six Dynasties in China. There is also 骚 (*sao*), as used in a long poem by Qu Yuan, which is characterized by the use of six-syllable couplets with the two lines of each couplet being connected by a meaningless syllable 兮 (*xi*). On the other hand, traditional Chinese literature does not possess the epic, formally described, although the form is the highest achievement in ancient Greek literature. From their Western rather than global perspective, Marx and Engels consider Homeric epics as the greatest works in the history of world literature.

As far as literary criticism is concerned, when we say why a work is of great originality and to what extent one work plagiarizes a preceding work or repeats it, we make such judgments from an international and cosmopolitan perspective according to some universally recognized criteria (see Wang, "'Weltliteratur'"). Thus literary cosmopolitanism has endowed us with a broad vision whether we recognize it or not. It enables us not to confine ourselves to a particular national cultural and literary tradition but to engage with excellent works in world literature. In this sense, any great literary work of originality should be absolutely original rather than restricted to a certain space and time. Mo Yan's works certainly belong to such literary works. On what scholarly basis can we make this statement? We cannot avoid evaluating individual works when doing literary studies, which will certainly refer to the relativity and universality of our evaluation. Starting from a national perspective, we often emphasize works' relative significance and their value within a given national cultural environment. Conversely, if we start from a cosmopolitan perspective, we will seek and therefore likely find their universal significance and value within a broad context of the literatures of the world and, to a certain extent, to redefine world literature.

World literatures and Chinese literature

While the ten forms I propose apply to world literature as a whole, I shift, nevertheless, to address them specifically in terms of the relationship between Chinese literature and world literatures. As is well known, China developed quickly in the Tang Dynasty (618-907) into one of the most powerful and prosperous countries in the world, both politically and economically as well as culturally and literarily. Chinese people at the time viewed their country as the 中央帝国 (Middle

Kingdom), while people of other countries, whether Eastern or Western, were viewed as 蛮夷 (barbarians), reminiscent of but developed independent of Aristotle's and Plato's thought. From a literary point of view, China was also regarded as a 诗的王国 (Kingdom of Poetry) with Tang poetry flourishing at a time when Europe was still in what has been called the Dark or Middle Ages. Such eminent Chinese poets of different dynasties as Qu Yuan (屈原) (340-278 BCE), Tao Yuanming (陶渊明) (365-427), Li Bai (李白) (701-762), Du Fu (杜甫) (712-770), Li Shangyin (李商隐) (812-858), Bai Juyi (白居易) (772-846), and Su Shi (苏轼) (1037-1101) (see Owen) all appeared much earlier than Dante, Shakespeare, or Goethe.

Unfortunately, because of later Chinese rulers' corruption and inability to govern the country well, it was not long before China became a second-class feudal and totalitarian country. Although for a long period of time, especially in the years before the Qing Dynasty (1616-1912) when China was isolated culturally from the outside world, it maintained close relations with the world in other arenas such as economics and Chinese literature still inspired Goethe. Indeed, this great European writer and thinker developed the concept of *Weltliteratur* with the help of his reading and dynamic understanding of Chinese literature in translation. After reading some Chinese literary works of minor importance through translation, Goethe put forward his utopian conjecture of *Weltliteratur*: "I am more and more convinced that poetry is the universal possession of mankind, revealing itself everywhere and at all times in hundreds and hundreds of men ... I therefore like to look about me in foreign nations, and advise everyone to do the same. National literature is now a rather unmeaning term; the epoch of world literature is at hand, and everyone must strive to hasten its approach" (Goethe qtd. in Damrosch 1; see also Habjan <http://dx.doi.org/10.7771/1481-4374.2346>). Unlike most European writers at the time, Goethe had a broad cosmopolitan vision of the literatures of all countries, owing in large part to his vast reading of non-European literary works in translation. In turn, Goethe himself benefited greatly from translation: it enlarged his reputation, moving from Germany to all of Europe and then to the whole world. When he was advanced in age, he was almost marginalized in German critical circles, considered by young avant-garde critics as conservative and old fashioned. Translations of his works, however, ensured his literary renown. And in the age of Eurocentric dominance, to be a famous European writer means to be a world-renowned writer. Moreover, his interest in Oriental literature, as well as the translation and reception of his works in Oriental countries, including China, solidified his fame in the East (see, e.g., Beecroft <http://dx.doi.org/10.7771/1481-4374.2334>).

Despite its relevance to the development of the field of world literatures (for a summary, see Tötösy de Zepetnek and Vasvári), Chinese literature has largely been marginalized on the map of world literatures and in comparative literature. In order to resume its literary and cultural traditions, in the twentieth century China launched a large-scale translation of Western cultural and literary works into Chinese, viewing it as the only way of unifying China with the world (see Wang, "On World Literatures" <http://dx.doi.org/10.7771/1481-4374.2336>). This process of Westernization through literary translation in China maintains today: numerous Western literary works are available in Chinese, while few excellent Chinese works are translated into other languages. There are chiefly three reasons for this: first, the absence and inability of excellent translation; second, the bias of Orientalism prevailing in Western literary scholarship, as well as mass media; and third, the shrinking of the literary market on a global scale. In its homogenizing of national cultures, globalization offers China an opportunity to bring its culture and literature to the world. Some Chinese scholars and translators, including myself, once thought that integrating Chinese literature into world literature in the shortest possible time was merely a matter of translating Western literature to Chinese. We seldom translated our own Chinese literature to major world languages, especially English, thus accounting in part for the current marginal position of Chinese literature in the world. Now, some contemporary Chinese intellectuals, including myself, are once again interested in cosmopolitanism and world literatures in this age of globalization, thinking it one of the most effective ways to promote Chinese literature and culture in the world.

Although cosmopolitanism has not yet attracted large critical and scholarly attention in Chinese academia, it is not unfamiliar to Chinese scholars. In the 1920s and 1930s, it came into China in the form of anarchism, attracting the attention of some young intellectuals. In literary circles, Ba Jin (巴金) and Junjian Ye (叶君健) were two eminent examples (see Wang, "World Literature"). Both learned Esperanto and expressed interest in it as they thought it might be a good way to integrate with the world. Ye even wrote his works in the artificial language and attracted attention from international Esperanto circles. Ye attained a much higher level of proficiency than Ba Jin, who quickly stepped out of the anarchist circles and engaged himself in the mainstream of modern Chinese literature. Ironically enough, Esperanto never gained as much popularity as English or any other major world language. Ba Jin then became a world-famous writer largely owing to translations of his works into other modern languages done by Sinologists and foreign translators. On the other hand, Ye failed to become as well known as Ba Jin and is known today in China primarily as one of the translators of Hans Christian Anderson's fairy tales and internationally for his novel *The Mountain Village* (1947), written in English. Their cases indicate clearly that any artificial world language cannot survive in face of the hegemonic languages such as English in the twenty-first century. Additionally, it is becoming clear that in the era of globalization, enthusiastically promoting Chinese must be done with the intermediary of English. It is with the recognition of the hegemonic power of English that we need to discuss the issue of cosmopolitanism again in the Chinese context with regard to world literature.

The current state of the book market is far from satisfactory in terms of the circulation of literary and academic works. Few British or U.S. bookstores carry books written by Chinese writers or scholars even in English translation, let alone in the original Chinese. In sharp contrast, nearly all bookstores in China carry as many foreign literary works as possible translated into Chinese. There are a number of publishing houses, such as Shanghai Translation Press (上海译文出版社), Yilin Press (译林出版社), and Foreign Literature Press (外国文学出版社), devoted almost entirely to the publication of translated foreign literary works, with Western literary works occupying the largest part of their titles. Such leading publishers in Beijing as the Commercial Press (商务印书馆) and the Sanlian Press (三联书店) make the most of their profits by publishing translations of contemporary Western literary works and those of humanities selling well. In contrast, books of the similar titles authored by Chinese humanities scholars hardly circulate even moderately. Today's young Chinese readers admire Western thinkers and writers much more than their Chinese counterparts. Why does this phenomenon occur in today's China and around the world? Does China lack excellent literary works or its own literary masters? The answer for anyone with some knowledge of contemporary Chinese literature and culture is obviously "no." I now offer the following three reasons in brief before extrapolating on them.

First is the prevalence and influence of the ideological bias of Orientalism among Western audiences. A long-lasting bias against the Orient and Oriental people, including China and Chinese people, persists. From my own observations, it is clear that those who have never been to China often view the country as, at best, exotic and, at worst, backward even now, and Chinese people as uncivilized in comparison with elegant Westerners. Thus excellent Chinese literary works are hardly expected. Xingjian Gao and Mo Yan are the rare exceptions. They are truly fortunate to have excellent English translators to promote their works in the world market. The effect of access to works is clear. It is an undeniable shame for a Chinese high school student to be unaware of such Western intellectual giants as Plato, Aristotle, Shakespeare, Goethe, Twain, Joyce, Eliot, Faulkner, or Hemingway. Their books sell well in China and are regularly anthologized in Chinese world literature anthologies. In contrast, it is quite natural for even Western literary scholars, let alone students and general readers, to be unaware of any or all of classical or contemporary Chinese authors. Second, largely because of the imbalance and even absence of excellent translations of Chinese literature, Chinese literature has failed to enter the world market. As we know, foreign language teaching in China has been a large educational enterprise with quite a few educational and commercial institutions reaping great profits. In recent years, along with the boom of Chinese language training worldwide, this enterprise has gradually been on the decline. Even so, English language training has been of great importance to China's high schools and universities: it is all but compulsory for the majority of university students in China. If they do not know English, they can hardly communicate with people of other countries, given that English has become a lingua franca in the age of globalization. And if university faculty members do not understand English, promotion is difficult.

Yet, the sad fact remains that most Chinese college students and teachers, including specialists in English, possess only enough reading proficiency to read English books and newspapers and only enough speaking proficiency to conduct simple communication with English speakers. Although many Chinese scholars have the ability to translate literary or theoretic works from foreign languages into Chinese, few could translate Chinese books into excellent and publishable foreign languages. Sometimes, their translations of great Chinese literary works into English or other major foreign languages either go unappreciated by native speakers owing to foreignizing elements or simply do not circulate in the target book markets. Many of the translated Chinese literary works published by China's Foreign Languages Press, for example, are chiefly circulated domestically rather than internationally. This finds particular embodiment in the sharp contrast of the circulation in the English-speaking world of the two major versions of the Chinese novel *The Story of the Stone* (红楼梦). Owing to the excellent English translation by David Hawkes, *The Story of the Stone* has been relatively popular in English-speaking countries. The other version, translated as *A Dream of Red Mansions* by Xianyi Yang and Gladys Yang, is mostly consulted by specialists of Chinese literature and translation studies but has not made a large impact in the book market in English-speaking countries. Third, owing to the market problem confronting all literary and scholarly production, it is difficult for Chinese literature to reach a world audience effectively, and this phenomenon is a paradox. We live in a postmodern consumer society today in which high-brow literature and cultural products are challenged by the rise of popular and consumer cultures. Since classical Chinese literary works of high aesthetic quality are far from such cultures, contemporary readers may find them unattractive even if English translations were available. If faithfully translated into English or other major foreign languages, they can hardly be appreciated by the international reading public, let alone be commercially successful like many Western literary or theoretical works in China. Contemporary Chinese literature may suffer from a related matter. Since classical Chinese literature developed largely in the absence of Western influence, contemporary Western readers may find it unpalatable and too distinct from the contemporary Western literature they are used to.

Chinese literary critics and scholars only contribute to this state of affairs. They often complain that China does not possess its own modern and contemporary literary masters like Proust, Eliot, Joyce, Grass, Faulkner, Hemingway, Kundera, García Márquez, or Naipaul. They aver that ours is an age of lacking literary and theoretic masters. Indeed, while Binzhong Zhu took the step of publishing a book-length analysis of Faulkner and Mo Yan, he commented on Mo Yan's works as inferior to Faulkner's based on the standards of the Western novel. We can conjecture from this that Mo Yan would fare better in scholarly analyses within the context of the Chinese novel. Thus many think that the Chinese should continue only translating literary masterpieces from Western languages to Chinese: to my mind, this would be tragic for Chinese writers and literary scholars.

There is hope, however, and the present volume *Mo Yan in Context: Nobel Laureate and Global Storyteller* (Duran and Huang) is a good example. The volume includes articles by scholars of comparative literature, sociology, philosophy, etc., who engage with Mo Yan's works in a constructive and global manner. Also, in the past decade both a Chinese-born Chinese national (Mo Yan) and a Chinese-born French writer (Gao) have been awarded the Nobel Prize in Literature. Thus we can point to the importance and success of translation and of Howard Goldblatt, who translated Mo Yan's works, and Mabel Lee, who translated Gao's works. Without superb English translations, in particular Mo Yan would most probably have missed the honor of the Nobel Prize. In this sense, we should say that his prize winning is a success of collaboration with the author as the nodal point amid a necessary global network of cosmopolitanites, including translators, publishers, nominators, readers, the media, etc. Mo Yan's winning of the Nobel Prize in Literature has been hailed enthusiastically by the majority of Chinese writers and ordinary readers as a good beginning for contemporary Chinese literature to be recognized by authoritative international institutions. It has also, in just this brief period, stimulated more people of the younger generation to be engaged in literary creation and studies. The popular and critical recognition of Mo Yan is founded on decades of practical, linguistic, and critical work. Howard Goldblatt was a trailblazer in starting to translate Mo Yan's works into English in the 1990s when Mo Yan was just beginning to be known domestically, far behind many of his contemporary fellow Chinese writers, such as Meng Wang (王蒙), Xianlang Zhang (张贤亮), or Anyi Wang (王安忆). Coincidently, some cosmopolitan Western literary critics and scholars took notice of his potential creativity as a promising writer. For example, Fokkema reread avant-garde literary texts from a Western and comparative perspective and in 2008 described "Chinese Postmodernist Fiction" in terms of three of its representatives, among whom Mo Yan comes first (151). Finally, the inclusion of Mo Yan's short story "Old Gun" in *The Norton Anthology of World Literature* for the first time in 2012 is a testament to its having started to establish its canonicity.

Some might say that Mo Yan is a typical Chinese writer: monolingual, so therefore nationalist. Such an assessment would derive from more of a comparative literature model than a world literature one, and it does not coincide with the core of cosmopolitanism, which does not require multilingualism. In a work whose title indicates his humility about his limited reception, 锁孔里的房间—影响我的10部短篇小说 (A Room Seen through the Keyhole: Ten Short Stories Which Have Influenced Me), albeit larger than that of the typical reader, Mo Yan pays tribute to the works of such Western and Latin American writers as Faulkner and García Márquez, writers who share his concern with cosmopolitan phenomena. Although Mo Yan sticks to his native county Gaomi in China's Shandong Province, as his literary model and fellow Nobel Prize in Literature awardee Faulkner does his fictionalized Yoknapatawpha County in the U.S. South, he deals with some of the fundamental issues and experiences shared by all human beings in the world. That is, from the very beginning, Mo Yan wrote both for Chinese readers and for all readers and lovers of literature throughout the world. In this sense, it seems that the more local a writer is, the more likely it is that his/her works may become more cosmopolitan with the help of translation. Thus we can see that cosmopolitanism and world literature do not contradict local, regional, or nationalist sentiment, except in its narrowest and most exclusive varieties.

Works Cited

Appiah, Kwame Anthony. *Cosmopolitanism: Ethics in a World of Strangers*. New York: Norton, 2006.

Bartoloni, Paolo. "World Literatures, Comparative Literature, and Glocal Cosmopolitanism." *CLCWeb: Comparative Literature and Culture* 15.5 (2013): <http://dx.doi.org/10.7771/1481-4374.2340>.

Beck, Ulrich, and Edgar Grande. *Cosmopolitan Europe*. Cambridge: Polity, 2007.

Beecroft, Alexander. "Greek, Latin, and the Origins of 'World Literature'." *CLCWeb: Comparative Literature and Culture* 15.5 (2013): <http://dx.doi.org/10.7771/1481-4374.2334>.

Brennan, Tim. *At Home in the World: Cosmopolitanism Now*. Cambridge: Harvard UP, 1997.

Calhoun, Craig. "Cosmopolitanism and Nationalism." *Nations and Nationalism* 14.3 (2008): 427-48.

Cao, Xueqin. *The Story of the Stone*. Trans. David Hawkes and John Minford. Bloomington: Indiana UP, 1973-1980. 5 Vols.

Cao, Xueqin. *A Dream of Red Mansions*. Trans. Xianyi Yang and Gladys Yang. Beijing: Foreign Languages P, 2001. 4 Vols.

Cheah, Pheng, and Bruce Robbins, eds. *Cosmopolitics: Thinking and Feeling beyond the Nation*. Minneapolis: U of Minnesota P, 1998.

Cheng, Chung-ying. "Developing Confucian Onto-Ethics in a Postmodern World/Age." *Journal of Chinese Philosophy* 37.1 (2010): 3-17.

Damrosch, David. *What Is World Literature?* Princeton: Princeton UP, 2003.

Duran, Angelica, and Yuhan Huang, eds. *Mo Yan in Context: Nobel Laureate and Global Storyteller*. West Lafayette: Purdue UP, 2014.

Fokkema, Douwe. "Chinese Postmodernist Fiction." *Modern Language Quarterly* 69.1 (2008): 141-65.

Fokkema, Douwe. "Towards a New Cosmopolitanism." *The CUHK Journal of Humanities* 3 (1999): 1-17.

Gao, Xingjian. *Soul Mountain*. Trans. Mabel Lee. Sydney: HarperCollins, 2000.

Habjan, Jernej. "From Cultural Third-Worldism to the Literary World-System." *CLCWeb: Comparative Literature and Culture* 15.5 (2013): <http://dx.doi.org/10.7771/1481-4374.2346>.

Kant, Immanuel. "Zum ewigen Frieden. Ein philosophischer Entwurf." *Kants Gesammelte Schriften*. Berlin: Königliche Preussisch Akademie der

Wissenschaften, 1931. Vol. 8, 341-86.

Marx, Karl, and Friedrich Engels. *The Communist Manifesto*. Ed. and trans. John E. Toews. New York: St. Martin's P, 1999.

Mitchell, Donald, and Angelica Duran. "A Textbook Case of Comparative Cultural Studies." *Mo Yan in Context: Nobel Laureate and Global Storyteller*. Ed. Angelica Duran and Yuhan Huang. West Lafayette: Purdue UP, 2014. 195–212.

Mo Yan. "Old Gun." *The Norton Anthology of World Literature*. Ed. Martin Puchner, Suzanne Conklin Akbari, Wiebke Denecke, Vinay Dharwadker, Barbara Fuchs, Caroline Levine, Sarah Lawall, Pericles Lewis, and Emily Wilson. New York: Norton, 2012. Vol. 5, 1172-88.

Mo Yan. *Red Sorghum: A Novel of China*. Trans. Howard Goldblatt. Harmondsworth: Penguin, 1994.

Mo Yan (莫言). 锁孔里的房间—影响我的10部短篇小说 (A Room Seen through the Keyhole: Ten Short Stories which Influenced Me). Beijing: Xinshije chubanshe, 1999.

Nussbaum, Martha, and Joshua Cohen, eds. *For Love of Country: Debating the Limits of Patriotism*. Chicago: U of Chicago P, 1996.

Owen, Stephen. *An Anthology of Chinese Literature: Beginnings to 1911*. New York: Norton, 1996.

Scholte, Jan Aart. "Globalization." *Encyclopedia of Globalization*. Ed. Roland Robertson and Jan Aart Scholte. London: Routledge, 2007. Vol. 2, 526-32.

Tötösy de Zepetnek, Steven, and Louise O. Vasvári. "About the Contextual Study of Literature and Culture, Globalization, and Digital Humanities." *Companion to Comparative Literature, World Literatures, and Comparative Cultural Studies*. Ed. Steven Tötösy de Zepetnek and Tutun Mukherjee. New Delhi: Cambridge UP India, 2013. 3-35.

Tu, Wei-ming. *Way, Learning, and Politics: Essays on the Confucian Intellectual*. Albany: State U of New York P, 1993.

Wang, Ning. "On World Literatures, Comparative Literature, and (Comparative) Cultural Studies." *CLCWeb: Comparative Literature and Culture* 15.5 (2013): <http://dx.doi.org/10.7771/1481-4374.2336>.

Wang, Ning. "Reconstructing (Neo)Confucianism in 'Glocal' Postmodern Culture Context." *Journal of Chinese Philosophy* 37.1 (2010): 48-62.

Wang, Ning. "'Weltliteratur': From a Utopian Imagination to Diversified Forms of World Literatures." *neohelicon: acta comparationis litterarum unversarum* 38.2 (2011): 295-306.

Wang, Ning. "World Literature and the Dynamic Function of Translation." *Modern Language Quarterly* 71.1 (2010): 1-14.

Wood, Allen W. "Kant's Project for Perpetual Peace." *Cosmopolitics: Thinking and Feeling beyond the Nation*. Ed. Pheng Cheah and Bruce Robbins. Minneapolis: U of Minnesota P, 1998. 59-76.

Yeh, Chun-chan. *Mountain Village*. New York: G. P. Putnam's Sons, 1947.

Zhu, Binzhong (朱宾忠). 跨越时空的对话：福克纳与莫言比较研究 (Dialogue Crossing Time and Space: A Comparative Study of Faulkner and Mo Yan). Wuhan: Wuhan daxue chubanshe, 2006.

Author's profile

Ning Wang teaches comparative literature at Tsinghua University and Shanghai Jiao Tong University. In addition to numerous articles in Chinese and English, his book publications in English include the single-authored books *Translated Modernities: Literary and Cultural Perspectives on Globalization and China* (2010) and *Globalization and Translation* (2004) and the collected volume *Translation, Globalization and Localization: A Chinese Perspective* (with Yifeng Sun, 2008).

Variation Study in Western and Chinese Comparative Literature

Shunqing Cao and Miaomiao Wang

Abstract

In "Variation Study in Western and Chinese Comparative Literature" Shunqing Cao and Miaomiao Wang present a theoretical and methodological framework designated as "variation theory." With the development of comparative literature in China, Chinese scholars are reconstructing the existing subjects and addressing the phenomenon of variation between literatures defined linguistically and nationally, not historically. Variation theory integrates transnational, cross-linguistic, cross-cultural, and cross-civilization variation, as well as images of Otherness. The framework is focused more on heterogeneity and variability than on universalism. As such, this framework promises to initiate innovation with regard to dialogues and cultural exchanges between East and West. Cao and Wang outline how dialogue and exchange contribute to the ongoing development of the theoretical foundations of a global comparative literature.

The study of the phenomenon of variation helps to account for the conflicts, differences, and similarities between Eastern and Western literatures and cultures. Both deconstruction and cross-cultural study emphasize differences and the problem of differences has become a core issue in current international and transnational research. While differences among cultures and literatures have been an issue in scholarship and scholars have designed many approaches, comparative literature and comparative cultural studies in particular can contribute to fostering dialogue (the latter is a framework developed by Steven Tötösy de Zepetnek since the late 1980s, with the most recent representative text being his collected volume *Companion to Comparative Literature, World Literatures, and Comparative Cultural Studies*). With the development of comparative literature in China since the 1980s, Chinese scholars have begun reconstructing existing theories and subjects, both homegrown and imported (see, e.g., Chen and Sheng <http://dx.doi.org/10.7771/1481-4374.2367>; Wang and Liu). Starting in the early 2000s, Shunqing Cao developed "variation theory," a framework and methodology that is making inroads inside and outside China (see, e.g., Wang, Miaomiao <http://dx.doi.org/10.7771/1481-4374.2370>; Wang, Ning <http://dx.doi.org/10.7771/1481-4374.2371>). Variation theory integrates contemporary theories about the exchanges of literary phenomena and interpretations between different cultures in a transnational, cross-linguistic, cross-cultural context, as well as with regard to the image of Otherness. This theory focuses more on the heterogeneity and variability than on universalism.

The type of cross-cultural study advocated here is related to the theory and practice of Chinese comparative literature and its resources. When the study of comparative literature with its Western background was introduced in Chinese scholarship, scholars noted that the discipline did not incorporate non-Western literatures and thus remained Euro- and US-American-centric: "while the French School conducts the study on the influences among different European countries by crossing the borderlines of countries and the US-American school further crosses disciplinary boundaries and conducts studies on the literatures of different countries which did not have any connections before, the Chinese School intends to connect Eastern and Western literatures and reconstruct the concept of world literature by crossing the wall between Eastern cultures and Western cultures, as well as breaking through the barriers formed by different cultures" (Cao, "Chinese School" 22; unless indicated otherwise, all translations are by Miaomiao Wang; see also Li and Guo <http://dx.doi.org/10.7771/1481-4374.2358>). As such, variation theory bypasses limitations in Western comparative literature. An especially important contribution of variation theory is its attention to cultural filtering, "the selection, modification, transplantation, and filtration of communicative messages by the recipients based on their cultural background and cultural tradition in literary communication. It is also a retroaction on the original information as a result of the creative acceptance by the recipients when one culture has influence on another" (Cao, "Theory" 184). In other words, cultural filtering is the mode of acceptance and comprehension of literary texts in heterogeneous cultures.

Three aspects of cultural filtering are particularly important. The first is the cultural background of the recipients: each recipient grows up in a specific time and space and thus is marked by a set of unique cultural, historical, and national characteristics. These characteristics are bound to play their roles in cultural communication (see, e.g., Morin). The second aspect is the subjectivity and selectivity in reader reception, which acknowledges that subjectivity is a basic prerequisite of cultural filtering and an admission of the possibility and necessity for recipients to select, deform, camouflage, permeate, rebel against, and create information in cultural and literary communication. In the course of cultural exchange, different recipients are influenced differently depending on the strength or weakness of the relationship between individuals and their cultures. Reader reception of course interacts with external forces such as the selection of types of text as determined, for example, by anthologies; the ways of reading taught; and translations, including the acceptance and influence of foreign cultures even within the same time and space. The third aspect is the reactions by the recipients: in cultural dialogue, influence acts and reacts through individual recipients. A prerequisite of cultural dialogue and communication is a diversity of opinions. To have cultural dialogue means to "permit contest, competition, and confrontation, which is to permit the conflicts between thinking, concepts, and views of the world in the diverse cultures" (Qin 21-22). Where there is translation, there is variation. When Chinese literature is introduced to the West, cultural filtering occurs as a result of cultural differences displayed in the form, content, and inherent ideas of the text. Victor H. Mair's translation of Chuang Tzu's (庄子) *Wandering on the Way* (逍遥游), a classic of Chinese literature, is a typical example. He translates 天 and 道 as "God." However, the Chinese original inscribes the Daoist concept as "heaven," which does not denote or connote the individual presence that the "God" of Judaism, Christianity, or Islam does: "The 天 in Chinese is neither a term for 'heaven' nor for 'God' and rather it is a term in-between, which combines both the connotation 'heaven' and 'God'" (Yao 47).

Another example that forefronts the aspect of cultural filtering described in variation theory is from the English translation of the fable "Dismembering an Ox by a Skillful Butcher" in Arthur Waley's *Three Ways of Thought in Ancient China*: "one has only to look at an ordinary Carver to see what a difficult business he finds it. One sees how nervous he is while making his preparations, how long he looks, how slowly he moves. Then after some small, niggling strokes of the knife when he has done no more than detach a few stray fragments from the whole, and even that by dint of continually twisting and turning like a worm burrowing through the earth, he stands back, with his knife in his hand, helplessly gazing this way and that, and after hovering for a long time finally curses a perfectly good knife, and puts it back in its case" (73). The cumulative effect of Waley's translation is to characterize the carver Pao Ding as meek: 怵然为戒 is translated as "nervous" (tense), 动刀甚微 as "some small, niggling strokes" (triviality of the skill), 为之四顾 as "helplessly gazing this way and that" (having no choice but to watch), and 踌躇满志 as "hovering for a long time" (shilly-shallying). This characterization opposes the image in the original work as super skillful, positive, and self-confident, virtually a master of his craft.

The differences just shown are representative of the great variation that occurs between Chinese texts and their translation to English. The mischaracterization of the butcher is particularly relevant in the Western reception of Mo Yan's work because of the reference to the character in *POW!* The meat-loving narrator of the novel, Luo Xiaotong, recalls the butcher Pao Ding early on in Mo Yan's novel: "Father made his living by his wits. In ancient times, there was a famous chef named Pao Ding who was an expert at carving up cows. In modern times, there was a man who was an expert at sizing them up—my father. In Pao Ding's eyes, cows were nothing but bones and edible flesh. That's what they were in my father's eyes too. Pao Ding's vision was as sharp as a knife, my father's was as sharp as a knife and as accurate as a scale" (27).

Anglophone readers who had read and accepted Waley's translation might be led to think that the narrator is undercutting his father's prowess, when instead he is expressing great filial pride. They would then also miss the reference to Pao Ding as the pinnacle of butchering expertise much later in the novel when a minor official introduces Luo Xiaotong's father, Luo Tong, as "the plant manager, an expert on meat. He has an unerring eye, like the legendary chef Pao Ding" (Mo Yan, *POW!* 236). The degradation of meat production at the factory contrasts with the high quality of the ancient butcher and chef, which Mo Yan highlights by again having the minor official call Luo Tong "Pao Ding" (236): "Pao Ding ... it's up to you to see that no water is injected into the meat" (236). Luo is evasive in response to the praise because he knows that the meat is not only injected with water but also human urine.

Likewise, variation arises when Western literature, specifically Anglophone literature, is introduced to Chinese, as is clear from observing Chinese translations of Anglophone works, as in the case of Charles Dickens. His *David Copperfield* has many Chinese translations, each accompanied by a number of variations ranging from language to culture. The most famous Chinese translations of the novel are 块肉余生述 (The Life of an Orphan) translated by Shu Lin and Yi Wei, 大卫·科波菲尔 (David Copperfield) by Qiusi Dong, and 大卫·考坡菲 (The Personal History of David Copperfield) by Guruo Zhang. As expected, there are differences between the original works and the translations, as well as between the Chinese translations. Lin and Wei adopted the method of domestication to cater to the reading habits of Chinese readers at the time and replaced Dickens's original title *The Personal History of David Copperfield*, which their free translation renders as The Life of an Orphan. In addition, Lin and Wei delete what they consider unimportant information such as some interjections, onomatopoeias, titles, and content in relation to religion. Their most obvious alterations reflect their attitude toward women. In Dickens's original, the wife Emily asks her husband David to respect her: "It was because I honoured you so much, and so much wished that you should honour me" (330). Lin and Wei replace Emily's request for equality with the traditional Chinese ideal of the "husband guiding the wife." In turn, Dong attempts literal translation, and while his Europeanized sentences are similar in form to the original, the logic of the original is lost. Zhang's translation has long been referred to as a well-translated version characterized by a combination of literal translation and free translation. Yet variation persists especially in terms of the religious differences between Eastern and Western cultures. Such is the case, for example, with regard to the altar in David's wedding ceremony. Zhang's translation as "matchmaker God" (月老神前611) introduces a matchmaker like the one in China into the English text and this encourages a misreading.

Variation occurs also at the macro level. For instance, *A Personal History of David Copperfield* is regarded in the West generally as Dickens's representative work. Conversely, it is *A Tale of Two Cities* that is often included in Chinese textbooks of foreign literature. In the most recent *Concise Cambridge History of English Literature*, George Sampson asserts that *A Tale of Two Cities* lacks the author's typical style (9). Why would such deviation in evaluation occur? Western readers or at least anthologizers may be more interested in Dickens' style and narrative structures, while Chinese readers and anthologizers may put more emphasis on themes. As Zhongxiang Wang posits, *A Tale of Two Cities* is chosen as Dickens's representative work in China because of its "reflection on thinking development of the writer and generalization of depth and width of history spirit" (24).

Literary misreading

When cultural filtering occurs heavily in communication, cultural misreading will inevitably ensue: misreading is the ultimate product of the actions and interactions of various factors in the process of cultural filtering. A primary factor is the individual because first and foremost there is the subjectivity of the reader. Readers from different cultures interpret heterogeneous cultures with the understanding of dislocation according to their own cultural traditions and habits of thinking, which is bidirectional. From the perspective of the relations between the leading role translators play in the process of translation and the original work, when translators encounter the original work, whose composition is activated by intervention, they will also absorb the original work in an open schema. Second, variation occurs owing to not only the difference of geographical space but also to dislocation across history.

A good example of misreading in Anglophone literature is the misreading of the description of the "delight" the narrator of Shakespeare's "Sonnet 130" takes "in the breath that from my mistress reeks" (112). Regarding "reeks," editor Stephen Booth writes that "a modern reader must be cautioned against hearing this word as a simple insult" given that in Shakespeare's day "reek" could have meant simply to "emanate" rather than to "stink" (454). A key example in Chinese literature can be found in a line by the Chinese monk Han Shan of the Tang Dynasty. A denotatively accurate rendering of the line "炼药空求仙" (Han Shan qtd. in Xia 1662) is to go into remote mountains to beg the immortal to produce the elixir. Beat poet Gary Snyder translates it as "tried drugs, but couldn't make immortal" (12). Snyder transforms the meaning of the character 药 rendered as "life-prolonging herb" or "elixir" as "drug" involving heroin or marijuana as possible meanings. At the hands of Snyder, Han Shan becomes a forerunner of the Beat Generation rebelling with decadent thoughts.

Variation stems from the diversity and asymmetry between two languages: to be freed from the restrictions and constraints of language means a kind of innovation and "the subtle differences experienced in different languages' world" into others (Xia 572), and thus translator Yuanchong Xu notes the inevitability of variability in Chinese-English translation: "Chinese is the character of comparative art, which is characterized with fuzziness. When translated into English, it is hard for the translator to indicate the 'subtle differences,' which needs a translator's creativity. Creativity will involve originality and variation, so translation is the process in which variation happens" (138). Such variation is increased when poets-as-translators bring their own creative penchants to bear on their translations. *Analects of Confucius* includes the adage that "to learn and at due times to review what one has learnt, is that not after all a pleasure" (学而时习之，不亦说乎 2457). Ezra Pound renders it as "to study, with the white wings of time passing is not that our delight" (34). He divides the single character 習 into what in Chinese would be rendered as two characters 羽 (wing) and 白 (white). His quest for imagery overrides his quest for accuracy of the original meaning. He does so again in the Confucian adage "after setting the object of pursuit, one will be able to calm down" (定而后能静 1673), which he renders as "having this orderly procedure one can grasp the azure, that is, take hold of a clear concept" (Pound 99). Again, the single character 静 would be rendered as two characters: 青 (azure) and 爭 (grasp). In *Investigations of Ezra Pound, Together with an Essay on the Chinese Written Character by Ernest Fenollosa*, Pound wrote that the "Chinese character is based upon a vivid shorthand picture of the operations of nature," and "a large number of the primitive Chinese characters, even the so-called radicals, are shorthand pictures of actions or processes," and that the radicals of the synthetic character show that "two things added together do not produce a third thing but suggest some fundamental relation between them" (8-10). In Pound's misunderstanding, Confucius becomes a forerunner of imagist poetry, the effect of which radiates throughout the West. It is also along this line that traditional Chinese poetry, especially with Pound's translations and transformation of Chinese Tang poetry, is often understood as imagist poetry. However, as André Lefevere has noted, "a direct presentation of cultural context is often essential if we are to avoid an assimilation to our own norms, and this requires us as readers to accept the translation's mediating role: 'When we no longer translate Chinese T'ang poetry "as if" it were Imagistic blank verse, which it manifestly is not, we shall be able to begin to understand T'ang poetry on its own terms'" (78).

Images of Otherness

In variation theory the image of Otherness refers to the literature of one country that is introduced in another country, necessarily attended by deep-seated variations through culture filtering, translation, and acceptance, reflecting the assimilation of the cultural rules of the national literature and its literary discourse and making the national literature of a country part of the literature and culture of the recipients' countries (see, e.g., Andraș). From the perspective of the image of Otherness, we can understand the phenomenon encapsulated by the statement proposed by Chinese scholars that "not all translated literature is foreign literature." It is with this perspective of variation theory that we now turn to Mo Yan's work as a representative case.

Mo Yan is the most successful contemporary Chinese writer in terms of the number of translations of his works into foreign languages and his global reception. With at least *Big Breasts and Wide Hips*, variation is performed by translator Howard Goldblatt working from a unique original, as he notes: "Some changes and rearrangements were effected during the translation and editing process, all with the approval of the author" (xii). In most Chinese-to-English translations, however, variation is primarily the product of the translator's Westernization of the original. In a creative rather than literal translation, Goldblatt revises parts of Chapters 19 and 20 of the English version of *The Garlic Ballads*. For example, in Chapter 19 defendant Zheng Changnian's son says "thank you for reminding me, Your Honor. I'll get right to the point. In recent years the peasants have been called upon to shoulder ever heavier burdens: fees, taxes, fines, and inflated prices for just about everything they need" (26) while the original reads "谢谢审判长的提醒，我马上进入实质性辩护。近几年来，农民的负担越来越重. 我父亲所在村庄，种一亩蒜薹，要交纳农业税九元八角。要向乡政府交纳提留税二十元，要向村委会交纳提留三十元. 要交纳县城建设税五元（按人头计算），卖蒜薹时，还要交纳市场管理税、计量器检查税、交通管理税、环境保护税，还有种种名目的罚款!" (340). While Goldblatt omits some details of Chinese law and policy with which Anglophone readers would be unfamiliar, his translation is successful because he uses the creative approach to adapt to the habits and tastes of Anglophone readers, and he is faithful to the art and aesthetic of the original form. Thus he employs creative discretion to help his readers accept and understand Chinese literature better.

Variation is less idiosyncratic or intentional in cases where translations are secondary translations, a centuries-long practice in which translations are based on other translations. Wolfgang Kubin notes that German translations of Mo Yan's work are based not on the original Chinese but on English versions. We observe then how contemporary English translations serve as the authority for Western language habits and aesthetic tastes (replacing the nineteenth-century predominance of French translations as the base). Mo Yan does not assume a regulatory role as other authors or publishers might. Instead, Mo Yan's translators are allowed to translate freely for their respective readers, and this way a dialogue ensues with and within successful variation (see Fu and Zhang <http://www.infzm.com/content/trs/raw/41156>).

The result of Chinese-to-English translations done by nonnative Chinese speakers is the insertion of a nearly invisible barrier based on the difference between Eastern and Western cultural psychology and patterns of narration. It seems fair to say that the widespread reception of Mo Yan's works owes much to the domestic appropriation conducted by excellent translators, rather than the exportation of native Chinese translators. Therefore, the translation of the national literature of a country is easily adapted to the recipient's country based on its language, culture, and readers' tastes. This is one major way that cultures can win nonnative readers' acceptance. And only when an effective transmission is achieved can the genuine charm of a culture and literature be circulated in the world. Estimating whether it can be defined as an image of Otherness lies in whether or not the rule of discourse changes.

Heterogeneity between Chinese and Western discourse

"Discourse Rule" is a useful term to refer to any one of the basic rules such as speculation, interpretation, and expression in specific cultural traditions, social histories, and formations of national cultural psychology. It influences theoretical thinking, the generation of meaning, and linguistic expression, which embody in discourse rules and speech methods in philosophy, aesthetics, and literary theory. Discourse rules generate historically and originate from different cultural systems resulting in heterogeneity. For example, a Chinese traditional discourse rule is the generation of meaning and style of language with Daoism as its core (see Cao, "Discourse" 5). Especially important for literary studies is the heterogeneity between the generation of meaning and style of language of the Western *logos* and Daoism. Take one line in *Lao Zi* for example: "Daoism produces one. One produces two. Two produces three. Three produces all things," and this is to say that everything is derived from Daoism (Lao Tze 44). Another passage of *Lao Zi* expresses an anti-logos stance on Daoism as origin and expression: "The beautiful words are not true, the true words are not beautiful, the way that can be spoken of is not the constant way; the name that can be named is not the constant name" (Lao Tze 3).

Daoism cannot be spoken as questioning, and the tension between unspeakable Daoism and Western *logos* causes the form of the generation of meaning and the style of language with Daoism as its core. Languages can communicate ideas of daily life, but when rising to the aspect of Daoism language is always poor even in its original: "The greatness of anything may be a topic of discussion, and the smallness of anything may be mentally imagined. But that which can be neither a topic of discussion nor imagined mentally cannot be said to have greatness or smallness" (Lin 99). No matter the greatness of the topic or the smallness of the imagined, Daoism is beyond topic and imagination and thus beyond language. On the one hand, the Chinese discourse rule with Daoism as its core emphasizes that meaning cannot be spoken. On the other hand, it uses implication and metaphor forming a unique way of expression. The speaker does not say, the reader does not speak, but the thought can be communicated. Attempting to convey this Chinese discourse rule is difficult because of the contradictory Western discourse rule of logocentrism characterized by scientific, systematic, and analytical verbal expression. There are many similarities between *logos* and Daoism, but among "being and invisible being," "speakable and unspeakable," and "language analysis and understanding" there are great differences, which in turn determine differences between Western and Chinese discourses (see Cao, "Tao" 54). Daoism and *logos* share the traits of being eternal and constant. Daoism tends to indicate invisible being, while *logos* tends to mean being. According to Heraclitus *logos* itself means being, although people do not understand it as such (see, e.g., Botten). Exploration, questioning, and analysis on being from *logos* makes Western culture, literature, and literary theory seem to be more precise and systemic, focusing more on the causality of logic and plot structure. Conversely, the invisible being from *Lao Zi* directs Chinese literary theory to emphasize spirit and neglect type. Another example of the image of Otherness is the Sinicization of Buddhism: "The process for Sinicization of Buddhism is simultaneous with the Buddhismization of China" (Zhang, Mantao 76; on the history of Buddhism and China, see, e.g., Mitchell and Duran). There are many aspects for the Sinicization of Buddhism including the translation of sutras, which was gradually Sinicized by methods of comparison and analogy to explain and understand the concept against a cross-cultural background. The Sinicization of Buddhism has gradually fused Buddhism and Chinese culture, forming Zen Buddhism.

In conclusion, variation theory represents the approximation of Chinese and Western thought, including literary and culture theory and translation theory and practice. Chinese ways of thinking and discourse rules can absorb and transform Western literary theories and vice versa. The most promising Chinese appropriation of Western literary theories will strive first to combine its own literary practice with traditional culture and cultural sources, understand native discourse rules, and consider its unique qualities in order to add value to Western literary theories. When compared with Western literary theories, we should aim at discovering similarities and differences between the two.

Works Cited

Analects of Confucius (论语译注). Ed. Liangnian Jin (金良年). Shanghai: Shanghai Gu Ji P, 2004.
Analects of Confucius. Trans. Arthur Waley. London: Allen and Unwin, 1938.
Andraş, Carmen Maria, ed. *New Directions in Travel Writing and Travel Studies*. Aachen: Shaker P, 2010.
Booker, Christopher. *Seven Basic Plots: Why We Tell Stories*. New York: Continuum, 2004.
Botten, Mick. *Herakleitos: Logos Made Manifest*. Peterborough: Fast Print, 2011.
Chen, Xiaoming, and Anfeng Sheng. "A Survey of Twentieth-century Literary Theory and Criticism in Chinese." *CLCWeb: Comparative Literature and Culture* 15.6 (2013): <http://dx.doi.org/10.7771/1481-4374.2367>.
Cao, Shunqing (曹顺庆). "比较文学中国学派基本理论及其方法论体系初探" ("Chinese School of Comparative Literature: The Essential Feature of Its Theory and a Tentative Study of Its Methodology"). *Comparative Literature in China* 1 (1995): 18-40.
Cao, Shunqing (曹顺庆). "道与逻各斯：中西文化与文论分道扬镳的起点" ("Tao and Logos: Origin of Division in the Culture and Literary Theory between the East and West"). *Literature & Art Studies* 6 (1997): 51-60.
Cao, Shunqing. *The Variation Theory of Comparative Literature*. Berlin: Springer, 2014.

Chuang Tzu. *Wandering on the Way: Early Taoist Tales and Parables of Chuang Tzu.* Trans. Victor H. Mair. Honolulu: U of Hawaii P, 1998.

Dickens, Charles (狄更斯). 大卫·科波菲尔 (*David Copperfield*). Trans. Qiusi Dong (董秋斯). Beijing: People's Literature Publishing, 1978.

Dickens, Charles (迭更司). 块肉余生述 (*David Copperfield*). Trans. Shu Lin (林纾) and Yi Wei (魏易). Beijing: Beijing Commercial P, 1981.

Dickens, Charles. *The Personal History of David Copperfield.* 1850. New York: Random House, 1950.

Dickens, Charles (狄更斯). 大卫·考坡菲 (*The Personal History of David Copperfield*). Trans. Guruo Zhang (张谷若). Shanghai: Shanghai Translation Publishing, 1989.

Han, Shan (寒山). 寒山诗注 (*Han Shan's Poems*). Ed. Xiang Chu (项楚). Beijing: Zhong Hua Book Company, 2000.

Fu, Ge (赋格), and Ying Zhang (张英). "葛浩文谈中国文学" ("Howard Goldblatt's Views on Chinese Literature"). *infizm.com* (26 March 2008): <http://www.infzm.com/content/trs/raw/41156>.

Lao Tse. *I Ching: Book of Changes.* Trans. James Legge. New York: Gramercy Books, 1996.

Lefevere, André. "Composing the Other." *Post-colonial Translation: Theory and Practice.* Ed. Susan Bassnett and Harish Trivedi. London: Routledge, 1999. 75-94.

Li, Qingben, and Jinghua Guo. "Translation, Cross-cultural Interpretation, and World Literatures." *CLCWeb: Comparative Literature and Culture* 15.6 (2013): <http://dx.doi.org/10.7771/1481-4374.2358>.

Mitchell, Donald, and Angelica Duran. "A Textbook Case of Comparative Cultural Studies." *Mo Yan in Context: Nobel Laureate and Global Storyteller.* Ed. Angelica Duran and Yuhan Huang. West Lafayette: Purdue UP, 2014. 195-212.

Mo Yan (莫言). 丰乳肥臀 (*Big Breasts and Wide Hips*). Beijing: Writers Publishing House, 2012.

Mo Yan. *Big Breasts and Wide Hips.* Trans. Howard Goldblatt. New York: Arcade, 2012.

Mo Yan (莫言). 天堂蒜薹之歌 (*The Garlic Ballads*). Beijing: Writers Publishing, 2012.

Mo Yan (莫言). *The Garlic Ballads.* Trans. Howard Goldblatt. New York: Arcade, 2012.

Mo Yan. *POW!* Trans. Howard Goldblatt. New York: Seagull, 2012.

Morin, Edgar. *Method: Towards a Study of Humankind.* Trans. J. L. Roland Bélanger. Bern: Peter Lang, 1992.

Pound, Ezra. *Investigations of Ezra Pound, Together with an Essay on the Chinese Written Character by Ernest Fenollosa.* Freeport: Books for Libraries P, 1967.

Sampson, George. *Concise Cambridge History of English Literature.* Cambridge: Cambridge UP, 2010.

Shakespeare, William. *Shakespeare's Sonnets.* Ed. Stephen Booth. New Haven: Yale UP, 1977.

Snyder, Gary. *The Gary Snyder Reader: Prose, Poetry, and Translations. 1952-1998.* Washington: Counterpoint P, 1999.

Tötösy de Zepetnek, Steven, and Tutun Mukherjee, eds. *Companion to Comparative Literature, World Literatures, and Comparative Cultural Studies*. New Delhi: Cambridge UP India, 2013.
Waley, Arthur. *Three Ways of Thought in Ancient China*. Stanford: Stanford UP, 1939.
Wang, Miaomiao. "Comparative Literature in Chinese: A Survey of Books Published 2000-2013." *CLCWeb: Comparative Literature and Culture* 15.6 (2013): <http://dx.doi.org/10.7771/1481-4374.2370>.
Wang, Ning. "Variation Theory and Comparative Literature: A Book Review Article of Cao's Work." *CLCWeb: Comparative Literature and Culture* 15.6 (2013): <http://dx.doi.org/10.7771/1481-4374.2371>.
Wang, Xiaolu, and Yan Liu. "Comparative Poetics in Chinese." *Companion to Comparative Literature, World Literatures, and Comparative Cultural Studies*. Ed. Steven Tötösy de Zepetnek and Tutun Mukherjee. New Delhi: Cambridge UP India, 2013. 239-53.
Wang, Yizhong (王易中). 编著，大智之门：孔子 "易·系辞" 解读 (Door of Wisdom: Interpretation of the Confucius's The Book of Changes). Taiyuan: Shan Xi Science and Technology P, 2011.
Wang, Zhongxiang (王忠祥). "论狄更斯的 双城记" ("On Dickens's *A Tale of Two Cities*"). *Foreign Literature Studies* 1 (1978): 24-31.
Xia, Yu (夏于). 全集注，唐诗宋词全集·第三部 (Collection of Tang and Song Poetry). Beijing: Beijing Hua Yi, 1997.
Xu, Yuanchong (许渊冲). 文学与翻译 (Literature and Translation). Beijing: Peking UP, 2003.
Zhang, Mantao (张曼涛), ed. 佛教与中国文化 (Buddhism and Chinese Culture). Shanghai: Shanghai Bookshop P, 1987.

Author's profile

Shunqing Cao teaches comparative literature and literary theory at Sichuan University. His interests in scholarship include comparative literature and literary theories. In addition to numerous articles and books, Cao's single-authored book publications in English include *The Variation Theory of Comparative Literature* (2014). Cao's most important contribution is the development of "variation theory" in comparative literature.

Author's profile

Miaomiao Wang teaches English language and literature at North China Electric Power University. Her interests in research include comparative literature and cultural studies. Wang's recent English-language articles include "Comparative Literature in Chinese: A Survey of Books Published 2000-2013," *CLCWeb: Comparative Literature and Culture* (2013).

A Textbook Case of Comparative Cultural Studies

Donald Mitchell and Angelica Duran

Abstract

In "A Textbook Case of Comparative Cultural Studies" Donald Mitchell and Angelica Duran posit that the cultural basis from which all literary works emerge includes a religious component given the historical perseverance of religious traditions. Hence, a basic understanding of the religious heritage and contemporary mix in Chinese culture is exigent to develop valid interpretations about literary works. Mitchell and Duran describe the changes made to the most widely used Anglophone introductory textbook on Buddhism, the third edition of Mitchell's *Buddhism: Introducing the Buddhist Experience*, based on the globalization of Buddhism in today's world. Religious interaction and influence is dynamic, no longer a one-way flow of Buddhism from Asia to non-Asian countries but rather a multidirectional flow between countries in all continents. Close readings of two religious figures demonstrate this dynamic with Mo Yan's Wise Monk Lan in *POW!* and the Swedish Pastor Malory in *Big Breasts and Wide Hips*.

We start with the argument that the cultural bases from which all literary works emerge includes a religious component given the historical perseverance of religious traditions. Hence, a basic understanding of the religious heritage and its contemporary expressions in Chinese culture is exigent to develop valid interpretations about literary works. In his 1982 *The Great Code: The Bible and Literature*, Northrop Frye demonstrated how strongly the sacred text of Judaism and Christianity, the Bible, pervades Western art and literature. Frye went to great lengths to emphasize that his study was "from the point of view of a literary critic" and was not a work of "theology," and to locate literary criticism as cultural and social criticism (xi). His emphasis was warranted because general readers and scholars at the time were still reluctant to engage with any talk of religion, wary that discussions merely doubled for evangelical attempts at conversion into a particular religion or equally untethered vendettas against religiosity. Such a response is understandable given the relatively recent development of the field of religious studies. While theology is a centuries-old field and presupposes that its scholars are believers, religious studies finds its beginnings in the nineteenth century when the Bible began to be analyzed historically and when Hindu and Buddhist texts were first translated into major European languages. Religions as cultural components recorded in literature significantly reduced the anxiety that discussions of religions tend to prompt since, as Donald Soetaert and Kris Rutten observe, "the concept of culture is often combined with literacy" (63). Literacy is based on written texts of all sorts and in turn, as Soetaert and Rutten note, extends to E. D. Hirsch's use of "cultural literacy to describe the level and breadth of knowledge citizens need to navigate in society," which is precisely our claim about what the knowledge of religious studies can provide to readers of literary works (63). This perspective is interdisciplinary in its best sense, or, as Rik Pinxten notes of his own work in anthropology, "comparative cultural studies adds a critical approach by contextualizing literature" (121). Indeed the major scholars who helped institutionalize religious studies in Western institutions employed phenomenological descriptions and interpretations emphasizing systematic and cross-cultural perspectives. For example, Mircea Eliade applied a historical perspective in *The Sacred and the Profane: The Nature of Religion*, William James philosophical and psychological ones in *The Varieties of Religious Experience: A Study of Human Nature*, and Emile Durkheim a sociological one in *Elementary Forms of Religious Life*.

We find T. Patrick Burke articulating this aim at objectivity in his *The Major Religions*, a popular textbook used in introduction to religious studies courses which cover both Western and Eastern religions. Burke distills the contentious history of the field of religious studies in his description of the field: "This book does not assume that the study of religions necessarily presupposes commitment to their truth or value. Our aim is simply to enable the student to become familiar with the basic information about the main religious traditions … As a general rule it is wise to suspend judgment until we are certain we understand the matter sufficiently. This applies to the theological beliefs, of course, but also to such matters as the Hindu caste system, or the fact that the major religions traditionally favor the male gender. The initial approach of the student should be to try to understand the reasons that may have led to the features he finds difficult to accept" (9). Even in his careful outline—in the textbook's second edition no less, when some corrections had been made—Burke provides readers with an unintentional instance of how fully religions participate in culture more generally: while Burke cites the favoring of "the male gender," he lapses into designating his imagined readers as a unified whole and as male in using "he," the unified male entity regularly positioned as the only or leading divine agent. This is not to nay-say Burke: his and other introductory textbooks on major religions are vital to procuring the promises of the "religious turn" in critical studies since the beginning of the twentieth century. Leaders in a variety of the fields participating in religious studies are bent on creating a basis and language upon which and with which global scholars can develop trenchant abstract theories as well as seek new modes for the real-world applications of their studies. In sympathizing with the dangers yet importance of Burke's project, we are also empathizing with it.

In 2002 Oxford University Press published its first major textbook on Buddhism: Donald Mitchell's *Buddhism: Introducing the Buddhist Experience*. The textbook covers the life and teachings of the historical Buddha, Buddhism in Southeast Asia that preserves the original forms of early Indian Buddhism, the development of the Mahayana Buddhist traditions of thought and practice in India, as well as the spread and development of Buddhism into Tibet, China, Korea, Japan, and the West. Over the years, the content of the textbook has evolved based on recent scholarship, as well as developments in Buddhist communities around the world. The changes in the textbook track the globalization of Chinese Buddhism that provide readers outside and inside of China the religious context for some elements in contemporary Chinese fiction. While Mo Yan is not a religious writer, his fiction does at times present cultural views, ideas, and values that have traditional Chinese Buddhist roots. It would be surprising if it didn't, given the broad reading he demonstrates in his works. Chinese literature can be traced back to ancient times, and in ancient times literature was infused with the religious foundations that marked all known civilizations. Sabina Knight's *Chinese Literature: A Very Short Introduction* does right by her Anglophone readers—mostly college students and general, educated readers—in repeatedly drawing attention to Chinese religious traditions in her impressive review of poetry, drama, historical narrative, and fiction.

A little closer at hand and more to the point, in this volume Chi-ying Alice Wang's "Mo Yan's *The Garlic Ballads* and *Life and Death Are Wearing Me Out* in the Context of Religious and Chinese Literary Conventions" demonstrates some of the rich relationship between Mo Yan's use of Chinese and non-Chinese religious traditions (see also Jinghui Wang). Understanding this relationship requires that readers and scholars possess the kind of basic knowledge to recognize when Mo Yan is swerving from traditional beliefs and thus being particularly playful or controversial, or when he is blending major global religions with native Chinese folk religions, or when he is introducing or reintroducing so-called religious texts into contemporary Chinese literary culture. For example, in *Life and Death Are Wearing Me Out*, Lord Yama figures as the wrathful and enigmatic leader of the underworld. Mo Yan seems to call attention to the Hindu, which is to say Indian, origin and usual depiction of Lord Yama later adopted by Buddhism in its popular forms in China by describing his attendants as "totally human in appearance, except, that is, for their skin, whose color was iridescent blue, as if treated with a magical dye" (6). The blue skin color tends to be more characteristic of Indian deities. Elsewhere, Mo Yan mentions in passing ancient literary texts that can be categorized with equal accuracy as religious texts, as when narrator Shangguan Jintong mentions "Laozi, the founder of Taoism himself" (325).

With just these compelling examples of the literary subtlety with which Mo Yan inscribes Chinese religions, we move to our next task of describing the updates of one particular branch of Chinese religion, Chinese Buddhism, in the three editions of the textbook, before we return in greater depth to two of Mo Yan's novels. We review the chapters on "The Chinese Buddhist Experience" and "Buddhism in the West" that the third edition of *Buddhism: Introducing the Buddhist Experience* retitles "The Globalization of Buddhism." We then align how global religions factor into two of Mo Yan's novels.

The first edition of *Buddhism: Introducing the Buddhist Experience*

In the first edition of the China chapter in the textbook, Mitchell followed the common practice of beginning with the introduction of Buddhism from India by way of the Silk Road in the first century CE, the early efforts to translate Buddhist texts from Sanskrit into Chinese, the influence of Taoism on these translations, and the later efforts in the fourth century to produce new translations that more closely followed the Indian textual tradition. The next section of the chapter presented how the schools of Indian Buddhism from the Abhidharma traditions to the Madhyamika and Yogacara traditions of Mahayana were formed in China. These schools are commonly referred to as "Indian Buddhism in China." While the development of these schools reflected certain values and assumptions of Chinese culture and thought, these elements were only hints of the more fully Chinese forms of Buddhism that would develop later. The chapter then turns to the actual schools of uniquely Chinese Buddhism. These schools define the Chinese experiences of Buddhism and would later spread to Korea, Japan, and Vietnam. Here we find the heart of East Asian Buddhism. The four schools covered in some depth in the chapter are Tiantai, Huayan, Chan, and Jingtu. They express the diversity of Chinese Buddhism from the scholarship and multiple practices of Tiantai and the extraordinarily complex philosophy of Huayan, to the meditative tradition of Chan and the devotional tradition of Jingtu. From the lens of the school approach to Buddhism, this section is the highlight of the chapter. It presents fully developed Chinese Buddhist thoughts and practices that contribute to Chinese culture. Therefore, numerous translations of original texts were presented in order to give readers direct access to the masters who formed these traditions through philosophy, metaphor, story, and example.

Although Mitchell had been trained as a philosopher and had taught Eastern religion courses for decades, he found himself entering into literary and linguistics terrain. These translations were difficult since many of the Chinese characters represent Sanskrit terms that had been presented in previous chapters on Indian Buddhism. But in China, they carried certain implications that were not found in India, meanings that give readers a better understanding of the Chinese experiences of Buddhism based on the values and assumptions of Chinese civilization. Even scant writings provide readers with the ability to see both the links with Indian Buddhism and the changes in perspective given how certain terms were used in Chinese Buddhism. It became clear over the six years between the first and second edition of the textbook that while the school approach to the story of Buddhism in China was helpful in giving readers a clear picture of the major formal schools of Chinese Buddhism, it was not so helpful in providing them with an understanding of how Buddhism exists today in Chinese culture. This was becoming more and more important given the growing prevalence in the mission statements of U.S. universities, particularly land-grant or public universities, about their aim to help foster global citizenship. Mitchell's own teaching experience dovetailed with that larger pedagogical development, since he was seeing more and more international, particularly Chinese, students in his classrooms and since he knew of the increased push for study abroad for native U.S. students.

The second edition of *Buddhism: Introducing the Buddhist Experience*

Given the need to help readers understand the more recent developments in Chinese Buddhism and their place in the culture of China today, the second edition expanded the China chapter. It included a discussion on the Qin Dynasty patriarch Zhuhong (袾宏) (1535-1615), who blended the Jingtu practice of devotion to Amitabha Buddha, the Chan practice of meditation, and the study of sutras as taught in Tiantai and Huayan. He also reached out to the laity, describing their strong devotional piety, lay activities outside the temple or monastery, and the study and distribution of Buddhist texts. These changes have helped to describe Buddhism in the daily life of Chinese Buddhists over the centuries and are thus responsive to cultural movements in China that stress the circulation of texts among all strata of the populous, not just the elite. But more important in understanding Buddhism in Chinese culture as a background for appreciating its literature, poetry, and the arts is Taixu (太虛) (1890-1947). He inspired a reform movement that had wide-ranging consequences and founded schools where modern secular subjects were taught along with traditional Buddhist scholarship in Western-style classes. Taixu supported lay study of Buddhist texts and doctrines and the publication of Buddhist books and periodicals. He founded new institutes or seminaries to train Buddhist monks and nuns as well as lay leaders and created new Buddhist structures to aid the needy in society. Finally, Taixu developed contacts with Buddhists in other countries and supported a kind of Buddhist ecumenism, one of the earliest global fellowships. The blending of the earlier reform of Zhuhung and the more recent reform of Taixu lay the groundwork for a new and broader understanding of Chinese Buddhism outside China. These innovations in the second edition of the textbook provide a truer contextual understanding of modern Chinese literature than the traditional schools of Chinese Buddhism.

Of signal importance in the second edition is the added essay "The Cultural Experience of Chinese Buddhism Today" by Wei Dedong from the Institute of Buddhism and Religious Theory at Renmin University in Beijing (see also his *The Essence of Buddhist Yogacara Philosophy*). Wei discusses how the heritage of Indian Buddhist customs, like the belief in rebirth, and China's own particular culture are carried forward in modernization movements in contemporary China. Wei's discussion gives readers of Chinese literature the context needed to understand the authors' descriptions of aspects of Chinese culture and daily life that have religious roots. For example, Wei presents temple rituals intended for liberating deceased loved ones called "worshiping all Buddhas for the attainment of rebirth" (267). Today, it is not uncommon for Chinese writers to refer to persons who have died but remain as ghosts or spirits needing to turn from this world and enter the Pure Land. Mo Yan does so, of course, in 蛙 (Frog). Mo Yan's title gains yet another resonance, to add to those provided by Lanlan Du's discussion "Abortion in Faulkner's *The Wild Palms* and Mo Yan's 蛙 (Frog)," if we know that the frog is a symbol of reincarnation as memorialized by the Japanese Zen poet Basho in his best-known *haiku*: "Old pond / frog jumps in – / Plop!" (215). Other examples include the tradition of pilgrimage to holy places in connection with the need for confession and forgiveness, the celebration of holidays, and actions that free people from evil karma or rescue persons from becoming hungry ghosts and enabling them to be reborn in the realms of humans or gods: all these activities can be found in Mo Yan's work.

In the concluding section of Wei's essay, he turns to the new forms of Buddhism in China due to modernization and globalization. These new forms pursue "Humanistic Buddhism" that follow the inspirations of Taixu and seek the peaceful development of Chinese society and the furthering of the public good through charitable activities such as disaster relief and provision of good education for youth living in poverty. These Buddhist organizations also have websites to introduce their work to the broader public. It is estimated that in 2012 there were 538 Buddhist websites in China. Wei points out that this renewal of Buddhism in China today has contributed to Chinese culture. For example, Buddhist themes are now pursued in Chinese art and literature. One example is the award-wining "Dance of the Thousand-Armed Guanyin" performed by the China Disabled People's Performing Art Troupe at the 2004 Athens Olympics and Paralympics. Another is the film 天下無賊 (*A World without Thieves*), released in 2004, which sold over one hundred million tickets in China (see Mitchell, *Buddhism* [2008] 272). It is about a pair of lovers who were thieves but changed their lives for the better because, as the female lover said, "I am pregnant and want to improve my child's karma." This film reminds one of the tragic relationships that conclude Mo Yan's *Life and Death Are Wearing Me Out*, especially given the provocative title to chapter 55, "Lovemaking Positions," with its evocation of Tantric Buddhism's sexual ethics. Again, we see how knowing about these beliefs—about Guanyin Bodhisattva and karma—can provide a necessary context for persons, both in China and elsewhere, to understand, appreciate, or even know what questions to ask about contemporary works of Chinese art and literature, such as the fiction of Mo Yan.

The third edition of *Buddhism: Introducing the Buddhist Experience*

In the third edition of the textbook, Mitchell added a new section to the China chapter on modern Chinese Buddhist movements and the book is co-authored with Sarah Jacoby (Northwestern University). This third edition has a number of firsts in textbooks on Buddhism: the textbook is the first on the topic to have a woman author, and it uses Pinyin rather than Wade-Giles for translating the sounds of Chinese characters into Latin script (while the latter matter may seem of little significance to some, it makes a social statement, much as does the use of US-American English in the Anglophone translations of Mo Yan's works by U.S. translator Howard Goldblatt).

For fully developed global and modern Chinese Buddhist movements, one has to look to Taiwan. The textbook used Wade-Giles and the name order popular globally only in this section in order for readers to find more information on these movements on the internet. Therefore, we do so in the following discussion. There are four major Buddhist movements in Taiwan sometimes called the "Four Kings of Taiwanese Buddhism." They include 1) Tzu Chi Compassion Relief Society (for these organizations, we follow their use of Wade-Giles), 2) Fo Guang Shan Buddhist Order, 3) Dharma Drum Mountain Buddhist Organization, and 4) Chung Tai Shan Monastery. The latter is a more traditional form of Chan monasticism that has numerous Chan meditation centers around the world, including eight in the U.S. The other three are more influenced by Taixu's Humanistic Buddhism. They have centers all over the world, too, and have played a role in the revival of Buddhism in China today. This is a kind of reverse flow in the movement of Buddhism. The Three Kings of Buddhism in Taiwan have roots in China and spread to other countries where they developed their social engagement, and then brought that experience back to the source of their own roots, namely, to China. These kinds of multidirectional flows of Buddhism are key components of the new Global Buddhism. They also parallel the multidirectional literary influence so rightly noted about Mo Yan's work.

The Chinese chapter of the textbook presents in some depth the three humanist Buddhist organizations. Cheng Yen (證嚴) is sometimes called the Mother Teresa of Buddhism, in reference to the Roman Catholic nun who won the 1979 Nobel Peace Prize. Cheng leads the Tzu Chi Compassion Relief Association that includes a network of hospitals, free mobile clinics, schools and a university, and an international relief network. The latter has carried out relief efforts in many countries, including China. Its first activity in China was in 1991 after the terrible flooding in central and eastern China. More recently, it provided food, blankets, and medical aid to survivors of the 2008 Sichuan earthquake. Tzu Chi now has over four million members and numerous centers throughout the world. Equally significant, they also have a publishing house that publishes books, magazines, and newspapers that share their values and cultural religious views with a broader audience. It is through this activity that persons in non-Asian countries can learn about the religious background of Chinese culture that is often expressed in contemporary Chinese literature. Literary scholars, especially those specializing in rhetoric and composition, are well aware that it is more accurate to say that online reading is replacing "reading," rather than the former lament that "reading" is diminishing among the younger generation. Hence, this mode of communicating Buddhism deserves attention.

The founder of Dharma Drum Mountain was Dongchu (東初), one of Taizu's disciples. When Dongchu moved to Taiwan, he founded the Chung-Hwa Institute of Buddhist Culture. Again, the focus was on teaching not only Buddhist doctrine but also culture and the arts. His Dharma heir was Sheng Yen (聖嚴), who built Dharma Drum Mountain, which includes a complex of monasteries, devotional temples, and educational centers. Dharma Drum has developed "six ethics of the mind," which present the traditional values of China in a modern and universal form: ethics for the family, school, environment, workplace, daily life, and a pluralistic society. Dharma Drum also has centers around the world where they express their values in different cultural settings while giving non-Chinese participants a better understanding of the Buddhist roots of Chinese culture.

Finally, we come to Fo Guang Shan to exemplify the recent developments of the ancient cultural component of religion. Leaving China for Taiwan, the founder Hsing Yun (星雲) decided not to propagate traditional Buddhism. Rather, given his experience of war and poverty and his study under Taizu, he wanted to revitalize Buddhism. He wanted to make it more responsive to the needs of the modern world. He created a modern form of Buddhism that teaches religious practice in ethical daily living while working for social change—building the Pure Land here on earth. He once wrote, "Master Taixu said that we can achieve Buddhahood only by fulfilling our humanity" (263). The globalization of this modernized form of Buddhism is carried out by its Buddha's Light International Society (BLIS). Here again the Buddhist roots of Chinese culture are emphasized. For example, next to the Fo Guang Shan complex is a massive new Fo Guang Shan Buddha Memorial Center. Besides the 108-meter-high statue of the Buddha, the eight multistory pagodas, and all the rich cultural artifacts within the buildings, there are murals on the walls of the complex. On the inside of the walls are murals of events in the life of the Buddha as understood in Chinese Buddhism. These murals are educational in that the stories they portray entail beliefs that are conveyed in Chinese literature and the arts. Also, on the outside of the walls are murals of stories and events in the history of Buddhism in China that also convey beliefs and values that are expressed in Chinese literature and the arts. As we shall see, this cultural educational style is also used in Fo Guang Shan centers around the world, thus providing a global vehicle for contextualizing the kind of fiction written by Mo Yan.

The globalization of Chinese Buddhist culture

Globalization is the result of a new interdependence of the cultures of the world owing to a number of factors such as global transportation, communication, and markets resulting in technological, economic, and social networks which transcend national and regional boundaries. The Internet and mass media have strongly influenced these networks as they penetrate the cultures of the world. In the past, cultures with their religions had geographical borders. Chinese Buddhist culture, for example, was primarily limited to China, Taiwan, and Vietnam. Globalization has allowed cultural boundaries to be penetrated by other cultures, creating global flows and interpenetration of religious ideas, practices, lineages, customs, literatures, and arts. In the past, there may have been different religions in a given society, but their relationships were fairly stable. Globalization has brought about new religious phenomena in all parts of the world. A new global pluralism of religions is now commonplace, and in it we find the globalization of Buddhism in general and Chinese Buddhism in particular.

This brief synopsis alone can go far in helping readers assess Mo Yan's depiction of specific characters correctly. For example, during a particularly violent scene in *Life and Death Are Wearing Me Out*, Shangguan Jintong hears his mother, Shangguan Lu, "utter loud prayers: Old Man in Heaven, Dear Lord, Blessed Virgin Mary, Guanyin Bodhisattva of the Southern Sea, please protect [my daughter] Niandi and all the children" (281). Readers are cautioned against reading this prayer as characterizing Lu as befuddled by the incredible trauma of the moment or as uneducated. Such blendings of various religious beliefs are part and parcel of all religions, especially so during the age of globalization. Indeed, Lu's knowledge of the major figures of folk religions, Christianity, and Buddhism attest to her transcultural awareness of various traditions that have made their way into even her small town in the Shandong Province.

In terms of Chinese Buddhism, the textbook presents how the different Buddhist traditions from India entered new cultural settings in China over a period of centuries, blending with concepts and values of Chinese culture. However, the globalization of Buddhism during the past half-century or so has been rapid and worldwide, with international and interregional flows producing Buddhist networks through which influence and change happens in all directions. What happens in Chinese Buddhist communities in one country can influence and shape what develops in Chinese Buddhist communities in other parts of the world; and these latter developments can in turn flow back to the country that originated them in the first place. This fact is in part due to how globalization enables any Buddhist group to become internationalized, to found temples, Dharma centers, and local communities in countries far from the group's place of origin. In doing so, Buddhist groups adapt by tailoring teachings to multiple cultures at the same time. This kind of globalization is something new in the history of the world (for an overview of this phenomenon, see Csordas).

When scholars of Buddhism first wrote about the flows of Buddhism outside Asia, they often used the term "West." They spoke about the "Westernization of Buddhism," the "Western transformation of Buddhism," "Buddhism in the West," or just "Western Buddhism." However, the "West" is not just a geographical term. It is used to refer to the "First World," namely, Western Europe, North America, and Australia, to the exclusion of not only Asia in the East but also Africa and South America in the South. In a broader sense, "West" refers to countries that are developed, urbanized, secular, and capitalist. The Second World and Third World are left out. Scholars today note that the globalization of Buddhism actually includes a diversity of non-Asian countries from "first" to "third" with the result being Global Buddhism. Further, the notion of "Buddhism in the West" implied one-directional flows of Asian Buddhism to the West, where it was modified to fit Western cultures. However, today scholars have shown that many modern forms of Asian Buddhism have developed due to colonialist incursions into Asia, or later non-Asian influences in Asia. This phenomenon produced a kind of "modern Buddhism" that has been exported to non-Asian countries only to be repackaged and returned to Asia and to other regions of the non-Asian world. For example, books written by Asian intellectuals influenced by the West, like D. T. Suzuki's *Essays in Zen Buddhism: First Series*, present a spiritualized, universalized, and purified Buddhism focusing on meditation and enlightenment, not on specific cultural beliefs, practices, devotions, rituals, rites, and ancestor worship stressed by traditional Asian Buddhism. This modern Buddhism in turn has had influence in parts of Asia and has become popular in many countries outside Asia. It was also easier to modify to fit different cultural situations since it left the original Asian cultures behind. Outside of Asia, this kind of sterilized modern Buddhism became known as "convert Buddhism" since it was not practiced by Asian communities. The latter kind of Buddhism became known as "immigrant Buddhism." What is interesting about the globalization of Chinese Buddhism from Taiwan is that, unlike reified "modern Buddhism," it does bring Chinese culture with it, and it is taken up by not just Chinese persons living in non-Asian countries but also by persons indigenous to those countries, too. The concluding chapter of the third edition of the textbook presents how Chinese Buddhism has spread to other countries and has educated non-Asian practitioners from those countries in the cultural aspects of China that are rooted in Buddhism. These involve inclusive cultural events that possess a particularly artistic bent.

Fo Guang Shan's Greater Boston Buddhist Cultural Center (GBBCC), for example, opened in 1999: today about half of their members are Euro-Americans. Their mission is to "express Buddhist teachings through cultural activities." This is the mission of almost all of the Fo Guang Shan centers around the world. They have educational courses and cultural events including Chinese art exhibitions, classes in the Chinese language, literature, crafts, painting, calligraphy, and flower arranging. In these cultural events and classes, the centers present the Buddhist ideas and practices that are behind different kinds of Chinese cultural expressions. The GBBCC has cultural outreach programs to public schools and student tours of their Center. Outreach to schools includes talks about Buddhism and Chinese culture. When students visit the center, they are taught calligraphy and shown the cultural artifacts and worship areas in the center. They have a regional summer camp for older youth. It is through these kinds of cultural activities that Fo Guang Shan brings to the U.S. and other countries an understanding and appreciation for the Buddhist heritage of China expressed in its present-day literature.

Another example is from Africa—a place that one does not think of as a site for Buddhist missions outside of Asia. In 1992, when Fo Guang Shan decided that the best activity they could do in Africa was to work with orphans, they founded the Amitofo Care Center organization, with a base in South Africa for this work. The first orphanage was established in Malawi with living quarters, a pre-school, an elementary school, a medical center, an activity center, and a vocational training center. The children live in "family units" with sixteen to twenty children, a caregiver, cook, and teacher. New orphanages are now in Zimbabwe, Swaziland, and Lesotho. Fo Guang Shan expects to open orphanages in all countries in Africa. In order to support this effort, Fo Guang Shan has opened an African Buddhist Seminary in South Africa. It has around three hundred Africans from different counties in training for two to three years at no cost. When they complete their training, they can choose to return home to work with centers there, or they can work at the orphanages. This seminary project has enabled Fo Guang Shan to staff its existing orphanages and to open ones in countries of its newer seminarians. The cultural training of the seminarians is central. While Fo Guang Shan inculturates itself in the African cultures, it also teaches Chinese Buddhism and its cultural expressions.

We can see in these two examples how global flows of traditional Chinese Buddhism into other countries bring about an adaption of ancient lineages to the conditions of contemporary non-Asian cultures. Innovations by Chinese Buddhist communities repackage Chinese cultural expressions in ways that speak to non-Asian cultures and provide more global understanding and appreciation for contemporary Chinese culture. The global spread of Chinese Buddhism today presents us with a fascinating story of the global weaving of new intercultural threads.

"The Cultural Experience of Buddhism in America Today"

At the end of the final chapter in the textbook is an essay entitled "A Cultural Experience of Buddhism in America Today" by Heng Sure (恆實) from the Berkeley Buddhist Monastery (410-15). Heng Sure points out that elements of Chinese Buddhist culture are replicated by immigrant communities in the U.S. *O-Bon* festivals that are celebrated in Japantowns. Chinese Buddhist organizations and temples like the ones mentioned previously celebrate the Buddha's birthday and other festivals, hold classes on Chinese Buddhist culture, and provide cultural sites, events, and activities for the general public. He then speaks about how a typical U.S. resident is affected by these popular cultural elements of Chinese Buddhism. Heng Sure grew up in the Midwest as a Methodist named Christopher R. Clowery (his birth name). He not only came to understand and appreciate Chinese culture but also converted to Buddhism and joined a Chinese order of monks. The present discussion is not interested in this kind of religious journey but in the ways in which the globalization of Chinese Buddhism has given persons around the world a context in which they can better understand contemporary Chinese literature. Heng Sure goes a bit further: he presents in his essay a connection between both his heritage culture (the U.S. culture of his birth) and his adopted culture (the Chinese culture of his choice), neither of which is forfeited. Some of his insights may be valuable to U.S. readers who not only want to understand what a Chinese author is saying about certain Buddhist beliefs and values but also compare them to the beliefs and values of U.S. culture. Such comparative religious exploration parallels with comparative literature in ways that can intersect and thereby engage in a deep level of comparative cultural studies.

We take two examples that often appear in Mo Yan's works: bowing or kowtowing and holding out a food bowl. Bowing is a pervasive practice in Chinese Buddhist culture. This is not part of U.S. culture and at first feels forced and uncomfortable. But the value here is a humble respect for others and for cultivating a nature that creates relatedness and care. It eliminates pride and makes room for connection and fellowship. Heng points out that for him this resonated with values that are part of U.S. culture informed not by Buddhism but by Christianity. Without advocating religiosity, many of Mo Yan's literary representations of bowing demonstrate the compulsion rather than joyous willingness to which this originally enlightening practice has degenerated at particular historical moments in twentieth-century China. Mo Yan's organization of material is often stunning by the ease with which he reflects the seamlessness of the religious and political under the umbrella of the cultural or literary. In *Sandalwood Death*, the fictional but verisimilar ritual of the executioners starts with lighting sandalwood incense, asking for the blessing of the "Patriarch" spirit, then kowtowing: he "went on down on his knees ... banged his head loudly against the brick floor." Then, after sacrificing a rooster, the narrator explains that he joins in and "[we] fell to our knees, and kowtowed three times" (38). Hours later, at the announcement of the entry of "His Majesty the Emperor!" the myriads of assembled women, eunuchs, and officials "sank to the ground" to kowtow (40). The mirrored enactment evinces and reinforces the hierarchical organization of both the spiritual and political system.

Another aspect is monks walking with alms-bowls through the streets. At first this might look like begging, but the deeper meaning is what is called being "fields of blessings." That is, the monks provide the laypeople the opportunity to practice generosity to a person in need of food. Such an act of loving care for those is need brings that person blessings. Heng Sure saw in this Buddhist custom a value that also resonates with the U.S. religious-based cultural value of helping those in need. Mo Yan provides numerous images of a character holding out a bowl, assuming at least a Chinese readership that will understand how the image reverberates with this common sight. At times, the image is used for comic effect, as when children are overly but charmingly greedy; at other times, however, it is used for tragic effect, as in *Big Breasts and Wide Hips*, when the already-paltry food rationing of six ounces is reduced to four ounces, and a number of starving females are reduced to trading sex for food from officials. The juxtaposition of the origins of the begging bowl and this image is indeed part of Mo Yan's artistic acumen that might go unnoticed by those unaware of the practices of Chinese Buddhism.

One could argue that the breadth of outreach of Chinese Buddhism on a global scale is narrow, providing only a few readers of contemporary Chinese fiction with a Buddhist contextual understanding of contemporary Chinese literature. However, the demographics tell a different story. Besides the Taiwan Buddhist movements described earlier, two large modern movements from Japan, the Rissho Kosei-kai and Soka Gakkai International, have a strong presence around the world today. Much of their beliefs and cultural forms relate to the Chinese Tiantai tradition. From Korea has come a new movement called Won Buddhism. And from Vietnam, Thich Nhat Hanh's Order of Interbeing has become popular, with 160 centers in Europe alone. Admitting and analytically exploring cultural overlap among countries that have fought violently over erstwhile geographical overlaps is a much more difficult pursuit in real life than it reads on the page. Scholars and citizens are invited to be humble about the influence they believe they can wield through their endeavors. Yet, with such humility, coupled with some knowledge of cultural and religious traditions, they may at least chronicle these developments and silently applaud positive ones wherever they crop up. Besides these newer movements, the more traditional forms of Chinese Buddhism or other national or regional forms of Buddhism influenced by China have developed a global presence. Chinese Buddhists arrived in Canada in the 1850s and were followed by Japanese Buddhists in the 1880s. Chinese immigrants have been in Australia and New Zealand since the mid-1800s, followed by Japanese and later by Koreans. Today, almost 7% of the New Zealand population is Buddhist and of these, 20% is Euro-New Zealanders. In Latin America, Buddhism goes back to the 1920s when Japanese immigrants arrived. At the start of the twenty-first century, Buddhism is the second largest religion in Brazil, with a strong cultural influence in the country. Sri Lankan Buddhists immigrated to Africa in the early twentieth century. They were followed later by Chinese, Japanese, and Vietnamese forms of Buddhism. While influence there is still small, it is growing owing to connections to East Asian Buddhist communities in Europe, especially France and Germany.

In the U.S., the first Chinese Buddhist temple was built in San Francisco in 1853. Twenty years later, there were hundreds of such temples in the West.

With changes to the immigration laws in the 1960s, traditional Chinese Buddhist communities experienced a large influx from China, Taiwan, and Hong Kong. By 2000 there were over two hundred Chinese Buddhist communities in the U.S. We have seen the same kind of growth with Japanese, Korean, and Vietnamese Buddhism. Most of these communities have outreach programs presenting East Asian Buddhist culture to Euro-Americans. As it turns out, then, the thousands of students who have read the China chapter in *Buddhism: Introducing the Buddhist Experience*, mostly U.S. natives, have in fact been learning about some threads of their own heritage no matter where in the world they have come from. They have also inadvertently been gaining the methodologies and knowledge base that can aid them in appreciating their own literature and Chinese literature in a more capacious way than they would have otherwise. One can see that as more modern Chinese literature is being translated and read by non-Asian readers, there are also more Chinese or Chinese-related resources available to provide firsthand experience of the religious contexts of what is being presented in this growing literature. As more university students take courses in religious studies and Asian studies, they gain the knowledge needed to understand better contemporary novels written by Chinese authors such as Mo Yan.

Mo Yan's Wise Monk Lan and Pastor Malory

Our analysis of two of Mo Yan's characters shows how some knowledge of global religions yields richer interpretations of contemporary literary works: Wise Monk Lan in *POW!* and the Swedish Pastor Malory in *Big Breasts and Wide Hips*. In *POW!* Wise Monk Lan possesses the major characteristics associated with Buddhism: serenity, silence, and physical austerity. The monk is introduced as "wearing a cassock that looks like it's made of rain-soaked toilet paper, which will crumble at the slightest touch, he fingers a string of purple prayer beads. Flies have settled on the Wise Monk's earlobes, but on his shaved head or oily face" (2) and is described often in such phrases as sitting "in a repose greater than the Horse Spirit behind him" (100). But the introduction is also infused with accurate references to the monk's wide-ranging experiences in the mundane world. He is someone "who has roamed the four corners of the earth, his whereabouts always a mystery, but who is, for the moment, living in an abandoned little temple" (2). Nonetheless, the amazon.com description of Wise Monk Lan as a "benign old monk" ignores his unusual form of "qigong breathing exercise" ("*POW!*" <http://www.amazon.com/Pow-Mo-Yan/dp/0857420763>). Qigong is a Chinese practice found in both Daoism and Buddhism, especially in the martial arts associated with Buddhism, and today some Chinese Buddhist groups outside Asia present it in their cultural classes having to do with health. In Qigong, breath, movement, and awareness align to cultivate and balance qi, or life energy, but the Wise Monk practices it in "a unique way" (75): "Folding up his body, he takes his *penis* in his *mouth* and rolls round on his wide bed like a wind-up toy with a taut spring. Steam rises from his shaved head in seven distinct colors. At first, I didn't think much of his trifling exercise regimen, but when I tried it I realized that rolling round on the bed is no big deal, nor is folding up my body that way, but taking my penis in my mouth—now that's a challenge" (75).

One wonders if Mo Yan is responding here to the new interest in Tantric Buddhism in China as presented in Mitchell's textbook. While this is not a Buddhist practice by any means, the sexual element reminds one of Buddhist Tantra. Wise Monk Lan's combination of his worldly travels and this practice aligns with the Buddhist temple god featured in the novel, the Wutong Spirit, the Meat God. The god of Wise Monk's temple is also highly sexualized. The narrator describes the large idol of the Wutong Spirit as follows: "First the face—a captivating face—then the neck—the spot where the human and horse necks ingeniously meet evokes seductive eroticism—and then lower, stopping at the unnaturally large genitals—testicles the size of papayas and a half-exposed penis that looks like a laundry paddle emerging from a red sheath" (173). The sexuality of Mo Yan's monk and Meat God is consistent with the earliest representations of divine beings. T. Patrick Burke notes that one of the earliest stone carvings of a pre-Vedic god has "buffalo horns rising out of his head, a fierce look on his face, sitting nude in what can only be the posture of a yogi, with a prominent phallus, the symbol of sexual potency, and surrounded by wild animals" (18). That sexuality represents potency and promise for the future and thus figures for religion itself.

This characteristic retains and develops with the character of Pastor Malory in *Big Breasts and Wide Hips*. With Lu, Pastor Malory fathers twins: son Jingtong and daughter Yunu. With the Muslim woman, he also fathers another son, who grows up to be a pastor as well. The main narrator Jingtong meets his half-brother at the very conclusion of the novel, described in a way that speaks to great characteristics of religion: "introductions were unnecessary, because even before she spoke our names, God had already revealed our origins to one another. This bastard son of Pastor Malory and a Muslim woman, my half brother, wrapped his hairy arms around me and held me tight. With tears filling his eyes, he said: 'I have been waiting for you for a very long time, my brother!'" (532). Religious studies scholars will recognize the novel's surprise ending as integrating the foundational, mythic ideal of human brotherhood found in the texts of many traditions. It coordinates in the Judeo-Christian tradition with the story of Joseph, who embraces his brother despite the brothers having left him for dead years ago, crying "*I am Joseph your brother*, whom you sold into Egypt" (Genesis 45.5). This mythic moment is as numbing for readers as it is for Jingtong. Pastor Malory had strongly embraced China, learning the language and fighting for citizens, both those who were members of his congregation and those who were not. Yet, he departs from practicing regulations for Christian clergy in engaging in sex with the Muslim woman and Lu, and for all Christians, in committing suicide. His transgressions, however, are assuaged narratively by the overwhelmingly positive nature of the concluding reunion, so welcome after the devastation of the Lu family and of the rural township. In Jingtong and the younger Pastor Malory is the expression of past romantic relationships and of the physical and mental strength of both sons to survive: this is the promise of a future that combines the two major Western-founded religions of Islam and Christianity into the East.

Similarly, *Buddhism: Introducing the Buddhist Experience* also presents the coming of Western religions into Asia and their new growth in China, especially Christianity. The background provided by that textbook as well as other nonfiction books under the keywords "religious studies" and "Asian studies" would at least enable readers of Mo Yan's novels to understand the religious roots of all major writings. This is not the case with just Mo Yan or just Buddhism. What Joanna Brooks writes of Christianity can be said of Buddhism and all other major religions: "Remembering the worldliness of religion is especially important" (951). The contextualization of contemporary Chinese literature for non-Chinese readers is certainly being expanded by scholarly textbooks as well as by cultural courses, expositions, lectures, and exhibits in Chinese Buddhist centers around the world. Looking at comparative literature in general, we can see that Frye was correct in saying that sacred texts and the traditions that express those texts pervade art and literature. In the globalization of the modern world, a global vision of world religions is important to contextualize our understanding of world literatures.

Works Cited

A World without Thieves (天下無賊). Dir. Xiaogang Feng (馮小剛). Shanghai: Huayi Brothers, 2004.

Basho. "Old Pond." *A Little Zen Companion*. Ed. David Schiller. New York: Workman, 1994. 215.

Brooks, Joanna. "Soul Matters." *PMLA: Publications of the Modern Language Association* 128.4 (2013): 947-52.

Burke, T. Patrick. *The Major Religions: An Introduction with Texts*. Malden: Blackwell, 2004.

Cheng Yen. *Three Ways to the Pure Land: Lectures by Dharma Master Cheng Yen*. Taipei: Tzu Chi Cultural Publishers, 2001.

Csordas, Thomas J. *Transnational Transcendence: Essays on Religion and Globalization*. Berkeley: U of California P, 2009.

Du, Lanlan. "Abortion in Faulkner's *The Wild Palms* and Mo Yan's 蛙 (Frog)." *Mo Yan in Context: Nobel Laureate and Global Storyteller*. Ed. Angelica Duran and Yuhan Huang. West Lafayette: Purdue UP, 2014. 63–76.

Durkheim, Emile. *Elementary Forms of Religious Life*. Trans. Joseph Ward Swain. New York: Macmillan, 1915.

Eliade, Mircea. *The Sacred and the Profane: The Nature of Religion*. Trans. Willard R. Trask. New York: Harcourt Brace, 1959.
Frye, Northrop. *The Great Code: The Bible and Literature*. New York: Harcourt Brace Jovanovich, 1982.
Heng, Sure, and Heng, Ch'au. *News for True Cultivators: Letters to the Venerable Abbot Hua*. Burlingame, CA: Buddhist Text Translation Society, 2003.
Hsing Yun. *Lotus in a Stream*. New York: Weatherhill, 2000.
James, William. *The Varieties of Religious Experience: A Study of Human Nature*. New York: Modern Library, 1902.
Knight, Sabina. *Chinese Literature: A Very Short Introduction*. Oxford: Oxford UP, 2012.
Mitchell, Donald W. *Buddhism: Introducing the Buddhist Experience*. Oxford: Oxford UP, 2003.
Mitchell, Donald W. *Buddhism: Introducing the Buddhist Experience*. Oxford: Oxford UP, 2008.
Mitchell, Donald W., and Sarah H. Jacoby. *Buddhism: Introducing the Buddhist Experience*. Oxford: Oxford UP, 2014.
Mo Yan. *Big Breasts and Wide Hips*. Trans. Howard Goldblatt. New York: Arcade, 2004.
Mo Yan (莫言). 蛙 (Frog). Shanghai: Shanghai Literature and Art P, 2012.
Mo Yan. *Life and Death Are Wearing Me Out*. Trans. Howard Goldblatt. New York: Arcade, 2008.
Mo Yan. *POW!*. Trans. Howard Goldblatt. New York: Seagull, 2012.
Mo Yan. *Sandalwood Death*. Trans. Howard Goldblatt. Norman: U of Oklahoma P, 2013.
Pinxten, Rik. "Comparative Cultural Studies and Cultural Anthropology." *Companion to Comparative Literature, World Literatures, and Comparative Cultural Studies*. Ed. Steven Tötösy de Zepetnek and Tutun Mukherjee. New Delhi: Cambridge UP India, 2013. 112-23.
"*POW!* By Mo Yan." *amazon.com* (2012): <http://www.amazon.com/Pow-Mo-Yan/dp/0857420763>.
Sheng, Yen. *Attaining the Way: A Guide to the Practice of Chan Buddhism*. Boston: Shambhala Publishing, 2013.
Soetaert, Donald, and Kris Rutten. "Comparative Cultural Studies and Pedagogy." *Companion to Comparative Literature, World Literatures, and Comparative Cultural Studies*. Ed. Steven Tötösy de Zepetnek and Tutun Mukherjee. New Delhi: Cambridge UP India, 2013. 63-74.
Suzuki, D. T. *Essays in Zen Buddhism: First Series*. New York: Grove P, 1929.
Wang, Chi-ying Alice. "Mo Yan's *The Garlic Ballads* and *Life and Death Are Wearing Me Out* in the Context of Religious and Chinese Literary Conventions." *Mo Yan in Context: Nobel Laureate and Global Storyteller*. Ed. Angelica Duran and Yuhan Huang. West Lafayette: Purdue UP, 2014. 123–37.
Wang, Jinghui. "Religious Elements in Mo Yan's and Yan Lianke's Works." *Mo Yan in Context: Nobel Laureate and Global Storyteller*. Ed. Angelica Duran and Yuhan Huang. West Lafayette: Purdue UP, 2014. 139–52.
Wei, Dedong. *The Essence of Buddhist Yogacara Philosophy*. Gaoxiong: Fokuangshan P, 2001.

Authors' profiles

Donald Mitchell is founder of the Religious Studies Program at Purdue University, where he taught philosophy and religious studies. In addition to numerous articles, his book publications include *Spirituality and Emptiness: The Dynamics of Spiritual Life in Buddhism and Christianity* (1991), *Masao Abe: A Zen Life of Dialogue* (1998), *The Gethsemani Encounter: A Dialogue on the Spiritual Life by Buddhist and Christian Monastics* (1999), and *Buddhism: Introducing the Buddhist Experience* (2003, 2008; and with Sarah H. Jacoby, 2014).

Author's profile

Angelica Duran teaches English, comparative literature, and religious studies at Purdue University. Her interests in scholarship include comparative literature, disability studies, and Renaissance British literature. In addition to numerous articles and chapters, Duran's single-authored book publications include *The Age of Milton and the Scientific Revolution* (2007) and her edited volumes include *A Concise Companion to Milton* (2007) and *The King James Bible across Borders and Centuries* (2014).

Epilogue

Soul Searching in Contemporary Chinese Literature and Society

Fenggang Yang

Abstract

In "Soul Searching in Contemporary Chinese Literature and Society" Fenggang Yang presents a brief overview of religion in China's recent past and contemporary situation. Based on his own life experiences in rural China and his education in China and the U.S., Yang discusses the status and history of religion during the Cultural Revolution, the 1980s and 1990s, and more recent developments of the interest in and the revival of religion in China. Yang's description includes attention to the role of writers such as Xingjian Gao and Mo Yan as prime examples in whose works religion plays a significant role.

To discuss the question of soul searching in Chinese literature and society, I will start with a brief biography situated in Chinese history. As the sociologist C. Wright Mills wrote, "the sociological imagination enables us to grasp history and biography and the relations between the two within society. This is its task and its promise" (6). Through a biographical account of the changes since the Cultural Revolution, I offer a personal observation of the quiet spiritual revolution that is like wildfire sweeping a vast land and a sociologist's reflection on the failure of Chinese literature to capture the spirit of the era yet its great potential to do so. This account includes a description of my rural upbringing, not all that distinct from Mo Yan's; my witnessing of the events in China in the late 1980s before moving to the U.S.; my experience of the freedoms my children have enjoyed in being raised in the U.S.; and my ongoing effort to bridge China and the U.S. through scholarship and scholarly networks.

My main point is that Chinese souls have been caged by traditionalism, modernism, Marxist-Leninist-Maoist atheism, and totalitarianism, and so are the souls of Chinese novelists. Although China is undergoing dramatic social changes and great spiritual awakening, producing great Chinese literature has been hampered. Yet, in or through literature, with Mo Yan's work as a key example, we have seen some souls slip out of the cage and wander, a bit in the dark but wander nonetheless: the oppressed souls of the class enemies of materialism, existentialism, and humanism; the lost souls of the youth (the Red Guards in the dim mist); and the "wanderer" of the 2000 Nobel Prize in Literature Laureate Xingjian Gao, in France now, on his way to Soul Mountain.

I was in college from 1978 to 1982, the second cohort after the universities were reopened after the Cultural Revolution. In fact, when I was in high school, I did not know there was such a thing called university. My first English sentence learned in high school was "Long live Chairman Mao!" But Mao died later that year, and our English class stopped right there. From elementary school to high school, we spent a lot of time learning to do farming, factory work, or military exercises instead of reading and writing. Growing up in a rural village in Hebei in northern China, I tried various ways to find books to read and would boast that I read all the books available in my village and the school. But the only available books I could find were Chairman Mao's *The Little Red Book*, a revolutionary novel called 小兵张嘎 (Little Soldier Zhang Ga) (Xu), and some novels of the socialist rural life by Ran Hao (浩然), such as the 1972 novel 艳阳天 (Bright Sunny Sky) and Nikolai Ostrovsky's Soviet novel 钢铁是怎样炼成的 (*How the Steel was Tempered*). We did not even have textbooks every semester, and the ones we did occasionally get, including textbooks of mathematics and biology, had a citation of Chairman Mao's words at the start of each lesson. As a matter of fact, I still remember what Mao said about farming: the eight characters constitution: 土肥水种密保管工 (eight factors from soil to labor).

During those childhood years, the best time was perhaps on a summer night sitting under the sky, fanning away mosquitoes, and hearing some senior villager holding a long tobacco pipe telling ghost stories. Ghost stories were the closest thing we had to religion back then. During the Cultural Revolution, religion was banned. There was not a single church, temple, or mosque open for religious services for Chinese in the whole country. All of the publications available to school students were cleansed of the so-called feudalistic superstitions and capitalist poisonous weeds. While religion was wiped out of society, ghosts, spirits, and gods were exorcised out of the literature, movies, mass media, and publications. Decades later, when I saw my U.S.-born children enjoying *Harry Potter* novels and films, I was happy and envious because when I was a child this was impossible for me to experience. My childhood was much too dry, boring, and lacking intellectual stimulation. There was no music either, other than revolutionary songs and operas. At school, if there was anything we learned about religion, it was the Marxist adage that religion is the opium of the people and that only oppressed and weak people would resort to superstitious beliefs. In the rural community in northern China where I grew up religion was not part of village life. Other than the few ghost stories told by elders, I can only recall one single occasion seeing some Daoist ritualists performing at a funeral. Upon hearing ghost stories or seeing a ritual, people, at least my peers, would simply laugh it off. We were taught at school that we must establish a "scientific" outlook on life, and it was believed that only science and technology and Mao Zedong's thought would make society progress toward the future beautiful communist society.

Upon entering university, I frequented the library and read almost all the Chinese classic novels I could borrow. While moving to read Western classic novels translated to Chinese, however, suddenly the novels and short stories by contemporary Chinese writers became interesting to me. One of the most fascinating was Ping Li's (礼平) 1981 novella 晚霞消失的时候 (When the Sunset Cloud Disappears), which portrays the protagonist, a Red Guard, as a man who struggles with notions of science and Marxist dialectic materialism for many years. Fortuitously, he runs into a Buddhist monk on the holy mountain of Taishan and engages in a long, enlightening conversation along the way hiking up to the top of the mountain. This novella instantly became politically controversial but popular among university students because of its departure from ideological orthodoxy. It also stirred heated debates among readers about science and religion. Religious clergy, once ridiculed and driven out of public sight, might hold some enlightening truths to the questions with which many young people were struggling. This idea itself was subversive at that time but stimulated truth-seekers to begin their search in religion as well as in other realms.

In 1991 the celebrated novelist Chengzhi Zhang (张承志), once a Maoist Red Guard himself, published the book 心灵史 (History of the Soul), which features his embrace of his rediscovered Islamic identity. Meanwhile, Xingjian Gao, until recently the best-known Chinese writer in the West and winner of the 2000 Nobel Prize in Literature, had also written novels in the late 1980s and early 1990s exploring spiritual themes in his novels such as 靈山 (*Soul Mountain*) and 一個人的聖經 (*One Man's Bible*). His characters were obviously spiritual seekers, but they commonly ended up hopelessly wandering without finding a spiritual home but finding a lot of sex. Indeed, throughout the 1980s and 1990s many Chinese intellectuals, novelists, poets, artists, and scholars have explored spiritual issues and sought religious answers. There have been some good articles published in China and the West on these issues, including Qiaomei Li's (李俏梅) "论中国当代作家的'宗教热'" ("On the 'Religious Fever' among Contemporary Writers of China"), Michelle Yeh's "The 'Cult of Poetry' in Contemporary China," and Rongan Cai's (蔡燊安) "宗教热: 灵魂的痛楚—对近年来美术创作流向的一种考察" ("Religious Fever: Pains of Souls—A Thought about a Trend of Art Creation in Recent Years") (see also Yang, "Between Secularist"). Clearly there was an enthusiastic search for spirituality and religion by Chinese intellectuals in the 1980s and 1990s.

Following the Cultural Revolution, in society at large all kinds of religions have been revived and are thriving in China. In 1987 I joined the faculty of Religious Studies at the People's University of China before coming to the U.S. in 1989. In the Introduction to the Study of Religion course I taught for a semester, to my surprise about 120 students of various departments were enrolled. Besides the curious and enthusiastic students, I also found devout believers at tourist or religious sites wherever I went. Through a series of fortuitous opportunities or by Divine Providence as one might say, I arrived at the Catholic University of America in Washington, D.C. in January 1989 and began my PhD in the sociology of religion. On 4 June of that summer, the Chinese communist authorities sent tanks into Tiananmen Square and crushed the democracy movement. After that, many Chinese students and scholars studying in the U.S. began to flock to Christian churches. Later I found the same change had happened within Mainland China. I have been drawn into this unprecedented cultural and social phenomenon of mass conversion to Christianity in the history of China and Chinese America and have conducted a number of empirical studies of it. Since 2000, I have been traveling to China every year to conduct research on Christians, Buddhists, Muslims, Confucians, and others. In my recent book *Religion in China: Survival and Revival under Communist Rule*, I summarize my empirical studies and theoretical development. My theories of the red, black, and gray markets of religion and the shortage in the economy of religion have caused me notoriety in China and elsewhere in the world.

By now it has become clear to me that 1989 is a watershed year in Chinese history in regard to the spiritual search and religious change. After the democracy movement was crushed, for example, a young couple who were Peking University professors quit and became Daoist-like hermits in the mountains, some college graduates became Buddhist monks, and many more college students, professors, and young professionals converted to Christianity. Of course, even more people dived into the ocean of market economy and became devoted to materialism, consumerism, and capitalism, which may be taken as substitutes of religion (see, e.g., Yang, "Lost in the Market"). The rise of Christianity is especially interesting and may bring profound changes in Chinese society and may also have long-term impact on other parts of the world.

In the 1980s Christianity spread fast in rural areas, and in the 1990s there was the rise of the so-called "cultural Christians" on university campuses by people who were attracted by the culture of Christianity, including its literature, philosophy, theology, arts, and history. Then, the market transition brought the phenomenon of Christian entrepreneurs, especially those in Wenzhou and other coastal regions. Further, in the twenty-first century there have been active Christian lawyers defending civil and human rights for marginalized people, artists creating paintings and sculptures with Christian themes, and Christian journalists taking positions in the mass media and press. Meanwhile, in China's emerging civil society Christian charity organizations have been active in providing social services, and Christian house churches in metropolises have challenged the Party-State to adapt and adjust. The Party-State tries hard to hold on to an outdated atheist ideology and suppress religion. Since 2005, in many metropolises some Christian house churches have formed large congregations and rented halls in office buildings for Sunday worship services. Many of the house-church members are university-educated young professionals. The Party-State has pressured these young professionals to join Party-State-controlled "patriotic" religious associations, but most of the house churches have refused to comply. Then, the Party-State began to crack down on the large congregations of house churches. For example, since the Easter of 2011, the Shouwang Church (守望教会) in Beijing has been evicted from its rental place and prohibited from entering the property it purchased. Also, its leaders have been under house arrest. However, every Sunday morning there has been a group of church members trying to gather at a square for an outdoor worship service. Every Sunday one to three dozen people would be rounded up and taken to the police station. The confrontation continues at the time of this volume's publication.

In brief, all kinds of religions are surviving and thriving in China. There has been a great awakening with various spiritual movements. In Europe and the U.S., dramatic social changes have generated some great novels that are both reflective of the era and inspirational in some eternally relevant spiritual dimensions. However, so far I have not seen an outpouring of Chinese novels like those in the modern West and I wonder why. I think it is because Chinese souls are in cages. There is the cage of modernism, the cage of Marxist-Maoist atheism, the cage of totalitarianism, and the cage of traditionalism. Chinese souls were caged especially during the Cultural Revolution. The forming of the modernist cage can be traced back to the May Fourth and New Cultural Movements about a century ago. These two cages are still in place today. In or through literature, we have seen some souls slip out of the cage and wander in the dark, as noted. Of particular interest here is the fact that Mo Yan's prolific novels have vividly portrayed some beleaguered souls as a result of the social and political struggles. Of equal interest is the fact that he has rarely mentioned any religious believer. What will emancipate the souls in bondage? Will the thriving religions in China emancipate the souls or enforce the cages? We have seen only a few glimpses of the searching souls in literature, but sociologists have observed and study the quiet spiritual revolution that is sweeping the vast lands of China like wildfire.

Works Cited

Cai, Rongan (蔡燊安). "宗教热：灵魂的痛楚——对近年来美术创作流向的一种考察" ("Religious Fever: Pains of Souls—A Thought about a Trend of Art Creation in Recent Years"). *Jiangxi Normal University Journal* 2 (2002): 74-77.

Gao, Xingjian (高行健). 一個人的聖經 (*One Man's Bible*). Taipei: Lianjing Publishing, 1999.

Gao, Xingjian. *One Man's Bible*. Trans. Mabel Lee. Sydney: HarperCollins, 2002.

Gao, Xingjian (高行健). 靈山 (*Soul Mountain*). Taipei: Lianjing Publishing, 1990.

Gao, Xingjian. *Soul Mountain*. Trans. Mabel Lee. Sydney: HarperCollins, 2000.

Hao, Ran (浩然). 艳阳天 (Bright Sunny Sky). Beijing: Ren min wen xue chubanshe, 1972.

Li, Ping (礼平). 晚霞消失的时候 (When the Sunset Cloud Disappears). Beijing: Zhongguo qing nian chubanshe, 1981.

Li, Qiaomei (李俏梅). "论中国当代作家的 宗教热" ("On the 'Religious Fever' among Contemporary Writers of China"). *Guangdong Social Sciences* 4 (1996): 106-11.

Mills, C. Wright. *The Sociological Imagination*. Oxford: Oxford UP, 1959.

Ostrovsky, Nikolai (Островский, Николай). *How the Steel was Tempered: A Novel in Two Parts*. Trans. R. Prokofieva (Прокофьева, R.). Moskva: Foreign Languages Publishing, 1952 [serial 1932-1934; book 1936].

Ostrovsky, Nikolai (奥斯特洛夫斯基, 尼古拉). 钢铁是怎样炼成的 (*How the Steel was Tempered*). Trans. Sha Mi (沙密). Chongqing: Guo xun shu dian, 1934.

Xu, Guangjao (徐光耀著). 小兵张嘎 (Little Soldier Zhang Ga). Beijing: Zhong guo shao nian er tong chubanshe, 1962.

Yang, Fenggang. "Between Secularist Ideology and Desecularizing Reality: The Birth and Growth of Religious Research in Communist China." *The Sociology of Religion: A Quarterly Review* 65 (2004): 101-19.

Yang, Fenggang. "Lost in the Market, Saved at McDonald's: Conversion to Christianity in Urban China." *Journal for the Scientific Study of Religion* 44 (2005): 423-41.

Yang, Fenggang. *Religion in China: Survival and Revival under Communist Rule*. Oxford: Oxford UP, 2013.

Yeh, Michelle. "The 'Cult of Poetry' in Contemporary China." *Journal of Asian Studies* 55 (1996): 51-61.

Zhang, Chengzhi (张承志). 心灵史 (History of the Soul). Beijing: Huancheng chubanshe, 1991.

Author's profile

Fenggang Yang teaches sociology at Purdue University. In addition to numerous articles in English and Chinese, his single-authored book publications in English include *Chinese Christians in America: Conversion, Assimilation, and Adhesive Identities* (1999) and *Religion in China: Survival and Revival under Communist Rule* (2012), and his recent edited volumes include *Confucianism and Spiritual Traditions in Modern China and Beyond* (with Joseph Tamney, 2011) and *Social Scientific Studies of Religion in China: Methodology, Theories, and Findings* (with Graeme Lang, 2011).

Selected Bibliography of and about Mo Yan's Work in Chinese and English

Angelica Duran and Yuhan Huang

Note

The bibliography does not include shorter texts or scholarly articles published in journals. In the case of Mo Yan's texts, titles are listed in chronologically ascending order to show the evolution of his oeuvre and in the case of secondary sources about his oeuvre items are listed alphabetically according to title. All translations from Chinese to English are by Yuhan Huang.

Mo Yan's novels published in English

Mo Yan. *Explosions and Other Stories*. Trans. Janice Wickeri. Hong Kong: Chinese U of Hong Kong, 1991.
Mo Yan. *Red Sorghum: A Novel of China*. Trans. Howard Goldblatt. New York: Viking, 1993.
Mo Yan. *The Garlic Ballads*. Trans. Howard Goldblatt. New York: Viking, 1995.
Mo Yan. *The Republic of Wine*. Trans. Howard Goldblatt. New York: Arcade, 2000.
Mo Yan. *Shifu, You'll Do Anything for a Laugh*. Trans. Howard Goldblatt. New York: Arcade, 2001.
Mo Yan. *Big Breasts and Wide Hips*. Trans. Howard Goldblatt. New York: Arcade, 2004.
Mo Yan. *Life and Death Are Wearing Me Out*. Trans. Howard Goldblatt. New York: Arcade, 2008.
Mo Yan. *Change*. Trans. Howard Goldblatt. London: Seagull, 2010.
Mo Yan. *POW!* Trans. Howard Goldblatt. London: Seagull, 2012.
Mo Yan. *Sandalwood Death*. Trans. Howard Goldblatt. Norman: U of Oklahoma P, 2013.

Mo Yan's work published in Chinese

Novels

Mo Yan (莫言). 红高粱家族 (*Red Sorghum*). Beijing: Jiefangjun wenyi chubanshe, 1987.
Mo Yan (莫言). 天堂蒜薹之歌 (*The Garlic Ballads*). Beijing: Zuojia chubanshe, 1988.

Mo Yan (莫言). 十三步 (Thirteen Steps). Beijing: Zuojia chubanshe, 1989.
Mo Yan (莫言). 酒国 (*The Republic of Wine*). Changsha: Hunan wenyi chubanshe, 1993.
Mo Yan (莫言). 愤怒的蒜薹 (The Garlic of Wrath). Beijing: Beishida chubanshe, 1993.
Mo Yan (莫言). 食草家族 (The Herbivorous Clan). Beijing: Huayi chubanshe, 1993.
Mo Yan (莫言). 丰乳肥臀 (*Big Breasts and Wide Hips*). Beijing: Zuojia chubanshe, 1995.
Mo Yan (莫言). 红树林 (Mangroves). Shenzhen: Haitian chubanshe, 1999.
Mo Yan (莫言). 檀香刑 (*Sandalwood Death*). Beijing: Zuojia chubanshe, 2001.
Mo Yan (莫言). 四十一炮 (*POW!*). Shenyang: Chunfeng wenyi chubanshe, 2003.
Mo Yan (莫言). 生死疲劳 (*Life and Death Are Wearing Me Out*). Beijing: Zuojia chubanshe, 2006.
Mo Yan (莫言). 蛙 (Frog). Shanghai: Shanghai wenyi chubanshe, 2012.

Collections of short stories, essays, speeches, and plays

Mo Yan (莫言). 透明的红萝卜 (The Crystal Carrot). Beijing: Zuojia chubanshe, 1986.
Mo Yan (莫言). 爆炸 (*Explosions and Other Stories*). Beijing: Jiefangjun wenyi chubanshe, 1988.
Mo Yan (莫言). 欢乐十三章 (Thirteen Chapters of Euphoria). Beijing: Zuojia chubanshe, 1989.
Mo Yan (莫言). 白棉花 (Cotton Fleece). Beijing: Huayi chubanshe, 1991.
Mo Yan (莫言). 金发婴儿 (The Golden-haired Baby). Wuhan: Changjiang wenyi chubanshe, 1993.
Mo Yan (莫言). 怀抱鲜花的女人 (A Woman Embracing Flowers). Beijing: Zhongguo shehui kexue chubanshe, 1993.
Mo Yan (莫言). 神聊 (Supernatural Talk). Beijing: Beijing shifan daxue chubanshe, 1993.
Mo Yan (莫言). 猫事荟萃 (The Cat Assembly). Beijing: Xinshijie chubanshe, 1994.
Mo Yan (莫言). 莫言文集 (Collected Works of Mo Yan). Beijing: Zuojia chubanshe, 1995. 5 Vols.
Mo Yan (莫言). 鲜女人 (Bright-Colored Woman). Beijing: Zuojia chubanshe, 1995.
Mo Yan (莫言). 会唱歌的墙 (The Singing Wall). Beijing: Renmin ribao chubanshe, 1998.
Mo Yan (莫言). 师傅越来越幽默 (*Shifu, You'll Do Anything for a Laugh*). Beijing: Jiefangjun wenyi chubanshe, 1999.
Mo Yan (莫言). 老枪，宝刀 (Old Gun, Treasured Sword). Shanghai: Shanghai wenyi chubanshe, 2000.
Mo Yan (莫言). 苍蝇，门牙 (Flies, Front Teeth). Shanghai: Shanghai wenyi chubanshe, 2000.
Mo Yan (莫言).初恋，神嫖 (First Love, Divine Prostitution). Shanghai: Shanghai wenyi chubanshe, 2000.
Mo Yan (莫言). 战友重逢 (Comrade Reunion). Beijing: Minzu chubanshe, 2001.
Mo Yan (莫言). 冰雪美人 (Snow Beauty). Beijing: Wenhua yishu chubanshe, 2001.
Mo Yan (莫言). 莫言中篇小说集 (Collected Novellas by Mo Yan). Beijing: Zuojia chubanshe, 2002. 2 Vols.
Mo Yan (莫言), and Lianke Yan (阎连科). 良心作证 (The Testimony of Conscience). Shenyang: Chunfeng wenyi chubanshe, 2002.

Mo Yan (莫言). 拇指铐 (Thumb Fetters). Jinan: Shandong wenyi chubanshe, 2002.
Mo Yan (莫言). 清醒的说梦者 (The Wakeful Dream Teller). Jinan: Shandong wenyi chubanshe, 2002.
Mo Yan (莫言). 罪过 (Sin). Jinan: Shandong wenyi chubanshe, 2002.
Mo Yan (莫言). 藏宝图 (Treasure Map). Shenyang: Chunfeng wenyi chubanshe, 2003.
Mo Yan (莫言), Yang Wang (王尧), and Jianfa Lin (林建法). 莫言王尧对话录 (Dialogue between Mo Yan and Yao Wang). Suzhou: Suzhou UP, 2003.
Mo Yan (莫言). 小说的气味 (Hallmarks of the Novel). Shenyang: Chunfeng wenyi chubanshe, 2003.
Mo Yan (莫言). 红蝗 (Red Locust). Beijing: Minzu chubanshe, 2004.
Mo Yan (莫言). 牛 (Bull). Beijing: Minzu chubanshe, 2004.
Mo Yan (莫言). 民间音乐 (Folk Music). Shenyang: Chunfeng wenyi chubanshe, 2004.
Mo Yan (莫言). 与大师约会:莫言短篇小说全集 (Appointment with Master: Complete Edition of Mo Yan's Short Stories). Shanghai: Shanghai wenyi chubanshe, 2005.
Mo Yan (莫言). 白狗秋千架 (White Dog and the Swing). Shanghai: Shanghai wenyi chubanshe, 2005.
Mo Yan (莫言). 北海道走笔 (Travels in Hokkaido). Shanghai: Shanghai wenyi chubanshe, 2006.
Mo Yan (莫言). 月光斩 (Moonlight). Beijing: Beijing shiyue wenyi chubanshe, 2006.
Mo Yan (莫言). 莫言讲演新篇 (New Collection of Mo Yan's Speeches). Beijing: Wenhua yishu chubanshe, 2010.
Mo Yan (莫言). 莫言对话新录 (New Dialogue with Mo Yan). Beijing: Wenhua yishu chubanshe, 2010.
Mo Yan (莫言). 变 (Change). Beijing: Haitun chubanshe, 2010.
Mo Yan (莫言). 用耳朵阅读 (Reading with Ears). Beijing: Zuojia chubanshe, 2012.
Mo Yan (莫言). 我们的荆轲 (Our Jinke). Beijing: Zuojia chubanshe, 2012.

Adaptations of Mo Yan's work to film

Red Sorghum (红高粱). Dir. Yimou Zhang (张艺谋). Beijing: Xi'an Film Studio, 1987.
Happy Times (幸福时光). Dir. Yimou Zhang (张艺谋). Nanning: Guangxi Film Studio, 2000.
Cotton Fleece (白棉花). Dir. Youqiao Li (李幼乔). Beijing: Anle Film Co., 2000.
Nuan (暖). Dir. Jianqi Huo (霍建起). Beijing: Aureape Ocean Park Co., 2003.

Studies in English about Mo Yan's work

"A Tribute to 2009 Newman Prize Winner Mo Yan." *World Literature Today* 83.4 (2009): 1-37.
Cai, Rong. *The Subject in Crisis in Contemporary Chinese Literature*. Honolulu: U of Hawai'i P, 2004.
Chan, Shelley. *A Subversive Voice in China: The Fictional World of Mo Yan*. Amherst: Cambria P, 2011.

Duran, Angelica, and Yuhan Huang, eds. *Mo Yan in Context: Nobel Laureate and Global Storyteller*. West Lafayette: Purdue UP, 2014.

Widmer, Ellen, and David Der-wei Wang, eds. *From May Fourth to June Fourth: Fiction and Film in Twentieth-Century China*. Cambridge: Harvard UP, 1993.

Studies in Chinese about Mo Yan's work

Chen, Xiaoming (陈晓明), ed. 莫言研究: *2004-2012* (The Study of Mo Yan: 2004-2012). Beijing: Huaxia chubanshe, 2013.

Ding, Boquan (丁柏铨), Depei Wen (文德培), and Chi Zhu (朱持). 中国新时期文学词典 (Chinese Literature Dictionary of the New Era). Nanjing: Nanjing UP, 1991.

Fu, Yanxia (付艳霞). 莫言的小说世界 (The Fictional World of Mo Yan). Beijing: Zhongguo wenshi chubanshe, 2012.

Guan, Moxian (管谟贤). 大哥说莫言 (Big Brother on Mo Yan). Jinan: Shandong renmin chubanshe, 2013.

Guo, Xiaodong (郭小东). 看穿莫言 (Looking through Mo Yan). Wuhan: Wuhan UP, 2012.

He, Lihua (贺立华). 怪才莫言 (Mo Yan: A Maverick Genius). Shijiazhuang: Huashan wenyi chubanshe, 1992.

Huang, Wenqian (黄文倩). 莫言丰乳肥臀论 (On Mo Yan's Novel *Big Breasts and Wide Hips*). Taipei: Wenshizhe chubanshe, 2005.

Kong, Fanjin (孔范今), Zhanjun Shi (施战军), and Xiaobing Lu (路晓冰), eds. 莫言研究资料 (Materials for the Study of Mo Yan). Jinan: Shandong wenyi chubanshe, 2006.

Li, Bin (李斌), and Guiting Cheng (程桂婷). 莫言批判 (Criticism of Mo Yan). Beijing: Beijing Institute of Technology P, 2013.

Liu, Zaifu (刘再复). 莫言了不起 (The Great Mo Yan). Hongkong: Xianggang zhonghe chuban youxian gongsi, 2013.

Liu, Zaifu (刘再复). 狂语莫言 (Passionate Words about Mo Yan). Hongkong: Mingbao chubanshe, 2013.

Ren, Xuan (任瑄). 高粱红了:对话莫言 (Sorghum Reddened: A Dialogue with Mo Yan). Beijing: Renmin ribao chubanshe, 2012.

Research Society of Mo Yan (莫言研究会), ed. 莫言与高密 (Mo Yan and Gaomi Township). Beijing: Zhongguo qingnian chubanshe, 2011.

Shao, Chunsheng (邵纯生). 莫言与他的民间乡土 (Mo Yan and His Folk Root). Qingdao: Qingdao chubanshe, 2013.

Wang, David Der-wei (王德威), ed. 说莫言 (On Mo Yan). Shanghai: Shanghai shudian chubanshe, 2013.

Wang, Meichun (王美春). 莫言小说中的女性世界 (The Female World in Mo Yan's Fiction). Chengdu: Sichuan UP, 2011.

Xiong, Zhiqin (熊志琴), ed. 论莫言生死疲劳:红楼梦奖2008得奖作品专辑 (On Mo Yan's Novel *Life and Death are Wearing Me Out*: Collective Essays of the 2008 Hongloumeng Prize). Hongkong: Tiandi tushu youxian gongsi, 2010.

Yang, Yang (杨扬), ed. 莫言研究资料 (Materials for Studies on Mo Yan). Tianjin: Tianjin renmin chubanshe, 2005.

Ye, Kai (叶开). 莫言评传 (Commentaries on the Life of Mo Yan). Zhengzhou Shi: Henan wenyi chubanshe, 2008.

Ye, Kai (叶开). 莫言的文学共和国 (Mo Yan's Republic of Letters). Beijing: Peking UP, 2013.

Zhang, Hua (张华). 莫言研究三十年 (Thirty Years of Study on Mo Yan). Jinan: Shandong UP, 2013.

Zhang, Ling (张灵). 叙述的源泉:莫言小说与民间文化中的生命主体精神 (The Origin of Narrative: Subjectivity in Mo Yan's Novels and Folk Culture). Beijing: Zhongyang bianyi chubanshe, 2010.

Zhang, Qinghua (张清华), and Xia Cao (曹霞), eds. 看莫言: 朋友、专家、同行眼中的诺奖得主 (Seeing Mo Yan: The Nobel Laureate in the Eyes of Friends, Experts, and Counterparts). Wuhan: Huazhong U of Science and Technology P, 2013.

Zhang, Wenying (张文颖). 来自边缘的声音:莫言与大江健三郎的文学 (Voices from the Edge: The Literature of Mo Yan and Kenzaburō Ōe). Beijing: Communication U of China P, 2006.

Zhang, Xudong (张旭东), and Mo Yan (莫言). 我们时代的写作: 对话酒国生死疲劳 (Writing of Our Age: Dialogue on *The Republic of Wine* and *Life and Death are Wearing Me Out*). Shanghai: Shanghai weiyi chubanshe, 2013.

Zhang, Zhizhong (张志忠). 莫言论 (On Mo Yan). Beijing: Zhongguo shehui kexue chubanshe, 1990.

Zhong, Yiwen (钟怡雯). 莫言小说: "历史" 的重构 (Mo Yan's Novels: Reconstructing History). Taipei: Wenshizhe chubanshe, 1997.

Index

Note: Page numbers in bold indicate the beginning of page spans for entire chapters and extended attention.

Acheng (阿城), 4
Aiken, Conrad, 72
Austin, J. L., 77

Book of Songs (诗经), 12, **123**
Brussig, Thomas, 154
Buddhism, **13**, 82, 124, **132**, **140**, 191, **198**, **205**, *See* religion
Burke, T. Patrick, 196, 209
Burt, Richard, 38, 41, 44, 45
Butler, Judith, 44

Calhoun, Craig, 168, 171
Cao, Shunqing, 13, **183**
censorship, 2, 31, **37**, 94
Chan, Shelley W., 6, 52
Chen, Thomas, 9, **37**
Chey, Jocelyn, 153
Chinese humor, 29, 96, 109, **153**
Chinese Writers Association, 79, 95, 150
Confucianism (儒家), 128, 140, 146, 172
cosmopolitanism, **167**
Culler, Jonathan, 78
Cultural Revolution (文化大革命), 25, 98, **107**, 140, 150, 155, 157, **215**

Damrosch, David, 9, 48, 124
Davis, Jessica Milner, 153
Derrida, Jacques, 78
Dickens, Charles, 186
Du, Lanlan, 10, **63**
Duran, Angelica, **1**, 12, 13, 14, **153**, **195**, **221**

Economic Reform (改革开放) or Opening-up Policy, 140, 148
Engels, Friedrich, 169
English, James F., 1
Englund, Peter, 123

Family planning (计划生育) or One-child policy, 5, 54, **63**, **86**, 95
Foucault, Michel, 70
Frye, Northrop, 195

Gaomi Township (高密), 12, 26, 29, **52**, 64, 77, **124**, 142, 149, 178
Gibbon, Edward, 27
Goethe, Johann Wolfgang von, 9, 172, 174, 176
Goldblatt, Howard, 6, 9, **23**, 39, 94, 116, 132, 160, 162, 189
Greene, Roland, 8
Griffin, Eric, 8

hallucinatory realism, 23, 32, 83, 96, 124, 155, *See* magic realism
Hayashi, Fumiko, **51**
He, Chengzhou, 10, **77**
Holz, Wolfgang, 115
Horiguchi, Noriko J., 10, **51**
Hsia, C. T. (夏志清), 154
Huang, Alexa, 6, 12, **153**
Huang, Yuhan, **1**, 11, 14, **107**, **221**

Jacoby, Sarah, 201

Knight, Sabina, 11, **93**, 161, 197

Lao Tse (老子), 141, 191
Liu, Xiaobo (刘晓波), 2, 31
Liu, Zaifu (刘再复), 116
Lu Xun (鲁迅), 127, 128, 159

Magic realism, 96, 124, 153 *See* hallucinatory realism
Mao, Zedong (毛泽东), 37, 39, 79, 94, 96, 97, 100, 101, 107, 109, 112, 129, 155, 156, 157, 216

Marx, Karl, 169
May Fourth Movement (五四运动), 124, 128, 147, 219
Mills, C. Wright, 215
Milton, John, 15
Mitchell, Donald, 13, **195**
Mitchell, W. J. T., 108
Mo Yan (莫言)
  "Abandoned Child," 94, 103
  Big Breasts and Wide Hips, 5, 24, 29, 32, **52**, 80, **85**, 97, 103, 162, 189, **207**
  Frog, 31, 54, 57, **63**, 85, 86, 87, 115, 150, 151, 200
  Garlic Ballads, The, 5, **27**, 30, **37**, 87, 97, **123**, 189
  Life and Death are Wearing Me Out, 5, 6, 29, 33, 57, **81**, 97, 100, 101, 103, **107**, **123**, **140**, 149, 154, **155**, 160, 197, 200, 203
  "Old Gun," 178
  POW!, 5, 14, 30, **157**, 185, **208**
  pseudonym "Don't Talk," 2, 94, 155
  Red Sorghum, 11, **25**, 52, 85, 95, 97, 99, 103, 148, 154
  Republic of Wine, The, 5, **28**, 84, 87, 93, 97, **154**, 161
  Sandalwood Death, 5, 30, 83, 84, 97, 114, 206
  Shifu: You'll Do Anything for a Laugh, 157, 159, 160
  "White Dog and the Swing," 88, 99
Moldenhauer, Joseph J., 69, 71

Naruse, Mikio, 56
Newman Prize, 2
Nobel Prize in Literature Laureates, 1, 4
  Faulkner, William, 5, 8, **63**, 83, 125, 176, 177, 178
  Gao, Xingjian (高行健), 2, 24, 37, 94, 157, 176, 178, 216, 217
  García Márquez, Gabriel, 5, 24, 32, 83, 96, 125, 148, 177
  Heaney, Seamus, 2
  Kertész, Imre, 2
  Müller, Herta, 30, 79
  Pamuk, Orhan, 1
  Steinbeck, John, 38
Post-Mao China, 26, 28, 37, 97, 107
Pu, Songling (蒲松龄), 81, 125, 147, 161

religion. 82, 114, **123**, **139**, 172, 186, **195**, **215**, *See* Buddhism
Roach, Joseph, 77
root-seeking (寻根), 4, 26, 125

Saussy, Haun, 9
Socialist Realism, 32, 116, 154
Strachey, Lionel, 154

Tiananmen Square Incident, 4 June 1989 (六四天安门事件), 14, 27, 218
Tötösy de Zepetnek, Steven, 3, 8, 183

Updike, John, 32

Variation theory, **183**
Volpe, Edmond, 72
Voltaire, 26

Waley, Arthur, 185
Wang, Chi-ying Alice, 12, **123**
Wang, David Der-wei, 2, 53, 85, 124
Wang, Jinghui, 12, **139**
Wang, Miaomiao, 13, **183**
Wang, Ning, 7, 13, **167**
Wedgewood, C. V., 25
Wei, Dedong, 200
Wells, Henry W., 125, 153
World literature, *Weltliteratur,* 9, **77**, 124, **167**

Yan, Lianke (阎连科), 37, **139**
Yang, Fenggang, 14, **215**